The
Happy Bottom
Riding Club

The
Happy Bottom
Riding Club

$\longleftarrow \bowtie \Longleftrightarrow \longrightarrow$

The Life and Times of
Pancho Barnes

Lauren Kessler

Random House
New York

Library of Congress Cataloging-in-Publication Data
Kessler, Lauren
    The happy bottom riding club : the life and times of Pancho Barnes / Lauren Kessler.
        p.   cm.
    Includes bibliographical references and index.
    ISBN 978-0-812-99252-6
    1. Barnes, Pancho, 1901–75. 2. Women air pilots—United States Biography.   I. Title.
TL540.B325K47   2000
629.13'092—dc21
[B]   99-39911

Random House website address: www.atrandom.com

Book design by Mercedes Everett

Title-page photo: Pancho Barnes, c. 1930. *Air Force Flight Test Center History Office, Edwards AFB Collection*

To

Don Hager

and, as always,

to Tom

It's so acceptably easy for a woman not to strive too hard, not to be too adventure-crazed, not to take too many risks, not to enjoy sex with full candor. . . . It isn't seemly for a woman to have that much zest.

—Diane Ackerman, *On Extended Wings*

Ah, hell. We had more fun in a week than those weenies had in a lifetime.

—Pancho Barnes

Acknowledgments

All books, I think, are beholden to the kindness of strangers. I am always amazed by this, amazed and delighted that so many strangers can be so generous with their time and themselves. This book would not have been possible without the help, interest, and encouragement of many people. Chief among them are Ray Puffer, historian at the Air Force Flight Test Center History Office, Edwards Air Force Base, my first and most enduring contact, who, from the very beginning, was kind, patient, knowledgeable, and good-humored; Jon Aldrich, antique plane enthusiast and collector, who not only gave me access to several boxes of Pancho's private papers but set me up in a room in his house to do my research; Tony King, a delightful man and wonderful storyteller who started working for Pancho in the late 1930s and talked to me for hours about the woman he clearly adored; Walt Geisen, a friend of Pancho's in her later life, who was as generous with his collection of tapes, private papers, and memorabilia as he was with his own time; and Carolyn Garner of the Pasadena Public Library, who helped me get my feet on the ground.

At the Air Force Flight Test Center History Office, Jim Young steered me to important material and gave up a corner of his big desk for me, and Cheryl Gumm paved the way for several important interviews. Also at Edwards, a few buildings away, Kathy Davis took the time to drive me out to Pancho's house in Boron; Linda Stowe answered questions and provided contacts; and archaeologists Rick Norwood and Barbie Stevenson Getchell made it easy for me to use the enormously valuable oral history projects completed under their supervision. Much of that work was done by interviewers Robert Mulcahy and Dana Kilanowski, to whom I also owe a big debt.

Screenwriter David Chisholm generously lent me an important taped interview and shared his insights into a story he knows well. Helen Ashford popped into my life on e-mail and proceeded to spend hours going through Southern California photo archives for me. Doug Keeney provided important and provocative leads. I must also acknowledge the help of Claude Hopkins and Mary Ellen Kennedy at the National Archives and Records Administration, San Bruno, California; Tania Rizzo at the Pasadena Historical Society; Phyllis Ashworth at the International Women's Air and Space Museum; Darla Bullard at the Ninety-Nines; Orité Renee Toulson at the Montgomery County, Pennsylvania, Orphans Court; Joy Werlink at the Washington State Historical Society; Larry Grooms, editor of the *Antelope Valley Press;* Dr. Peggy Baty, president of Women in Aviation, International; Bobbi Roe, editor of *Woman Pilot* magazine; and the folks at the History and Genealogy Department of the Los Angeles Public Library.

Many people generously sat for oral history interviews with me, in person and by phone. Without their stories, this one would not have been possible. I thank Carl Bergman, Richard Bortner, Bob Fetters, Mary Graham Fetters, Everet Forten, Helen Fulmer-Steager, George Griffith, Alfred Houser, Joseph McKinstray, Bob Logan, Grace Logan, Richard McKendry, Barney Oldfield, Rob Pollack, Pierre Poudevigne, Boardman C. Reid, Nancy Simonian, Otto Tronowsky, Bobbi Trout, Margorie Urick, Ray Urick, Elinor Wagner, Phyllis Walker, John Weld, Fay Gillis Wells, Dorothy Woods—and especially, as previously mentioned, Tony King and Walt Geisen.

My many faithful correspondents were no less helpful. I thank Jim

Bardin, Larry Burden, Tom Collins, D. Russell Crounse, Bruce Fraites, Richard Frey, Shirley Gillespie, Rob Hackman, General J. Stanley Holtoner, Betty J. Love, Luis Marin, Robert McDougle, Walt Neikamp, Jack Pollack, Lloyd Sims, Martin Snyder, Mary Swan, and Ray Young.

And those were just the strangers.

I must acknowledge my agent, Sandy Dijkstra, for being her wonderful, powerful self, as much a force of nature as Pancho ever was. I want to thank my editor at Random House, Bob Loomis, the master of his art, who is both kind and keen-eyed, a tough critic and a perfect gentleman. I know how fortunate I am to work with him.

Closer to home, I thank Dorothy Schick for lifting me off this earth in her Cessna Skyhawk and for sharing her books and her enthusiasm. I thank Carol Ann Bassett, Tom Wheeler, and Duncan McDonald for their encouragement and support. I thank Nancy Webber, Kellee Weinhold, Elizabeth Balder, and Rosemarie Eisenberg for getting me through the hard part.

And I thank, with head and heart, my husband, friend, and collaborator, Tom Hager, who spent long days in county courthouses and basement archives doing research for this book and even more days at home caring for the kids while I did the research, who edited the manuscript with the enthusiasm of a spouse and the sharp pencil of the fine editor and writer he is, who talked me through countless rough spots, literary and otherwise, who was, quite simply and quite wonderfully, always there.

Contents

Contents

Part Three
Ratlands

Prologue

Pancho needed to be persuaded. She was sitting in Walt and June Geisen's kitchen in Lancaster, California, a desert town two hours northeast of Los Angeles, drinking coffee and considering Walt's invitation. Pancho had been famous, but that was long ago. She had once owned a thirty-five-room mansion and a sprawling oceanfront estate and a 360-acre desert oasis. She had once owned Cadillacs and racehorses, cabin cruisers and airplanes. But now, in the winter of 1970, she was just an old woman living alone in a one-room shanty with her dozens of Yorkies and Chihuahuas.

When she got tired of her own company, she drove to the local post office or over to the county clerk's, stood at the counter, and talked to whoever would listen. Lately she'd been driving into Lancaster to stop by Walt and June's. Two or three times a week she'd show up at their door just before dinner and then act surprised when June asked her to stay for a meal. She was in some ways a pitiful figure, alone and broke and, if not looking for handouts, then certainly looking for company. But it was hard for Walt and June to feel sorry for Pancho, because once she sat down at the table and started talking, she was transformed. She told big, brawling, wonderful stories about the old days, stories about

Hollywood before color, before sound, stories about the Air Force before it was the Air Force, about people she had flown with and partied with and gotten drunk with, heroes and generals and millionaires and stars, people Walt and June had only read about. So the Geisens didn't feel they were doing Pancho a favor by giving her a free meal. They felt she was doing them a favor by sharing her past.

Pancho had known Walt for more than ten years. He was an aviation nut like her, a pilot who flew for fun, hopping in his Cessna on a Saturday morning to fly to Bakersfield for lunch or to just tool around in the big, open sky above the Mojave—bore a hole in it, as he would say to his flying buddies. Walt's work was with airplanes, too. He was an engineering supervisor at the GE Flight Test Center over at Edwards Air Force Base, just north of Lancaster. That's how Pancho knew him. Pancho's only son, Billy, worked under Walt. Over the years, Pancho and Walt had forged a casual friendship built on these not-quite-impromptu dinnertime visits. Pancho had always gotten along well with men and generally tried to tolerate the women they were married to. She actually liked June Geisen, who had raised sons and, perhaps because of that, seemed unperturbed by Pancho's X-rated jokes, indecorous yarns, and liberal use of four-letter words.

That evening in the Geisens' kitchen, Walt asked Pancho if she would be the guest speaker at the annual Experimental Aircraft Association banquet coming up next month. The local chapter was a large, enthusiastic group of men who, like Walt, lived and breathed airplanes. Pancho had been a social being to her core. She had, in her time, thrown three-day bacchanals, ridden a horse into a barroom, and hosted the biggest, loudest, wildest party the desert had ever seen.

But when Walt invited her to deliver the banquet speech, she hesitated. She felt suddenly and uncharacteristically shy. She had been out of the spotlight for so long. Who would remember her? she wondered. Who would care about her adventures so many years ago? Who would want to sit and listen? For all the friends she used to have, no one came by her little house up in Boron. All her old cronies, famous and otherwise, had died or moved away or, she figured, forgotten her. She hadn't been at a public event in close to fifteen years. And what, she wondered, would she wear? She was the least vain of women. Her standard attire ran to mud-caked jeans and old Western shirts. She had not worn a dress for years, never wore makeup, and rarely washed, let alone styled, what was left of her hair. But she knew she couldn't stand up in front of all those guys, those local pilots and engineers and aircraft industry bigwigs, those men in their suits and ties with their wives in high heels and cultured-pearl necklaces, she couldn't stand up in front of all of them and not look good.

But Walt succeeded in persuading her to deliver the banquet speech anyway. The thought that she might be, if only for an hour or so, the center of attention again was too appealing to ignore. The next day, she phoned a local woman she knew, and they spent most of the week figuring out what Pancho would wear. She had a theatrical sense of color that ran to eye-popping purple and grass green, oranges and reds and yellows, big colors that announced one's presence with a shout and a bang, not the kind of colors most seventy-year-old women would wear. Pancho's friend was amazed when the outfit they came up with actually looked good. It was a wild green and purple paisley print tunic, long-sleeved and high-necked, falling straight and slim over her nonexistent hips. She wore it over a pair of simple black slacks.

Pancho dressed carefully that evening, January 16, 1971. She applied eyeliner and lipstick, amazed that she still knew how. She tried to do something with her wisps of graying hair, but gave up and stuck her favorite wig on her head instead, the big, black, curly one that gave her an abundance of hair but also gave her that odd, surprised look old women have when they wear big, dark wigs. Still, she looked good when she showed up at Walt and June's house that night.

When they got to the Elks Lodge in Palmdale, they found an overflow crowd, maybe 120 people. Those who couldn't be accommodated in the banquet room sat or stood in the bar. They had all come to see and hear Pancho Barnes. Many of them had been surprised to read her name on their invitations. They knew her by reputation, of course. Everyone who knew anything about the history of aviation knew about

Pancho Barnes. And they knew *of* her because, even in this place known for its eccentric desert characters, Pancho had loomed larger than life. She had been the talk of the Mojave since the 1930s. But most of the people who showed up that night thought she had died years before.

When the meal was almost over, Ted Tate got up to introduce her. Ted was doing PR for General Dynamics over at the base. Although he had encountered Pancho years ago in her heyday, when he was a young man on the fringes of the fun, he had just recently engineered a friendship with her. He couldn't get enough of her stories. He was enamored of, almost obsessed with, the romantic life Pancho talked about having lived, a life that it was no longer possible to live. Ted had a smart and beautiful wife and four children, but he had begun to spend all his free time with Pancho. He would go over to her place and take her driving across the desert in his hopped-up T-Bird with the top down. They would sit on corral fences, eat at greasy spoons, and roar around the desert, Ted driving, Pancho talking. He was so full of her stories, so much a fan, that Ted didn't really know how to introduce her. There was too much to say. Besides, he figured she could say it better than he could. So he made it short:

"Here she is," he said. "I love her."

Pancho walked to the podium, smiling in her big black wig and loud paisley tunic. Her face was deeply lined, forty years of desert living etched around the eyes and mouth. She had always been a homely woman, and age did nothing to improve her looks. She looked all of her seventy years, but she also looked healthy and alive, energetic, ready to rumble, as in the old days. She grabbed the sides of the stand and waited for the applause to stop, not wanting it to, of course. She had no idea what she was going to say. She hadn't prepared a speech. But talking was what she did best, so she trusted herself. When the applause died down, she launched into a story about Frank Clarke and Paul Mantz, legendary Hollywood stunt pilots and rivals. She had flown with both of them. It seemed that Clarke, who had been the dean of the movie pilots until Mantz showed up, had once placed a curse on his rival, putting an evil spell on Mantz's airplane for good measure. The audience listened intently as Pancho gossiped about these two famous men, about the movies they flew in, the stunts they performed with airplanes that were now certifiable antiques. No one picked up a fork to finish dessert. The story ended with Mantz crashing in his Lockheed and Clarke convinced his curse did the trick. The audience laughed, on cue, and before Pancho had a chance to wonder what she would say next, someone yelled out: "Tell us about the air races, Pancho."

Pancho smiled. She had a big, wide smile that dimpled her cheeks. Her voice was clear and strong, accentless, as California voices are. The events she talked about were fifty years in the past, but she remembered every date, every stop she made during the first cross-country race ever flown by women. Single-engine biplanes that didn't go as fast as the cars her audience drove to the Elks Lodge that night. Flying without instruments. Landing on unlit scraped-dirt runways. Pancho had them hanging on every word. Amelia was there, she told the audience, knowing that they would know who Amelia was.

"Tell us about how you got the name Pancho," someone yelled from the back of the room.

"Tell us about the time you tested the Lockheed," someone else yelled.

"Tell us about Howard Hughes."

Pancho couldn't believe it. These people *knew* her. They knew her history; they knew her stories. It had been so many years since she had driven in and out of Edwards Air Force Base with her special permit, the guards waving her through, the commanders opening their doors and sitting with her to chat. It had been so many years since her Wednesday night dances had attracted four hundred fun-starved officers and their wives, so long ago that her sprawling desert resort had been the unofficial headquarters for a generation of hotshot pilots and jet jockeys. But these people in the room knew about her. They were shouting out their requests for stories like an audience at a concert calling for their favorite songs.

"Okay, I'll tell you about Hughes," Pancho said, launching into a story about the making of *Hell's Angels,* Hughes's 1930 aerial master-piece, and how a young starlet named Jean Harlow got her break. She told them about how she had flown for Hughes, the only woman in the sky, and how she and Hughes had later squared off, fighting over the services of Frank Clarke, and how Hughes had pulled rank and won, but not without a few concessions forced by her.

"Howard was a great person," she said deadpan, waiting a beat, a comedian setting up the punch line. "Of course, he was young then, and he hadn't gotten . . ." She paused. "Strange." The audience laughed and clapped. Here was a woman who had hobnobbed with Howard Hughes, and she was standing right in front of them at the Elks Club podium. Pancho looked out into the audience, and she knew then that she had them, just as in the old days. They would listen for as long as she could talk. She could be as outrageous as she wanted to be now.

"Ya know," she said, leaning forward into the microphone, lowering her voice as if confiding in all 120 people simultaneously, "those stunt pilots were real embarrassed by the name of one of those early movies, *Cock of the Air.*" She let that sit for a moment. The audience tittered. Those who knew the legend of Pancho knew she had a legendary dirty mouth. "Yeah," she said, "they wanted to rename it *Penis of the Ozone.*" For a heartbeat, the room was silent, as the men decided whether they should laugh in front of their wives, and as the women decided whether they should show their husbands they understood the joke. Both concluded in the affirmative, and the crowd erupted into a full thirty seconds of uncontrolled guffaws. Pancho soaked it up, like the desert floor after a cloudburst.

"What else?" she said, when the audience had quieted. "Anyone else have any suggestions? Or are you getting tired of listening to me?"

"No!" "No!" "No!" A half-dozen or more voices yelled from the audience. Then someone called for another story of the old days, and Pancho was launched again, weaving detail and dialogue, inserting a few well-placed profanities, pausing at all the right places, building to a punch line. Again, laughter. Then another request. Then another. After an hour, it was she who tired of the stories, not the audience.

Ted Tate came up to the podium to bring the evening to a close, beaming at Pancho, reaching forward to clasp her hands. He stood next to her and leaned into the microphone, his head almost touching hers. Pancho's face was flushed. At that moment, she was as happy as she had ever been.

"Let's give a standing ovation to the first lady of flight," he said, looking at Pancho, then out into the room. And they did—Walt and June and all the other plane-crazy husbands and wives who worked at Edwards and flew on weekends and loved the desert, as Pancho did, for its vast, cloudless, horizon-to-horizon skies, skies made for flying.

Part One

—◄◈►—

High and Mighty

1

To Whom the Future Belongs

Every Sunday, the old man would take his granddaughter on another adventure. They trekked by mule up the San Gabriel Mountains, cheered in the stands at Buffalo Bill's Wild West Show, sat side by side on a hard bench under the Ringling Brothers big top watching a parade of trained elephants, toured alligator farms and ostrich ranches, visited expositions, horse shows, and amusement parks. The old man was tall and spare, with a strong jaw and chiseled face, still handsome in his late seventies. He had dark, deep-set eyes, a well-tended silver handlebar mustache, and the bearing of a man who knew he was somebody. He was. He was Thaddeus Sobieski Constantine Lowe, Civil War hero, pioneering balloonist, renowned inventor, promoter, and showman, known nationwide as the man who had created the grandest, most astonishing, most popular tourist attraction in turn-of-the-century Southern California.

Holding his hand was his eight-year-old granddaughter Florence, his favorite among many. She was an energetic, excitable girl with a moon face, a short neck, and little legs already muscular from years of horseback riding. She was brash and adventurous, maybe even foolhardy and a bit wild, and he loved her for it. He loved her pluck, her physical bravery, her feistiness. To her mother, Florence was an unruly, undisciplined, and uncivilized child. To her grandfather, she was a kindred spirit.

This Sunday, January 16, 1910, the old man was taking his granddaughter to the first aviation exhibition in America, a ten-day extravaganza, half demonstration, half competition, and all showmanship. Fliers from the United States and abroad had come to Dominguez Field in the rolling hills just north of Long Beach to pit their skills and their fragile, homemade machines against one another. Who could fly the fastest, the highest, stay in the air the longest, carry a passenger and still remain aloft? The machines were delicate, like birds, with fine, light wooden skeletons and skins of linen stretched tight and varnished to stiffness. The aviators were young and daring, their sense of adventure eclipsing their common sense.

Just six winters ago two Midwestern brothers, bicycle makers by trade, had become the first to show that heavier-than-air, motorized flight was even possible. On a beach in North Carolina, flying into a stiff twenty-one-mile-per-hour headwind, Orville, the younger brother, kept their contraption in the air for a thrilling twelve seconds, covering 120 feet. Later that morning, just before gusty winds so damaged the tiny airplane that the brothers had to quit for the day, older brother Wilbur flew for fifty-nine seconds, covering 852 feet. Two years later, in Dayton, Ohio, a much-improved version of the Wright brothers' machine flew $24\frac{1}{2}$ miles in thirty-eight minutes. Overnight, aviators captured the American imagination. They were hailed as the Wizards of the Air, heroes who were, as a historian of that time wrote, "breaking gravity's absolute grip on our dreams."

The old man and his granddaughter sat in the stands set up at the edge of the grassy field watching the aviators compete for fabulous prizes: $3,000 for the fastest ten laps around the field, $1,000 for the man who could fly three laps while carrying a 150-pound passenger. There were biplanes and monoplanes, experimental aircraft made and flown by aviation pioneers like Glenn Curtiss and Lincoln Beechy, men who were not yet famous but soon would be.

There were also airships and balloons on the field, dirigibles of all sizes, the old technology, big, slow, graceful, and quiet, billowing in the wind, next to the new, clumsy, and loud. The old man, Thaddeus Lowe, was there to see both. He had brought with him the design for a new airship, a revolutionary—or crackpot, depending on whom one asked—idea for an enormous passenger balloon that could circle the globe. He called it the Lowe Planet Airship. The design showed a huge gondola with luxury hotel appointments, an elegant dining salon, and an observation deck. The old man imagined entertaining passengers with in-flight magic-lantern shows. He was about to apply for a patent.

But it was clear to him that Sunday to whom the future belonged. He looked out at the field, at Glenn Curtiss circling the air in his Curtiss biplane. Then he looked down at eight-year-old Florence by his side. Her face was uplifted. Her eyes were riveted to the sky.

"Everyone will be flying airplanes when you grow up," he told her. "You'll be a flier, too."

She believed him. Grandpa Lowe knew everything. When she grew up, she wanted to be just like him.

Thaddeus Lowe was born on a modest farm in 1832 in Jefferson Mills, New Hampshire. Although apprenticed out to a Boston bootmaker to learn a useful trade, he was, as a boy, fascinated by science, not shoemaking. Soon after arriving in Boston, he conducted his first experiment in aviation by placing a tomcat in a wire cage suspended from a huge kite he had constructed. The cat, airborne for an hour, lived to tell the tale.

Lowe stayed as an apprentice out of duty to his parents. But as soon as his time was up, he set himself on another path entirely, hiring on as a laboratory assistant to a traveling chemistry show. The show was part vaudeville, part rudimentary science, with Lowe standing behind a table stocked with bottles of colored liquids that he combined to dramatic effect. It was during one of his chemistry shows in New York that the young man, who now styled himself a "Professor of Chemistry," looked out into the audience and into the eyes of Leontine A.

Gachon, the smart, cultured, adventurous nineteen-year-old daughter of Parisian expatriates. One week later, on February 14, 1855, the two were married. For the next decade, while Leontine was busy birthing and mothering the first seven of the ten children the couple eventually would have, Thaddeus took to the skies.

He made his first balloon ascent, rising to two hundred feet, in 1857. He loved ballooning for the sheer adventure of it, the thrill of being airborne, the quiet drama of floating across a vast landscape, seeing vistas no man had ever seen before, the skill and sangfroid needed to navigate the thing and bring it back safely to earth. But ballooning also appealed to his scientific side. He studied air masses and wind currents, concerned himself with complex questions of engineering and gas technology, plotted lengthy journeys, drew up plans for enormous airships. Within two years, using funds from the chemistry show, he had completed work on an airship five times bigger than any previous balloon. He was convinced he could cross the Atlantic in it, but on his first two attempts, one from New York, the other from Philadelphia, it never got off the ground.

Out of personal funds but undeterred, Thaddeus turned to individual investors, persuading them of the "mercantile and pecuniary benefits" of a transatlantic crossing. Their money funded his next attempt, an ascent from Cincinnati bound for Philadelphia to test the existence of the upper air currents Thaddeus believed would whisk his ship across the ocean. Eight hours and 350 miles later, blown off course by prevailing southerly winds, he landed in a field outside Unionville, South Carolina, where the excitable local residents proclaimed him "an inhabitant of some ethereal or infernal region." One man suggested that he should be "shot on the spot where he had dropped from the skies." This turned out to be the least of Thaddeus's troubles.

The Professor, a Yankee, had set down his balloon deep in the heart of Dixie only days after the firing on Fort Sumter, and the shotgun-toting natives accused him of being a Union spy. Thaddeus mollified them slightly by producing from his pocket a clipping from the Cincinnati newspaper that announced his flight. Then he left, hastily and on foot. He may not have planned to be on a mission for the Union, but immediately upon returning to Cincinnati, he justified the suspicions of the Southerners he had encountered by telegraphing President Lincoln with information gained on his trek through Dixie. It was from Thaddeus Lowe that Abraham Lincoln first learned of the Tennessee legislature's vote for secession.

The war put his personal ballooning plans on hold, but it also presented tremendous opportunities. Thaddeus rushed to Washington, D.C., to convince Army officials of the importance of ballooning to the war effort. When talk got him nowhere, he ascended in his balloon from the lawn outside the Smithsonian, and on a clear June day in 1861, high above the capital, he sent the President the first telegraphed dispatch from an aerial station. He could see for fifty miles, he told Lincoln, tapping out the message in Morse code from the basket suspended from his balloon, the wire dangling beneath him a thousand feet: THE CITY WITH ITS GIRDLE OF ENCAMPMENTS PRESENTS A SUPERB SCENE. Soon thereafter, the Secretary of War engaged his services.

During the next two years, Thaddeus and his team of fifty men and five balloons made more than three thousand ascents, tracking troop movements, reporting on Confederate positions, and filing reconnaissance reports in the Yorktown and Williamsburg campaigns and at the battles of Fair Oaks, Chancellorsville, Mechanicsville, and Chickahominy. Ballooning was such an uncommon activity that Thaddeus attracted the fire of Union troops as well as Confederates, becoming known as "the most shot at man in the war." Unfazed, he lined his observation basket with sheet metal and went back to work.

He was the first person to telegraph a dispatch directly from a balloon to field headquarters, the first person to take aerial photographs, and the pioneer of aerial mapmaking. He and his men were credited with saving the Union Army on two occasions. Operating independently of the military, with no rank or position, dressed not in Union blue but in the high silk hat and black frock coat that were the upper-class costume of the day, Thaddeus Lowe was, as his granddaughter Florence later so proudly claimed, the father of the United States Air Force.

After the war, the large and still expanding Lowe family settled in Norristown, Pennsylvania, where Thaddeus proceeded to make a fortune with his inventions and patents, including the first practical means of making ice, and a refrigeration unit used in steamships and railway cars for the transportation of perishables. He also invented a process for manufacturing artificial gas and crisscrossed the country selling gas plants to cities with no natural gas. That is how, in 1886, he found himself in the West, in the quiet agricultural village of Pasadena, which, like the rest of Southern California, was teetering on the edge of the biggest land boom in American history.

Moneyed Easterners were just discovering the pleasures of Pasadena, particularly during the warm winter months, and a number of elegant resort hotels were under construction. But the year that Thaddeus Lowe came west to sell the city an artificial-gas plant, the main avenues were still dusty dirt streets that wound their way through lush orange groves. Hundreds of acres of vineyards and apple and orange orchards thrived in the fertile soil. The open plains that swept north to the feet of the San Gabriel Mountains were copper and gold with poppies, dotted with baby blue-eyes, buttercups, and wild mustard. The six-thousand-foot San Gabriels, with their soft folds and crenulations, their muted, ever-changing colors, the palest of greens, tawny brown, dusky purple, were a dramatic backdrop for the emerging town. "If there be an Elysium on earth," wrote a visitor from the East when she saw Pasadena for the first time, "it is this, it is this."

Thaddeus Lowe thought so, too. In 1888 he brought his family west and, soon thereafter, commissioned the construction of a 24,000-square-foot mansion on South Orange Grove Avenue. It was a broad, quiet, majestic street on a gentle rise above the thriving center of town. Fast becoming known as Millionaires' Row, it was the showplace of Southern California, with more than a hundred millionaires living on neighboring ten-acre estates, one mansion more impressive than the next. Here lived the Libbys of Libby, McNeil & Libby, the Warners of Borg-Warner, the Merritts of U.S. Steel, the Wrigleys of chewing gum fame, the beer tycoon Adolphus Busch, the Cravens of

Liggett-Myers Tobacco, the Harknesses of Standard Oil—and the Thaddeus Lowes.

The Lowes' was one of the earlier mansions on the street, a massive three-story home with bay windows, porticoes and wide wraparound porches, an enormous basement museum to house Leontine's collection of African baskets, and a five-story circular tower to serve as Professor Lowe's private astronomical observatory. The *Pasadena Star* called it "the finest residence in the state." The Lowes moved in and quickly became social leaders and lavish entertainers.

Other wealthy men in their fifties came west to retire. Thaddeus founded the Pacific-Lowe Gas and Electric Company, the Citizens Ice Company, and the Citizens Bank of Los Angeles. He dabbled in real estate. He bought and resuscitated Pasadena's failing Opera House. Then, in the winter of 1891 he began the most ambitious, creative, and, some thought, crazy engineering project Southern California had ever seen: a narrow-gauge railroad winding along the spine of the San Gabriels that would offer travelers breathtaking vistas, the kind of views one could not get otherwise—except by ascending in a balloon.

From the beginning, the scheme presented almost insurmountable challenges, and that's what appealed to Thaddeus most. Dozens of canyons and gorges had to be spanned by bridges. The slopes of the San Gabriels were so steep that the grading had to be done by hand, with supplies packed in by mule. One slope was so precipitous, rising at a sixty-degree angle, that no ordinary railway could mount it. Thaddeus hired the man who had designed the San Francisco cable car system to create a special conveyance.

On July 4, 1893, Professor Lowe's railroad officially opened for business. The Incline Cable Car, decked with flowers, palm fronds, and red, white, and blue bunting, glided noiselessly up a 1,500-foot incline as a band played "Nearer My God to Thee" and thousands of spectators in straw boaters cheered and waved pennants. At the bottom of the incline, Thaddeus had built an expansive three-story hostelry with a dining room that could seat eighty and a public hall for dances and concerts. Outside the hotel and its attached outdoor pavilion, more than a thousand steps linked wooden walkways that traversed streams, skirted waterfalls, and hugged boulders down the side of Rubio Canyon.

At the top of the incline, on Echo Mountain, Thaddeus was busy constructing an even more impressive resort that would feature a four-story, seventy-room grand hotel with its own bowling alley, billiards room, and barbershop. There would be two ornamental fountains, a casino, a dance hall, a zoo, and a metal-domed observatory. The *Los Angeles Times* reported an opening day crowd of as many as six thousand, adding, "The financial success of the undertaking is assured."

A month later, Pasadena officials proclaimed the first-ever civic holiday, Lowe Day. One illustrious speaker after another touted the railroad as the engineering feat of the century and Thaddeus Lowe as the man of the hour. One speaker hailed Thaddeus as a greater genius than Ben Franklin. Another called the project "so unique in its general character . . . so bold in its conception . . . [that] it . . . annihilates space and defies the laws of gravitation as to literally bring the mountains to our door."

Still, Professor Lowe set his sights higher. Beyond Echo Mountain was a peak just recently renamed Mount Lowe in his honor. His railroad must go there. Thaddeus had thus far funded the entire project from his own fortune and the private investments of friends. But the Mount Lowe section of the track proved to be exorbitantly expensive. He tried to sell construction bonds to fund it, but by the end of 1894, the Panic of 1893 had finally hit California, and he had so few takers that he began liquidating his own businesses to meet the financial obligations of the railroad. He sold off his real estate. He mortgaged the Pasadena Opera House. He mortgaged his South Orange Grove Avenue mansion. Two years later, more than a half million dollars in debt and paying ruinous interest rates of 10½ percent, he lost the family's home. Soon he was defaulting on the interest payments, and in 1899, six years after the lavish grand opening of Mount Lowe Railroad, he lost it all.

In 1895, while Thaddeus Lowe was still in control of his empire, his favorite son, the seventh of his and Leontine's children, married Florence Mae Dobbins. Thad Junior was nominally involved in his father's business ventures but seemed mostly to lead a Teddy Roosevelt–inspired life as a sportsman and outdoor adventurer. He bred horses and rode superbly. He hunted. Florence Mae was thick-necked and plain-faced, the daughter of another wealthy family who, like the Lowes, had come west, also from Philadelphia, the decade before. Her father, Richard J. Dobbins, was a noted architect, the designer of the official buildings of the 1876 Centennial, a wealthy Philadelphian who invested his fortune wisely and conservatively. His wife, Caroline, was a shrewd, straitlaced Episcopalian who ran the family with an iron hand. They and their entourage of servants came west by private railroad car and built a mansion near the Lowes'.

For Thad Junior and his family, the match with Florence Mae was a fine one. The Lowes were marrying into more than money. They were marrying into old money and Daughters of the American Revolution–Main Line Philadelphia respectability. But the Dobbinses had some doubts. Although Professor Lowe was, at the time of the betrothal, arguably the leading citizen of Pasadena and still a man of great wealth, Caroline and Richard considered him "more or less a promoter." He was nouveau riche and, besides, had made his money too publicly and with too much fanfare. Richard Dobbins might have voiced stronger objections, but he was quite ill and died before the marriage.

Whatever her doubts, Caroline not only sanctioned the union but also gave the couple a two-story house in neighboring San Marino as a wedding gift. The young couple's first child, William Emmert, born a year later, was an aristocratic-looking boy with fine, delicate features and a frail constitution. Thad Junior had wanted a rough-and-tumble son who would ride and hunt with him, but young William was taken over by his mother and maternal grandmother, protected from the rigors of childhood, given piano and violin lessons, and educated by private tutors.

The son Thad Junior wanted was finally born five years later, on July 22, 1901. But it wasn't a male child. It was a sturdy, energetic, athletically inclined daughter. Named Florence Leontine after her mother and paternal grandmother, she inherited her broad shoulders, short, thick neck, and overly round face from the Dobbins side. From the Lowes she got her brashness, her sense of adventure, and her theatricality. From the beginning, Thad Junior and his father, old Professor Lowe, treated her like a boy.

The years after little Florence's birth were hard ones for the old man. He had lost his railroad. He had lost his mansion on South Orange Grove Avenue. Although he had not given up—he continued to work on wild, visionary ideas like the Lowe Planet Airship and an aerial, peak-to-peak tramway in the mountains—he was now in his mid-seventies, and there was little hope, given his past financial problems, of raising funds for a major project. But here was little Florence, fearless, with the fierce energy and insatiable curiosity of the young. She was his antidote to old age and disappointment. He loved to spend time with her, and she, in turn, idolized him. They were inseparable for the first ten years of her life.

But in the fall of 1911, while visiting one of his daughters in Norristown, Pennsylvania, Thaddeus Lowe fell and broke his hip when crossing the railroad tracks. (The irony was lost on his family.) The fracture refused to mend; he was bedridden in his daughter's home and too weak to return to California when he received another blow: the news of Leontine's death in May 1912. His condition worsened, although he was finally transported back to Pasadena later that year. Then, on January 16, 1913, at the age of eighty, old Professor Lowe died. Florence was then eleven and a half, old enough to understand the hole her grandfather's death would leave in her life.

Twenty years before, Thaddeus had been one of the richest men in one of the richest towns in America. When he died, his entire estate consisted of four Civil War medals, a sword and scabbard, a pistol, a watch, two gold-headed canes, and a single share of stock in the Pasadena Land and Water Company. The estate's total value was $299. After the funeral costs, his children were left with a $700 debt.

The legacy he left his favorite granddaughter, Florence, was not money but rather a way of living in the world. He was a man of bold vision, with a flair for the dramatic, who did not know, or chose to ignore, when enough was enough. He was a man inspired by challenges that dissuaded others and should have dissuaded him. He was, as a California historian once wrote, "supremely interested in doing the things that everybody said could not be done." He was a true showman, from his days as a touring, crowd-pleasing Professor of Chemistry to his years of elaborate business ventures and lavish living. He put on a great show at great expense.

Thaddeus Sobieski Constantine Lowe was that most American of characters: both a self-made and a self-*un*made man. His granddaughter would follow in his footsteps.

2

An Overexuberance of Spirit

Old Professor Lowe may have outrun his fortune by the time little Florence was born, but Thad Junior had grown up on Millionaires' Row, in a world of liveried servants and lavish parties. In his twenties and early thirties, he had managed a business that sold his father's patented odorless Lowe Heaters from a retail outlet in Pasadena's Opera House. He had been part of the excitement of Mount Lowe Railroad and its many development schemes. Those businesses were gone, leaving Thad with neither occupation nor livelihood. But he did have a wealthy wife, and, courtesy of the Dobbins money, he was able to continue living the life of landed gentry. He raised Thoroughbreds and harness horses on the estate grounds and bred bantams for cockfighting. He went deer hunting up in the Sierras and fishing in the wild mountain rivers. On farmland in Cherry Valley, east of Los Angeles, he raised registered dairy cows and experimented with cheese making, bred goats and chickens, and conducted amateur horticultural research. He and his wife, Florence Mae, were pillars of Pasadena society. He was a member of the building committee that erected the impressive new St. James Episcopal Church. She was the founder of the St. James Women's Guild.

Their new home reflected their place in the Southern California aristocracy. Caroline Dobbins had at first built her daughter and son-in-law a modest house in San Marino, an enclave of large estates bordering the city of Pasadena. Eight years later, when little Florence was two, Caroline replaced that home with a three-story, thirty-five-room mansion more befitting her daughter's station. The new place featured eighteen-foot ceilings, English wood paneling, hand-carved moldings, and a massive crystal chandelier. A harpsichord chime called the family to meals. Upstairs, the baths were marble and the spigots were silver. Outside, a spacious patio surrounded a circular pool dotted with water lilies. The estate had tennis courts, stables, and a three-quarter-mile exercise riding ring.

It was here, on South Garfield Avenue in San Marino, that Florence lived her Gilded Age childhood. The family took their breakfast in the breakfast room, their lunch in the luncheon room, and their dinner in the formal dining salon, butlers standing by their elbows to serve from sterling silver platters. Surrounded by a battalion of servants who kept the house and the estate running smoothly, Florence never had to pick up after herself. She never had to draw her own bath or brush her own hair. Instead, she was coddled by maids and doted on by her father and grandfather. She got what she wanted when she wanted it.

When she was three, her father bought her a pony. By the time she was four, she was a competent rider. For her fifth birthday, Thad presented her with a Thoroughbred. That year she won the first of her many equestrian trophies, competing at the first annual Pasadena Horse Show. Her father taught her to handle harness horses. He hired an instructor from Anaheim to teach her how to ride five-gaited horses, another instructor for reined and hackamore horses, and a third for jumping horses. Florence could ride on her parents' estate as well as on Grandmother Dobbins's land, where there was also a stable of fine horses and trails ran up the hills and down the arroyo.

It was in many ways the kind of life little girls dream of, a pampered, carefree, storybook girlhood. But not far beneath the surface, there were problems. While the old Professor took her on junkets every weekend, and her father enthusiastically oversaw her education on horseback and encouraged her love of animals, Florence got scant attention from her mother and Grandmother Dobbins. They were busy tending to and hovering over her older brother, William Emmert, who battled illness all through his childhood, finally succumbing to leukemia when Florence was twelve. Even when the women weren't consumed with caring for William, they spent little time with Florence. She was a mystery to them, a little girl who had no interest in being a little girl, a little girl who would rather wear muddy riding clothes than beautiful frocks, who would rather go fishing with her father than learn embroidery from her mother.

Florence wanted her mother's attention, as all children want their mother's attention, but as a little girl, she didn't know how to get it. She couldn't compete with her brother—that, she realized early on—but she also couldn't seem to find any place in her mother's heart. What she was good at, what she loved, the kind of girl she was, either by genetic predisposition or by encouragement, her mother didn't understand or even like. Florence felt the distance and the disapproval, and she mirrored it. The life she saw her mother and grandmother leading was so much less interesting than the life her father and grandfather led. Why would she want to be like the women, fussing with their clothes, arranging dinner parties, sitting quietly to drink tea, overseeing servants, when she could be riding and fishing, running through the hills, rolling in the grass with her dogs? Florence rejected her mother's life even as she sought her mother's love. The two, mother and daughter, had little to bind them but this, their mutual rejection, and their silent longing for each other's respect. Florence grew up a rough-and-tumble child ignored by her mother and encouraged, then indulged, and finally spoiled by the men in the family, who could not set limits for her, or did not know how to.

In a time and place where beauty mattered, she was also not a pretty girl. The upper-class world she was born into valued sweet-tempered young ladies with alabaster skin, delicate features, elaborate upswept hairdos, and wasp waists. Florence had none of these. She was swarthy and rugged, with skin that tanned to bronze and straight, almost black hair that she wore short and slicked back. Like her mother, she had a big nose, fleshy cheeks, and a short, thick neck. "Poor Florence," her cousins would say behind her back, "she has that *neck*." She had the broad-shouldered, slim-hipped body of a boy. She looked good in jodhpurs and odd in a dress.

As she grew older, Florence saw herself as she was. She was a smart girl, smart enough to know that society gave a homely girl only two choices: She could retreat into herself, shoulders hunched, eyes downcast, taking up as little room and making as little noise as possible, a walking apology for her lack of conventional beauty, timid, grateful for any attention others might give her. Or, with apologies to no one, she could come out swinging. Early on, she made her choice.

She grew up tracking mud and manure across the imported carpets and through the elegant rooms of the family mansion, terrorizing the servants who attempted to rein her in. From the stableboys, she learned to spit and curse. She grabbed any opportunity to defy convention. At a horse show in Sacramento, she took an instant dislike to one of the other girls, the daughter of the governor of California, a young lady too prim and proper for Florence's tastes. They were both to compete in a jumping event the following day, Florence astride a stallion named Dream of Love, the governor's daughter riding a mare called Lover's Dream. At midnight that night, Florence, naked except for her fancy English riding boots, mounted her horse. She roared through the stables and around the arena, yelling, "Oh Lover's Dream, slow down, slow down!" Everyone who heard her—and she made sure everyone heard her—thought she was the governor's daughter. Immensely pleased with herself, she put the horse away and enjoyed the rest of the competition.

At age eight, after being tutored at home for a few years, Florence started school. At Pasadena Elementary, a public school across the street from the California Institute of Technology, she fit in well with her classmates. She was the only girl among twenty-three boys. She tried to outrun and outshout them in the fields, spitting, cursing, roughhousing, and initiating or joining in their pranks. The rougher the game, the better she liked it. She was popular with the boys, the center of attention. Her behavior became so outrageous that even her mother, who generally ignored her, and her father, who indulged her, realized that something must be done. But they didn't know how, or didn't care, to do it themselves.

In a large, pretty house on a tree-lined street just off Orange Grove Avenue, Miss Mary L. Ranney had just opened a private girls' school with twenty-one pupils, all daughters of Pasadena high society. The parents of the first pupils wanted their daughters to get a basic education before they were sent off to finishing school. Miss Ranney, a forward-thinking English major from the University of Chicago, had other ideas. She wanted the girls to go on to college. At Miss Ranney's, soon to be known as Westridge School for Girls, the pupils dressed in uniforms of white middy blouses and long dark skirts. They studied French verbs on the front porch and read history on the stair landing.

Very little of this interested Florence, but she buckled down during her first year, eighth grade, and maintained a B average. The next year, her grades fell to D's and F's, and she started getting into more and more trouble, along with her cousins Dean and Carolyn Banks, whose estate bordered the Lowes'. The three secreted themselves in the basement of the mansion or out in the stables, experimenting with smoking and drinking and managing to get into whatever mischief they could. Thad and Florence Mae could have paid attention to what their daughter was doing. They could have confronted her. They could have established rules and made an effort to enforce them. Instead, they transferred her to a stricter school, a Catholic boarding school, hoping the more confining atmosphere would keep her in check.

Ramona Convent, run by the Sisters of the Holy Name, was set high on a hill in neighboring Alhambra. It had been started when a wealthy local family with a misbehaving daughter couldn't find a nearby Catholic school. Rather than send the girl far away, they donated land to the church and helped establish the convent. Not every Ramona student was there because her family believed she needed a firm hand, but many were.

The school served 150 boarders, mostly the daughters of wealthy local families, but the nuns also took a number of day students. They created a strict environment and expected the convent girls to look and act like Victorian ladies. Students wore white uniforms with high-collared, puffed-sleeved blouses and floor-length skirts. The nuns gave lessons in courtesy, deportment, and manners. Merits and demerits were carefully recorded on each student's report card. Good behavior earned a student a ribbon of merit or a pin of recognition. If the reward system didn't work, parents were called in. If a girl didn't start behaving quickly, she was asked to leave.

The nuns maintained high academic standards as well, teaching English, math, history, and foreign languages in addition to religion. To cultivate the finer instincts, there were piano lessons, choral practice, and instruction on the hand painting of china.

Florence became a Ramona boarder for the 1916 and 1917 school years; Carolyn Banks was also enrolled. Florence was not an eager student. In a photograph taken of her class, the young ladies sit primly facing forward, their hair prettied with bonnets and bows, their eyes looking into the camera, at once demure and expectant, their hands clasped on their laps. Florence sits at an angle. One of her arms is flung over a porch railing. Her dark hair is slicked back straight from her brow. She casts a sidelong glance at the camera, her lips curled in a small, wry smile.

During her second year at Ramona Convent, she ran away on horseback to Tijuana. She loved excitement. She loved making waves, loved knowing that her school friends were talking about her, whispering about her behavior, as envious as they were scandalized. She also knew she had grabbed her parents' attention in a big way. This was bolder than flunking classes, bigger than sneaking cigarettes with her cousins. She waited for the reaction from her distant mother and her overindulgent father. She must have been disappointed when all they did was find another school for her, enrolling her as a full-time boarder.

Bishop School in La Jolla, Florence's fourth school in eight years, was run by the Episcopal church. The girls lived two to a room on the second floor of a long concrete building. In warm weather, they slept on cots set side by side on an awning-shaded porch. The accommodations were far more rustic than Florence was used to, but it was the social rituals of her new home that she found the hardest to accept. There was hymn singing in the living room after dinner, Sunday tea in the parlor, white-glove dress-up luncheons in the village, and chaperoned visits to the cove for discreet bathing. There were little crustless sandwiches eaten at proper picnics, the girls shading their faces from the sun with bonnets and umbrellas. There was the election of the May Queen, with prancing around a beribboned pole.

Florence was assigned to room with Ursula Greenshaw, two years her senior, a superior student whom the headmistress had handpicked to help set an example for girls who, like Florence, found it difficult to comply with the rules and standards of Bishop School. Greenshaw, who went on to graduate from Vassar and then earn a medical degree, tried her best to be a suitable role model, but Florence was Florence; Ursula could only look on with a mixture of disapproval and detached amusement. Living with Florence for two years was an education.

Having grown up in an Episcopalian household, with her grandmother Dobbins, her mother, and her father all pillars of the church, Florence had little trouble with the religious reverence required by the school. It was everything else she rebelled against—all social conventions, and especially all attempts to encourage femininity. During one visit, Florence's mother brought her a box of delicate, hand-sewn lingerie imported from France. Florence saw it not as a thoughtful gift, which it may or may not have been, but rather as another rejection of who she was, a frilly symbol of her mother's dissatisfaction. She waited until her mother left the room, then kicked the box and sent it flying. Sometime later, when she was looking for a rag to polish her riding boots, she rummaged around for the box, grabbed the lingerie, and used that.

Florence loved pranks, the bigger, the more shocking, the better. One night Ursula came into their room and stumbled over a body sprawled on the floor. When she switched on the light, she found her roommate lying in a pool of blood, a suicide note pinned to her blouse with a dagger. The blood, it turned out, was only red ink, but in those first few seconds of shock when Ursula stared speechless at her roommate's body, Florence enjoyed herself immensely.

Another time, Ursula opened the door to find Florence's favorite horse, Dobbins, calmly standing in the middle of the dorm room. When Florence was ushered into the headmistress's office to explain, she feigned surprise and innocence, expressing sympathy for the horse, which her parents had brought from San Marino to be stabled in the nearby village. "Poor Dobbins," she told the headmistress. "He must have been so lonesome that he even came upstairs to find me." Florence's interests during her Bishop School days, her roommate wryly noted, "were largely confined to horses."

She managed to make it through two years at the boarding school, thanks mainly to the position of her family, and in June 1919 she joined her class for graduation ceremonies. The speaker that year was a man barely ten years older than the girls he was addressing, a man just at the beginning of a promising career in the Episcopal church. His name was Calvin Rankin Barnes. He had a strong jaw, a high forehead, and classic, even features. The girls whispered to one another as he took the podium: What a fine man he was, how handsome he was. Florence barely noticed. To her, the graduation ceremony meant only one thing: freedom. Now she could do what she really wanted to do. Or so she thought.

3

An Imaginable Future

What eighteen-year-old Florence wanted to do was become a veterinarian. She loved horses and had been around them all her life. She loved herding cattle with her father at their Cherry Valley ranch. She loved dogs. But when her mother heard of these intentions, she moved quickly to divert her daughter into a more ladylike enterprise. Florence enjoyed drawing and sketching, a hobby she picked up from her father, who amused himself with pen-and-ink landscapes. She was therefore promptly enrolled in the Stickney School of Art, a high-toned Pasadena institution that attracted accomplished visiting artists to further the artistic aspirations of wealthy local matrons. There Florence studied painting, for which she had some talent but little passion. She was eighteen, living in her parents' home with no money of her own. She had little choice but to go along with her mother's decisions, even as she continued to resist the role her mother so fervently wanted her to play, that of a Pasadena debutante.

Childhood rebellion was one thing. It might be dismissed as an overexuberance of spirit, the uninhibited romping of an overindulged little girl. But as she grew older, her brash ways became increasingly unacceptable to her mother and increasingly at odds with decorous, stiff-necked Pasadena society. Her parents conferred about Florence's future, searching once again for a way of dealing with their daughter's rebellion without dealing with their daughter. Where school had failed, perhaps marriage would succeed. At any rate, if she was married, she would no longer be the Lowes' responsibility.

It was Caroline Dobbins who came up with what she thought would be a good match for her granddaughter: The rector of St. James Episcopal Church in South Pasadena. He was an attractive young bachelor whose intelligent sermons and charming manners were the talk of the congregation, particularly the young, unmarried women. His bearing was noble. His comportment was beyond reproach. He was C. Rankin Barnes, the same man who had delivered the speech at Florence's graduation ceremony.

A more upright and solid citizen would have been difficult to find. The dutiful son of a minister—his father was rector of San Diego's largest Episcopal church—he had graduated from Berkeley and gone east to seminary school. Back in California, he had served as a vicar at one church before assuming his position at St. James a year before. In Pasadena and South Pasadena, St. James was the society church. The same people who rode at the Hunt Club and danced at the cotillions and frequented the Cal Tech lectures sat in the pews of St. James every Sunday morning. Caroline Dobbins was a major donor to the church. Her money would finance an impressive new bell tower. The Lowes were prominent members of the congregation.

The Reverend Barnes did not have money. He did not have the social standing of the best families of Pasadena. But he had the prestige of his position and the kind of staid respectability the Lowes hoped would rub off on their daughter. Here was a man who just might be able to keep Florence under control. Caroline approached the young rector with an offer of an arranged marriage, and, after a brief period of deliberation during which he must have considered Caroline Dobbins's stature in the church, he saw the wisdom of the union.

Florence could not have been thrilled at the prospect of marriage, but she had her own reasons to agree. She knew that while she was still in her parents' household she would never be allowed to be whoever it was she wanted to be. With a new husband, even one so upright and proper, she might have a fighting chance to exert her independence. Florence was also, underneath her brashness, a young woman still looking for the approval of her mother. William Emmert had been her mother's favorite. Perhaps marrying the kind of man her brother might have become would bring her closer to her mother, bring her the love and acceptance she would never admit she needed.

Marriage was also one of her few imaginable futures. Florence was a young woman with wealth and standing but limited options. Careers were almost unheard of for women of her time and class. Her mother had already rejected her idea of becoming a veterinarian. What else was there but marriage? The question remaining was to whom. Florence may not have been as captivated by the Reverend Barnes as some of the other young ladies in the congregation, but she took note of his good looks and saw how others respected him. She admired him, too, and during their carefully orchestrated seventeen-month courtship, she even began to think they had something in common.

Intent on seeing the match work, Florence's mother arranged early-morning horseback rides for her daughter and the Reverend Barnes. Before breakfast, when the air was fresh and clear, the two set off across the Lowes' estate, following bridle trails through the tall oaks. They rode in companionable silence, she relaxed and loose in the saddle, he stiffer, less comfortable. But they were outdoors, on horses, and Florence was happy and willing to believe it would always be this way. When they returned to the house, the servants had an elegant breakfast waiting. They ate while Florence's mother hovered over them, sparking conversation. Her mother had never before paid such attention to Florence, and she reveled in it.

Florence was still going to classes at the Stickney School of Art, painting in oil and studying under Guy Rose, an artist of some repute in America and Europe. But in the fall of 1920, at her mother's request, she left Stickney. She would be too busy with wedding plans to continue her lessons. There were bridal gown fittings, trousseau fittings, luncheons, showers, and teas. Becoming Mrs. C. Rankin Barnes would take all her time.

If she had serious doubts about the marriage, they were lost in the swirl of wedding activity eagerly generated by her mother. For the first time in many years, perhaps even since her daughter, at three, learned to ride a horse, Florence Mae felt part of her life. Their interests had been as different as their personalities, the mother a proper society woman concerned with maintaining decorum and doing good works, the daughter a headstrong tomboy with a passion for horses and pranks. But now they had a common goal: the planning and execution of a wedding worthy of the Pasadena Lowes. It took them many months.

Meanwhile, Florence and Rankin were whisked from party to party—a theater outing thrown by friends in Los Angeles, intimate dinners, a formal luncheon at the Valley Hunt Club, hosted by the Lowes. Florence's cousins and friends threw her showers. Her former classmates at Westridge School for Girls gave a tea in her honor. The excitement continued through the mild California fall and early winter, until just after the new year. At noon on January 5, 1921, at the altar of St. James Church in South Pasadena, the groom's father officiated as Florence Leontine Lowe and Calvin Rankin Barnes exchanged vows.

St. James looked more like a greenhouse than a church that after-noon, with massive floral arrangements banking an altar draped with white roses. Sweet pea and heather adorned the pews. Palm fronds and ferns decorated the walls. The bride and her party cradled enormous bouquets of roses and lilies of the valley. Florence wore a tea-length white satin gown with organza ruffles and a boat neck that had the un-fortunate effect of setting off her least attractive feature. She wore a stiff, crownlike headpiece from which flowed yards and yards of tulle netting that arranged itself like fog around her feet. The groom was in his ministerial best, facing his father and flanked by his tuxedoed younger brother. Outside the church, all the chauffeured automobiles in town were lined up for blocks.

After the ceremony, the guests made their way to the Lowes' mansion for an elaborate reception. As the orchestra played in the dining salon, a stag line formed in the foyer to kiss the bride. Except for a few pecks planted on her cheek by her fiancé, Florence had never been kissed before. The men on the stag line took their responsibilities seriously, delivering impassioned, openmouthed kisses that took the new bride by surprise. Apparently, there was more to men than she had thought. The party continued throughout the long afternoon with champagne toasts from handblown crystal goblets, music, dancing, and platter after platter of hors d'oeuvres carefully selected by the bride's mother. Finally it was time to toss the bouquet and disappear upstairs to change into the blue two-piece suit that the tailors had spent weeks shaping to her broad-shouldered measurements.

The couple drove to San Bernardino that evening, where they stayed at the Riverside Inn. As her mother had instructed her, Florence retired to the bathroom connected to their suite and carefully dressed herself in a handmade lace and satin nightgown, part of the trousseau she and her mother had spent months putting together. She thought it was almost too beautiful to wear to bed, more like a ball gown than sleeping attire. She was uncomfortable and nervous anyway on her wedding night, but the nightgown made the feeling worse. Florence had always worn plain cotton pajamas.

When she emerged from the bathroom, her husband, equally nervous, looked her over from head to foot, admired her nightgown, and then asked her if she would mind taking it off. He had never seen an unclothed woman before, he told her, and he figured his wedding night was a good time to start. Florence might have seen the humor in this had she not been so completely mortified. She quickly slipped into the large bed, turned away from her husband, and refused to let Rankin touch her. The two lay stiff and awake waiting for their first night together to end.

The next day, they boarded the *Southwest Chief* to the Grand Canyon and, in their sleeping compartment with its separate upper and lower berths, were spared second- and third-night attempts at intimacy. But the following evening, when they had arrived at their honeymoon destination and had dined formally at the hotel Florence's mother had selected, Rankin steered his bride back to their room. It was a long walk.

"We have been married now for four days," he informed her after he closed the door behind them. "Please take off your clothes and get into bed."

Florence put on another one of her fancy trousseau nightgowns, got into bed, and waited with her eyes closed, as awkward and embarrassed as she had been on the first night. Rankin was no better. He fumbled around under her nightgown. She thought he seemed like an inexperienced doctor. Finally, after a few more minutes of fumbling, Florence felt a pain between her legs. She opened her eyes and saw that her husband looked pale and miserable, more pained than she was.

"I do not like sex," he told her. "It makes me nervous. I see nothing to it, and I do not wish to have any more of it."

Florence got out of bed, took off her nightgown, and rinsed the blood from it in a basin. Then she put on a pair of pajamas she had sneaked into her trousseau and climbed back in. Neither of them ever talked about that night, nor did they repeat it.

After their honeymoon, the couple moved into the modest rectory attached to St. James. For a young woman accustomed to life in a thirty-five-room mansion where servants outnumbered family, the church's small quarters were an unhappy, unsettling change. The Reverend and Mrs. Barnes would be living on a stipend of $1,800 a year. There would be no servants. Florence would have to cook and care for her own home, duties she knew little and cared less about. She had not thought of this during the courtship, had not considered what being married actually meant when one's husband had little money. At home now in the rectory, she was just beginning to understand what life might be like when she discovered she was pregnant. Rankin seemed happy. Her mother was overjoyed. Florence, nineteen years old and six weeks married, was less sure.

Through the spring and summer, as her belly grew, so did her ambivalence concerning motherhood. She stayed away from Rankin and the rectory, spending most of her time on her parents' estate, where she rode horses, always accompanied by her favorite dog, a big German shepherd named Nix. At least pregnancy had this benefit. She was living her old life again. When she got too big to ride, she allowed her mother to interest her in hand-sewing a layette for the baby. Florence Mae was concerned and attentive, and it helped pass the time. When the days grew uncomfortably warm and humid, she took up temporary residence at her mother's summer house in Laguna Beach on a cliff overlooking Emerald Bay. Her grandmother Dobbins had bought twenty acres out there years before and had built both herself and her daughter homes on the promontory to catch the cooling sea breezes. Florence stayed there through the worst heat of the Southern California summer.

On October 9, 1921, nine months and a day after her first and only intimacy with her husband, she gave birth to a nine-pound boy at Pasadena's Good Samaritan Hospital. It was not an easy birth—after a long labor, doctors had to pull out the baby with forceps—but William Emmert Barnes, named after Florence's long-dead brother, was a healthy child. Some women gaze into the eyes of their newborns and feel a bond closer than any other they will ever feel. But the birth of a child does not automatically transform every laboring woman into a loving mother, and it did not transform Florence into one. She had never been mothered by her own mother. She had grown up encouraged in male pursuits, disdainful of women's roles, and accountable to no one. She had married without love and had conceived without passion. When she looked at William Emmert—Billy, she would call him—she saw a responsibility she was temperamentally unwilling and emotionally unable to accept. In the hospital, the nurses took care of him, except at feeding time, while Florence spent her days of recuperation worrying about Nix, the big police dog that had been her constant companion.

She missed him terribly, she told the nurses. She needed him with her, she told her mother. She became more and more agitated. Nix was her link to her old life. She needed him to help her remember who she was, now that she was suddenly also someone else, a mother. After some hasty negotiation, the hospital superintendent, bowing to the wishes of her wealthy clientele, allowed Nix to stay in the room. Florence would lie still, her arm hanging down out of the bed, her fingers trailing back and forth, Nix nuzzling her hand with his wet nose. He was alert to any visitors and retreated under the bed only after he saw that his mistress was in no danger.

Florence worried about what Nix would think of the baby. When she felt well enough to leave her bed, she put the infant on a blanket and let the dog nose him over. Florence Mae looked on, horrified. The dog could have killed little Billy easily and swiftly. But Nix sniffed a few times and returned to Florence's side. Perhaps he realized that Billy was not and would never be a serious competitor for his mistress's attention.

When she left the hospital, Florence went to her parents' home, not her husband's. At the Lowes', she slept in her own room, attended by servants. Billy was cared for by nurses her mother hired. But Rankin wanted her back. She was his wife, and she and Billy should be with him in the rectory. He was determined that she live the life of a minister's wife, on a minister's salary.

4

Becoming Pancho

That she settle into a quiet, predictable routine, days filled with caring for an infant and keeping house, weekends ordered by the social obligations of a minister's wife—this was asking too much of twenty-year-old Florence Lowe Barnes. This new life made little sense to her. Not that she thought of her situation that way. She was not a reflective person. She was a doer. What she felt, nursing Billy in the small living room of the St. James rectory, was a restlessness so intense that she could barely contain it.

For a short while, she tried to play the part she had been assigned. As was expected of the minister's wife, she taught a Sunday school class. But when her group of nine-year-old boys proved resistant to her teachings, she bribed them with pocketknives to learn the catechism. She acted as a hostess at various church-related ladies' affairs, but often ended up scandalizing members of the congregation by telling risqué stories of her teenage adventures, her conversation interspersed with mild profanity. She did this intentionally. She did it to shock, to separate herself from the good, sober Episcopalian women sitting so straight in their chairs, drinking their tea from china cups. She did it to keep her sense of self intact.

As the months went by, she discovered something about her husband that she hadn't suspected. She had known that women liked him. She'd known since she heard the whispers of her classmates the day he delivered her high school graduation speech that women found him handsome. What she hadn't known, and now came to realize, was the extent to which Rankin enjoyed the attention of his female parishioners. He would receive a call late at night. One of his congregation, invariably a woman, needed him. There was a problem she needed to talk to him about, a spiritual crisis she was experiencing, some difficulty only he could help resolve. Could he come right over? Yes, Rankin would always say, he'd be there immediately. He told Florence to dress and get the baby ready, and together they drove in their little car to the house of the troubled woman. Florence was directed to wait in the car; she never came inside. She was needed to provide Rankin with an out. "If any of the women wish to make an advance toward me," he told her, "I will tell them my wife is out waiting in the car." Rankin thrived on the attention of his female parishioners but in no way wanted to compromise his position with unseemly entanglements.

Florence saw that her husband was busy and popular, that the life he lived brought him distinction and prestige. He was satisfied. She, increasingly, intensely, was not. Once again, as she had done during her pregnancy, she began to spend more time at her parents' estate, with her horses and her big dog Nix. She began to look around for something that would relieve the boredom of her life, something that would offer the fun, the excitement—and the money—she was used to.

She found it a few miles to the southwest, in Hollywood, in the fast-paced world of the motion-picture industry. By the early twenties, the movie colony was already well established. United Artists, Metro-Goldwyn-Mayer, and Universal topped the list of almost two dozen enterprises clustered between Hollywood Boulevard and Melrose, devoted to making everything from serials to two-reelers to million-dollar feature-length extravaganzas. The studio system was already firmly in place, but the industry was young, fluid, dynamic. It was still a seat-of-the-pants operation where today's prop boy could be tomorrow's director. Some studios produced elaborate costumers shot on location, like M-G-M's *The Arab*, starring the exotic Ramon Novarro. Others, like Universal, specialized in cheap-to-script, cheap-to-shoot Westerns, known in the trade as horse operas. At Universal, they also called them red feather releases, and they shot them in the nearby Calabasas Hills, terrain that looked more like the snakebit Arizona Territory than like Southern California. Successful horse operas depended on well-trained horses, and here Florence found her niche.

It happened that she knew one of the top directors at Universal at the time, the immensely talented and equally dictatorial Erich von Stroheim. Before his 1919 debut as writer-director-star of Universal's highly successful sex farce *Blind Husbands*, he had worked in stables in and around La Jolla, where Florence met him while she was a boarding school student. It was probably through this connection that she landed her first Hollywood job, renting out her gray gelding Platinum King for cowboy movies. Behind the camera, sitting on her little black horse Buster, Florence whistled and coaxed PK through the scenes. There was nothing the horse wouldn't do for her. She had trained him so that he would gallop up to a stagecoach, keep pace with it, allow an actor to drop down into the saddle, and then gallop away, all with perfect timing for the camera. Eventually she was allowed to shoot second camera on quickie horse operas, traveling all over the Calabasas Hills with a heavy Bell & Howell on her shoulder. She doubled as a horseback rider in some scenes. She worked as a script girl. In *The Lighthouse by the Sea*, filmed at Laguna Beach, she doubled for the actress Louise Fazenda, landing the job through the director, Malcolm St. Clair, a Pasadena society friend of the family. Even Nix landed a few roles.

Florence was caught up in the excitement of making movies. She was a minor player, but the line between minor and major players was blurry in those days, especially in the world of quickie Westerns. She began to meet fascinating people, from the cinematographer Gordon Pollack, who intrigued her with his discussions of Freudian psychoanalysis, to the suave stuntman John Weld, who loved to party almost as much as she did, to the darkly handsome actor Ramon Novarro. She worked in the movies only a few days a month, but those few days changed her life dramatically. But even more than the fun she had, even more than the friendships she made, what attracted her was the money.

Florence was paid a hundred dollars a day for working with horses, plus extra when she doubled or helped shoot the movie. With this money, she immediately hired a cook, a housekeeper, and a full-time nurse for the baby. Now life began to resemble her carefree childhood again. When she wasn't out in the hills making movies, she would leave Billy with his nurse and go riding on the bridle paths at her parents' and grandmother's estates. She spent a great deal of time jumping, which was her specialty, and rejoined the horse show circuit. There her equestrian talents landed her a job as a riding double for the evangelist Aimee Semple McPherson. As an adjunct to her preaching at the International Church of the Foursquare Gospel, McPherson made the rounds of the horse shows, roping in sinners by parading around the arena in sidesaddle-riding attire and a high silk hat on a dapple-gray gelding named Radiant. She would circle the ring once, stopping often to lean down and talk with people, then lead Radiant out of sight into an entrance tunnel where Florence, dressed in an identical riding habit and silk hat, would switch places with her. Astride Radiant, Florence galloped around the ring in perfect form as the crowd applauded her skill. McPherson paid her well for the stunt.

At the Los Angeles Ambassador Show, the most elegant of the upper-crust equestrian events, men in tuxedos and women in evening gowns sat in decorated boxes to watch Florence and other top riders coax their horses up and over the challenging obstacle course. Florence's mother came to the shows, gasping audibly each time her daughter rode a horse over a jump. Florence could hear it from the stands, and it annoyed her every time.

Her relationship with her mother, never close, was newly strained now that Florence made little attempt to play the minister's wife. Still, when Florence Mae, not yet fifty years old, suffered a stroke and died suddenly in the spring of 1923, her daughter was distraught. The shock was amplified when Thad quickly attached himself to an energetic outdoorswoman only three years older than his daughter. Florence's health was shaken. At first, the doctors called her problem a "nervous breakdown," because that's what women were said to be having in those days when they took to their beds. Later they said the trouble was a serious heart condition that she probably would not survive. In fact, undiagnosed like her mother, Florence was already suffering from severe high blood pressure. It caused weakness and palpitations and kept her in bed, attended by a full-time nurse.

She had always been proud of her physical strength, bragging to her girlhood friends about how fast she could run, bragging to her movie acquaintances about the heavy equipment she could carry. She had taken her physical strength for granted, just as she had long depended on her strength of will. She could not believe either would fail her, even as she lay grieving for her mother and seriously ill, immobile in her childhood bed. She had an abiding confidence in herself that Grandfather Lowe had seeded and nourished. She called on that confidence when, after weeks of lying in bed being told she was critically and perhaps fatally ill, she simply stopped listening, got up out of her sickbed, and ran away from home.

That was how she thought of it, even at age twenty-two, that she was running away from home. She went alone, traveling across the United States by train, writing only sporadic postcards home. At first, when she exerted herself at all, just climbing stairs or walking the length of the train, she was pale and breathless. But she kept on the move, increasingly enjoying her solitary cross-country adventure, and slowly, her strength returned. She was convinced she had cured her incurable heart disease, and this gave her more confidence than ever. It may be that she reduced the stress in her life and thereby lowered her blood pressure. When she finally returned to Pasadena some months later, she was as healthy as she had ever been and ready to resume the exciting life she had begun to create for herself.

Now that life would be richer materially, thanks to the money and property she would inherit from her mother. Florence Mae's personal estate included the San Marino mansion and the Laguna Beach house—both of which her mother, Caroline Dobbins, had given her—plus various pieces of real estate in and around Los Angeles that she had acquired herself. As the only child, Florence inherited these substantial holdings immediately upon her mother's death. But there were greater riches to come, because Florence Mae had been in line to inherit one-fifth of her own father's estate after Caroline Dobbins died. Now that future share went to Florence. She was not yet a millionairess, but she was independently wealthy. With her money and her servants, her health and her self-confidence, it seemed she could do anything she wanted.

Hollywood continued to interest her, not for the hundred dollars a day anymore, but for the excitement, for the physical challenge, and for the company of men. She had spent very little time and shared very little intimacy with her own husband, but she realized, from watching others, from their easy way together, from their talk, their touches, their jokes, that there was far more to such relationships than she knew. She thought about sex, about why other people seemed to enjoy it so much while her own experiences were limited and so negative. All around her, Victorian morals were under assault. The new young women of the Roaring Twenties acted like Florence in many ways: They wore pants, they smoked in public, they were brash and assertive. But they kissed their men casually; they threw petting parties, the new indoor sport of the Jazz Age; they flaunted their sexuality. "I've kissed dozens of men," one of F. Scott Fitzgerald's heroines brazenly confessed, "and I suppose I'll kiss dozens more." Florence had kissed one man, and had not had much fun doing it. But she still remembered the thrill of those stag-line kisses at her wedding. Leaving Rankin at the rectory and Billy with his nurse, she went looking for, as she put it, "someone to discover all the mysteries with."

She had attached herself to a group of Pomona College students, friends of one of her cousins. She invited them to the newly inherited Laguna Beach house, a perfect spot for long weekends of drinking, dancing, and necking. One of the students in particular, a young man named Bill, appealed to her. Like Florence, he was both inexperienced and eager not to be. So, while the Reverend Barnes tended to his church duties, Florence dated Bill. They went on short trips together. They spent a great deal of time at the beach house, holding hands, kissing, and talking about—but not engaging in—sex. Florence thought she was in love with Bill and would have sought a divorce had she not felt it would ruin Rankin's career. They may have had an odd and emotionally distant relationship, but Florence liked her husband and still had great respect for him as a church leader. She may also have understood what a peculiarly enviable position she was in: She was a married woman, with the protection of that status if she needed it but none of its responsibilities and few of its limitations.

A year went by before she agreed to go on an overnight trip with Bill to his fraternity cabin on Mount Baldy. Later Florence would not remember what the cabin looked like or whether she and Bill had anything to eat or drink or what they talked about. But she would remember, in detail, their lovemaking. He undressed her slowly, kissing her closed eyes, kissing her shoulders, touching her gingerly, soothing her as if she were a frightened colt. He took her out to the porch, where she stood naked under a full moon in the mountain air, then picked her up in his arms. "I'm going to carry you across the threshold," he told her.

On a bunk in the cabin, he wrapped himself around her, and she finally discovered, after four years of marriage, the joy of sex. They showered together, then went for a midnight hike, then came back and did it all over again. This time Bill did not have to take as long. Florence felt "absolutely heavenly, happy, relaxed, as if I had won a battle or whipped the world." On the way down the mountain the next morning, she could hardly keep her hands off him, and by the time they got to the arroyo near Azusa, they had to turn off the highway. There in the hot sand, just out of view of the road, they made love again. It was only when they were driving through the streets of South Pasadena, a few blocks from the rectory, that Florence allowed herself to remember that she had a husband and a young son. When she thought of them, she thought of them in quotes—as her "so-called family," she said to Bill.

She couldn't go home yet. Bill turned a corner and they drove around all day, stalling, thinking and talking, returning to the rectory long after dinner. There Florence parked Bill in the guest room and went to confront her husband. Rankin greeted her with characteristic equanimity, filling her in on news of the church, the parish, and the household. Florence listened without hearing. When he had finished with his small talk, she told him where she had been the night before, about the cabin on Mount Baldy, and about Bill and her. She didn't spare him much, but she did spare him their tryst in the hot sand of the arroyo.

At first, Rankin didn't believe her. He knew that Florence liked to shock people. Maybe this was her idea of a joke. She insisted, quietly, that it was true. She told him that she knew what she had been doing was wrong but that she wasn't sorry. He had been pacing back and forth as she spoke. Now he sat on a chair and put his face in both hands and sobbed.

"Get rid of him," he told her after he'd gained control of himself. "I never want you to see him again." Taken aback by Rankin's emotional response, feeling guilty if not sorry, she gave him her word.

Early the next morning, she got Bill out of bed and drove him back to campus. They did not see each other for many months—that promise to her husband, she kept—but they wrote every day, their secret letters ferried back and forth by Florence's cousins. She filled her time with horseback riding and shows, with her few days a month of movie work, with as much activity as she could arrange. She was, she now discovered, a woman of strong sexual appetites. Without fulfillment, she found herself in a state of almost unbearable tension.

The day Rankin left for New Orleans on an extended trip for church business, Florence got in her car and drove directly to Pomona, where Bill was still taking classes. He packed his clothes and came back to the rectory with her. There were no neighbors to see them. The church was not in a residential area. Florence's mother was dead, and her father and his new young wife were living far away, on Lake Arrowhead. The only one around to register disapproval of the arrangement was little Billy's nurse, Miss Ketchum, an avid churchgoer and a great admirer of the Reverend Barnes. Soon after Bill moved in, Miss Ketchum packed up little Billy's things and took him out of the rectory and to the house she had previously shared with another of the reverend's admiring female parishioners.

It took Florence four days to realize that her child had been taken away. She and Bill drove to Miss Ketchum's and demanded that Billy come back with them. He had been raised from infancy by his nurse and barely recognized his mother, but he was a dutiful boy, and he went along. But once she had him, Florence had little idea of what to do with him. For a few days, she acted like an overindulgent aunt, buying him cap pistols and every toy he demanded, letting him camp out in the rectory, treating him to a wild and glorious time. But before the week was out, Miss Ketchum was back. She would look the other way with Florence and her lover. She would leave them alone. She couldn't bear to be separated from Billy, and she couldn't stand the thought of the harm his mother was doing him.

Bill and Florence continued their affair for months, quickly changing their living arrangements when Rankin returned. Bill moved to a little house Florence owned, and she visited him there most nights. During the day, they both worked as electrician's helpers for the studios on Poverty Row in Hollywood. In between times, she played at being Mrs. Barnes, society woman and minister's wife. The reverend probably knew of their relationship. It had hurt to find out about it at first, but it was not a hurt that went deep, that cut to the heart. Rankin did not love his wife that way. His feelings were, instead, hurt pride, embarrassment, fear of scandal. Yet as long as Florence could keep her secret life secret, keep her lover away from the house, away from Billy, and away from the small piece of her life that she shared with Rankin, the charade suited them both. For Rankin, life was smoother and less complicated without Florence. For Florence, life was far more exciting without Rankin. But both knew, without discussing it, that divorce was not an option.

With the tacit consent of her husband, with her money and her inherited property and her newly awakened sexuality, Florence began to live an even more exuberant life. At the San Marino mansion and at her oceanfront house, the parties became bigger, louder, longer. During the summer months, the house at Laguna Beach became increasingly popular with the Hollywood set. Florence had many friends in the movie industry now, and they freely availed themselves of her hospitality, enjoying the sea breezes, the free food, and the abundant liquor. Bill was still around, but so was the dashing silent screen actor Ramon Novarro, who lavished Florence with his attention. For a while, a strapping young man from Iowa camped out at San Marino, too. He was playing football for USC on scholarship and having trouble making ends meet. His name was Marion Morrison, and he kept a German shepherd named Duke by his side. Florence's social life was becoming increasingly raucous and increasingly public. Things were getting out of hand. Pasadena was talking. Mrs. Barnes was encouraged to take a long voyage.

In mid-January 1927, she boarded the steamship *Finland* with a first-class ticket for an extended cruise of South America. It was to be a white-glove luxury trip, a floating vacation from her indecorous life, but Florence quickly remade the voyage to her own liking. The ship had barely cleared port before she found herself attracted to a tall, sun-burned Texas oilman named Don Rockwell. They would be friends, fellow adventurers, and lovers for most of the journey. Together they explored the sights of the port cities—Balboa, Panama, Lima, Santiago, Buenos Aires, Rio de Janeiro, Trinidad, and Havana—but they also made their own adventures. When the transfer from one ship to another was delayed, the two, along with a small group of like-minded shipmates, found a tugboat to take them upriver and deep into the jungle. At other ports, Florence and her new friend strayed far from the tourist areas, exploring a leper colony, a snake farm, and the red-light district. They party-hopped through Buenos Aires and Rio.

Don Rockwell had never met a woman like Florence. She was no beauty, but she was so uninhibited, so sexually charged, that she seemed to create a force field of energy and excitement around herself. She was his "jungle kitten," as he wrote in this poem for her:

> *With her tawny satin hide*
> *She would cuddle by my side*
> *Like a jungle kitten purring in the sun*
> *She was heathen; she was hot*
> *She was all that I am not. . . .*
> *With her eager lips and arms*
> *Always quick to prove her charms . . .*

It was not a lovely, lyrical shipboard romance, Florence was quick to tell a friend. It was "an outrageous, vulgar love affair." The two-month cruise, meant to remove her from a life that was becoming too exciting, had the opposite effect.

By early March, the ship was back in the United States, docked in New York harbor. Rather than take the train back west immediately, the two stayed to explore Manhattan together, spending weeks in Greenwich Village among the artists, thinkers, and dissidents who congregated there. When she finally arrived home, Florence had made up her mind about a few things. She immediately arranged to have her parents' San Marino mansion redecorated in Spanish style to reflect her love of the countries she had just visited and her desire to entertain even more lavishly. The newly refurbished home featured a dramatic entryway, flagstoned floors, and ceilings with hand-carved hardwood beams. In the enormous dining room stood an antique Spanish refectory table thirty feet long. In the foyer, there were two Spanish saddles detailed in sterling silver. It was, everyone agreed, one of the showplaces of Southern California, and Florence would be living there. There would be no more pretense of living at the rectory.

She loved her new house, but even before the transformation was complete, she was on to something else.

One evening, she and a few friends were sharing travel stories around the bar in the basement of her Laguna Beach home when someone suggested that they all hire on as crew aboard a South America–bound vessel. It was one of those late-night, alcohol-fueled schemes that usually go nowhere, only this time it went somewhere. The group—a Paramount stuntman, an M-G-M cameraman, a local actor, a Los Angeles lawyer, a Pasadena architect, and a Hollywood dentist, along with Florence, the only woman—located a banana boat, the M/S *Camina*, that regularly sailed from Southern California down the Baja Peninsula and the west coast of Mexico.

Florence went down to the docks at San Pedro to sign on, her hair stuffed under a dirty watch cap that was pulled down over her eyes. She was wearing a man's work shirt a few sizes too large and a pair of grease-stained dungarees. She got on the crew as "Jacob Crane." Her own group of adventurers knew she was a woman, of course, but what the rest of the crew saw was a short, narrow-hipped boy who smoked incessantly, drank whisky (and plenty of it) straight, and cursed like a sailor.

The boat departed San Pedro harbor at dawn and, as soon as it cleared port, the crew took down the U.S. flag and hoisted the colors of Panama. That's when Florence and her friends learned that there were guns and ammunition in the cargo hold, bound for an obscure band of Mexican revolutionaries fighting in the Gomez-Serrano Rebellion. As it turned out, though, it wasn't the payload that got the *Camina* in trouble. It was the chaos that came in the wake of the rebellion.

At the seaport of San Blas, on the west coast of Mexico south of Mazatlán, the ship, having delivered its cargo, was seized by local port authorities. The situation was complicated. Forty bandits were holding the town hostage, demanding an enormous bribe to end their siege and the blockade of the busy harbor. With the rebellion going on elsewhere, there were no federal troops available to defend the town, but the townspeople were not about to give in. From the days of the Spanish conquest, San Blas had been one of the wildest, deadliest seaports on the Pacific. They were used to handling trouble. Soon after the *Camina* made the mistake of dropping anchor in the harbor, armed guards from the town boarded the ship and impounded it, bringing with them all the town's money and valuables, which they hoped to hide from the bandits. The days stretched into a week, then a month, then six weeks, and still the *Camina* was held in the harbor at gunpoint. Some of the crew began to sicken with malaria. Florence was ready to jump ship but could find no one who wanted to risk the bandits in town and the revolutionaries in the countryside.

Late one evening, Florence watched from the shadows as the helmsman huddled with some of his mates. His name was Roger Chute, and he had taken a leave of absence from his job with the California State Fisheries Lab to go on this adventure. Florence saw him giving his personal possessions to the other men and guessed he was getting ready to escape the boat in one of the dinghies. She demanded to come along. Chute, who had discovered a while ago that she was a woman and had the typical sailor's prejudice against women on ships, had not been a friend. He flatly refused. Florence insisted. And so it went until the woman who was used to getting her way got her way.

They escaped at dawn, leaving the rest of the crew on board, rowing to shore, and then setting out along a century-old jungle trail, Roger Chute on an underfed white horse, Florence on a small burro, the proceeds of some fast trading with the locals. All day they worked their way through the dense countryside, fording and swimming rivers as they came to them, trying to avoid both robbers and revolutionaries. At one point, Florence looked up at Roger astride the white horse and had to smile. They were in danger, but she couldn't help it: She was having fun.

"If you don't look just like a modern-day Don Quixote riding such a skate," she teased him.

He looked down at her on the burro and laughed. "In that case, you must be his companion, Pancho."

"You mean Sancho," she corrected him. "Sancho Panza."

"Ah, what the hell, Pancho or Sancho, you fit the bill," Roger said. "From now on I'm calling you Pancho."

They laughed about it and kept riding. But the name stayed in her head. She said it to herself, over and over, "Pancho . . . Pancho . . . Pancho Barnes." She liked how the two names sounded together, a pleasant contradiction, she thought, upbeat, punchy, a name people would notice, not like Florence. It fit her. She liked it.

Together, she and Roger rode east for days until they hit Mexico City, arriving just in time for Cinco de Mayo. There were huge bonfires, noisy parties, and revelers everywhere, but gringos weren't safe on the streets. U.S.–Mexican relations were strained, and Americans were not popular south of the border. But Pancho and Roger had come too far and risked too much to stay holed up in their cheap rooms during the country's biggest, wildest celebration. They went out to mingle in the local cantinas.

Florence was still dressed in her sailor's clothing and so attracted no special attention, but the two were soon recognized as Americans. They noted the hostile looks and the finger-pointing and quickly adopted the strategy of pretending to be Germans, who seemed to be enjoying popularity in the city. As they sat across from each other at a little table in the cantina drinking beer, Roger loudly recited the opening line from a German song, and Pancho countered animatedly with a line from "Lorelei." Then they slapped each other on the back and laughed heartily, as if they had just shared a wonderful joke. The ruse worked several times during the long, drunken evening.

From Mexico City, they tramped cross-country on foot more than two hundred miles to Veracruz, where they caught a steamer to Puerto México, a small port on the Gulf. The ship was so loaded down with its cargo of chickens, cows, and pigs that the deck was almost flush with the water.

While gathering shells a few days earlier, Roger had brushed against some coral. On the boat, Pancho saw that the scrapes on his legs were now ugly wounds, with red streaks running up his calves that Pancho recognized as a telltale sign of blood poisoning.

There was no doctor at the port, but they learned that there was a small field hospital a few miles inland, at a refinery. The situation was quickly becoming desperate. Roger was alternately feverish and racked with chills, his face pale, his energy sapped. There was no transportation to the refinery. They would have to walk. It was a long two miles, with Roger leaning almost his full weight on his friend. Pancho so prided herself on her strength that she had a hard time remembering she was a five-foot-four-inch woman, but she remembered it during that hike inland.

At the hospital, Roger was treated and she was given instructions on how to drain and cleanse the wounds and told to change the dressings daily. Roger was in pain, but with his infection arrested, they moved on, catching a boat to Campeche on the Yucatán Peninsula, bumming inland to Mérida and then to visit the ruins. By now, the little money they had was gone, and Roger's legs were not healing fast enough. At the American Embassy, an official arranged passage for them on the *Rajah,* a ship to New Orleans. But their adventure was not over yet.

From New Orleans, they walked, hitchhiked, and hoboed west, running afoul of the law in Austin, Texas, where they were picked up for vagrancy. The police gave them twenty-five cents apiece for a bunk and told them to get out of town the next morning. When they finally made it back to Southern California in November 1927, almost seven months after first setting foot on the *Camina,* they were mud-caked, sun-blackened, dog-tired, and the closest of friends.

For Roger Chute, it had been a glorious adventure in an already adventuresome life. He could not remember ever having had so much "real, heart-deep pleasure as on that filthy, sublime, painful, jubilant, comic, exotic, infected, goddamn beautiful bummatory expedition," he wrote a few years later.

For Florence Lowe Barnes, it was something more. She had played at being an adventurer before this, defying convention, going her own way, riding her horses, traveling across America by train, taking the South America cruise. But in all this, she had never been far from family, from comfort and wealth, from a clean berth or a first-class cabin.

In Mexico, on foot in the backcountry, on tramp steamers in the Gulf, eating what could be scrounged, sleeping on a serape laid on bare earth, she had lived like a peasant, not a society woman, and she had not only survived, she had had the time of her life. Money was wonderful, she loved having it, but the Mexican trip taught her she could live without it if she had to. For a private-school-educated Pasadena debutante and San Marino chatelaine, even one as independent-minded as she, this was a life-changing lesson. Always confident in her abilities, especially in her physical strength, she had now actually field-tested them, and she knew she could handle the toughest of situations. When she presented herself at the rectory door that November, her short hair slicked back with gardenia oil, her face as brown as leather, huaraches on her feet, she was a different woman, with a different name. She was Pancho Barnes.

5

Flying

In the late spring of 1927, while Pancho was riding a burro across the Sierra Madre, another audacious explorer, a traveler of a different sort, was piloting a monoplane across the Atlantic. When Charles Augustus Lindbergh completed the first nonstop transatlantic flight in history on May 21, he became not just a hero, not just an immediate celebrity, not just an instant legend, but the most famous human being on earth. Afterward, when he crisscrossed the United States on a Guggenheim-funded tour to promote aviation, stopping at countless cities and towns along the way, thousands and thousands of people came to pay homage to the future.

The next spring, a tall, slender, sandy-haired woman who looked enough like Lindbergh to be his sister flew from Newfoundland to Wales in twenty hours and forty minutes. Although she was a licensed pilot, Amelia Earhart went as a passenger on that flight, a stunt orchestrated by her husband-to-be, the New York publisher G. P. Putnam. Shrewdly, he labeled her "Lady Lindy" and set in motion a public relations juggernaut that made her Lindbergh's equal in the pages of the daily newspapers if not also in the skies.

She may have been aviation's first bona fide national heroine, but

Earhart—who was known simply by her initials, AE—was hardly the first or the best of the female fliers. More than a decade before AE went along for the famous transatlantic ride, a young stunt pilot named Ruth Law flew nonstop solo from Chicago to New York. Before her, there was San Francisco journalist Harriet Quimby, the first American woman to receive a pilot's license (in 1911), who flew the English Channel, and her friend Mathilde Moisant, the second licensed woman, a fearless pilot who set altitude records, put on exhibitions throughout Mexico, and narrowly escaped death on more than one occasion. There was "Queen Bess"—Bessie Coleman—the first African American woman aviator, licensed two years before AE, who toured the South as a flying daredevil.

There were others, too, wing walkers and parachutists, barnstormers and record breakers, both female and male, who flew their tiny open-cockpit planes in the years immediately before and after World War I. But it was not until Lindbergh and Earhart in the late 1920s that America became plane crazy. Long Island, especially Roosevelt Field, was one center of activity. So was Dayton, Ohio, hometown of the Wright brothers. In the West, aviators were drawn to Southern California with its open land and clear skies. There, by the middle and late 1920s, dozens and dozens of little airfields were being carved from farmlands and orchards, with thousand-foot dirt runways and shacks for hangars: Arcadia, Alhambra, Baldwin Park, Culver City, Crawford out in Venice, Rogers at Wilshire Boulevard and Fairfax, Martin Brothers in Santa Ana, Metropolitan in Van Nuys—the biggest, eighty acres surrounded by chicken farms where the owner raised banana squash between the runways. Kids rode their bikes out to the airstrips after school to gawk at the World War I Jennies and the pilots in their greasy overalls hunkered down in the shade under the wings. Crowds came out on the weekends to see the pilots loop and spin and dive. Daredevils and would-be record breakers came from all over the country to fly the skies of Southern California. AE said the flying conditions in and around Los Angeles were the best she'd found anywhere. Ruth Elder, a fiercely competitive long-distance flier, thought Los Angeles was "the aviation center of America." Bobbi Trout, a local girl who set out to break every record she could, said of Southern California: "The flier learns here as nowhere else the meaning of the joy of flying."

In the spring of 1928, Pancho was ready for a new adventure. The Mexico trip had been wonderful, exciting, memorable. She continued to regale her friends with her tales of adventure, embroidering them in the telling, conscious of herself as the main character in a dramatic narrative she could shape and reshape. She started up her parties again in the newly redecorated San Marino mansion. She rode her horses. But she was bored.

Her cousin Dean Banks had just started taking flying lessons at an old balloon field in nearby Arcadia and asked her if she wanted to come along. Equally interested in new adventures and in not allowing Dean to get too much ahead of her in anything, she readily agreed. Although she had not considered the idea of taking flying lessons before that moment, now, suddenly, it seemed like the best idea in the world.

The airfield wasn't much, a narrow dirt strip with two ancient, cavernous balloon hangars, a mooring mast, and a few pilots tending to World War I–vintage planes. Dean introduced her to Ben Caitlin, his teacher, who had learned to fly in France during the war. He stared at her. Her hair was still cut short, as it had been in Mexico, and she was wearing old riding clothes. Her arms and shoulders were hard and visibly muscled, like a man's.

"So you want to learn how to fly?" he said. He made his living giving flying lessons, but women were not his favorite pupils.

Yes, she said.

"Now, when is it you wanted to start learning?" he asked.

Pancho didn't hesitate. "Well, right now is okay," she said.

Caitlin reached into the front cockpit of one of the planes, grabbed a leather helmet and a pair of goggles, and tossed them to her. Moments later, they were airborne, Pancho strapped in in front, Caitlin at the controls in back. She had been in an airplane once before, years ago. When her mother was still alive, the family had taken a scenic boat trip to Santa Catalina. You could see the island from Grandmother Dobbins's house up on the cliff above Laguna Beach. The water was rough that day, the crossing uncomfortable, and Pancho, as seasick as she would ever be, refused to get back on the boat to go to the mainland. She spotted a tiny plane that had just landed with a passenger, ran over, and chartered it for a quick, uneventful return flight.

Her first flight with Ben Caitlin that spring morning was uneventful, too. She liked the fast taxi down the dirt strip, dust flying everywhere, and she liked suddenly, effortlessly being lifted above it all, the engine loud in her ears, the wind whipping at her face. But before she had a chance to feel airborne, they were down again, and Ben was jumping out of the cockpit. They agreed to another, longer flight the next day.

The morning was bright and clear. Ben took the little plane up to a thousand feet, then banked it sharply to the right, dipping the wing straight down. The horizon disappeared; the earth tilted to meet them. Pancho felt her body being pulled, its weight straining against the seat straps. Ben straightened their course, but before Pancho could get her bearings, he pointed the nose up and looped the plane in a long, slow outside circle, turning the world upside down. They flew belly up for what seemed like a long moment. When they were right side up again, Ben rolled the plane, wing over wing, first to the right, then to the left, until Pancho didn't know what was earth and what was sky anymore. He climbed again, put the plane into a stall, and spun it straight down in a tight spiral. The earth came at them, spinning like a platter. In a few hundred feet, the nose of the plane would bore a hole in the ground. At what looked like the last possible moment, Ben pulled out of it, straightened out, and landed on the little airstrip.

When they had taxied to a stop, he yelled up to her, grinning, "Still want to learn how to fly?" He had, in aviation parlance, "wrung her out good." He expected to see her pale and shaken, queasy, finished with flying. But there she sat, grinning back, her face flushed, her eyes a little wild, riding the last wave of an adrenaline rush so exquisite that it was almost painful to feel it ebb away.

"Hell, yes, I want to learn how to fly," she told him.

He shook his head, trying to figure her out. "I suppose I'll have to teach you," he said. "But I have to tell you, I've had thirty-three women students and not a single one of them has ever soloed."

Pancho came to the airfield several times a week from then on. Ben charged her five dollars for a fifteen-minute lesson. They wore no parachutes because Ben couldn't afford them. In the cockpit, there wasn't much to learn. The only instrument was an oil gauge. Pilots looked over the side to judge altitude. They dipped a string in the gas tank to gauge fuel level. They hung a key chain from the control board to show them if they were flying straight. In the cockpit, life was simple: stick and rudder, up and back, left and right. The planes stayed in the air, when they stayed in the air, by quick thinking and guts. Flying was 85 percent man and 15 percent machine, Ben always told her. There was no talking tube between the two open cockpits, so Ben instructed by hand signals: Hand up meant "Point the nose of the plane up"; hand down, nose down. Hand out to the side meant "Pick that wing up"; hand on the right cheek meant the plane was skipping or skidding to the right and needed correction.

Ben started by teaching Pancho how to fly straight and level, pointing to a road below so she could orient herself. It didn't take her long to catch on, tracing the road from above, holding the nose level by gauging the horizon line and keeping her eye on the key chain. Next he started her on turns, then figure eights. Each day was a new challenge; each day, another thrill. Ben had never had a female student so quick to learn and so fearless as Pancho, so eager, so filled with pleasure in the act of flying.

When the lesson was over, Ben would take the plane up around twelve hundred feet and perform aerobatics—wingovers, loops, barrel rolls, slips, stalls, and spins. He wasn't trying to scare her anymore. He was just having fun. He was also showing her how it felt when an engine stalled out, which happened often in those tiny planes, and what to do when the ship started spinning. One evening at dusk, they were fly-ing back in after another lesson when, with Ben at the controls, the plane went into a dizzying spin and came down to within fifty feet of the ground before Ben pulled it out and landed. As soon as they stopped taxiing, he jumped out of the cockpit and leaned against the side of the plane. Pancho joined him.

"Well, Ben, I've got to the point where nothing worries me any-more," she said, laughing. "You were pretty low that time but, you know, I'm just so used to these maneuvers that I never get scared." Ben didn't say anything, so she looked at him more closely. His breathing was quick and shallow.

"We damn near got it," he said. "The rudder stuck, and I kicked it and fought it all the way down. I just kicked it hard enough and got it loose. But we almost spun in." Pilots always talked about spinning in, never about crashing. After that, Ben didn't spin anymore. A few days later, the owner of the airplane they were using, a man named Jimmy Rosen, spun in. The ship was demolished, and Jimmy was killed in-stantly. A while later, another flier crashed into the old balloon mooring mast. His plane ricocheted and bounced onto the Pacific Electric rail-road tracks that bordered the airfield, cutting down twenty-eight power poles along the way. Crashes were commonplace, although it was equally commonplace for a pilot to walk away from a wreck. The planes flew only ninety miles an hour, often less, and were easy to jump clear of. The dirt runways and pasturelands where the pilots set down were forgiving. Pancho didn't think about the danger, or if she did, it was only to acknowledge that it was the danger that heightened the thrill.

By early summer, she was ready to learn how to land. The Arcadia airstrip was short, with a nasty prevailing crosswind and a stand of tall eucalyptus trees on the east end. A few of the trees had been topped and trimmed to leave space for an airplane to slink through on its ap-proach, but the clearance was tight. A pilot had to sideslip a plane through the gap in the trees, left wing pointed down, then quickly straighten out before setting the ship down. The landings looked spec-tacular, but to Pancho, who learned the graceful maneuver easily, they were just normal procedure. By summer she was also ready to own her own plane. Barnstormers were paying $600 for World War I–surplus Jennies. Amateur pilots might spend $1,000 for a decent little plane. But Pancho was accustomed to getting the best. In early July, she bought a used Travel Air biplane for $5,500, five times what an average family made in a year.

Now she was spending all her time out at the airfield with Ben, her cousin Dean, and the pilots who flew in and out of Arcadia. Her mother's money supported her. Servants kept the San Marino house running. A nanny took care of her son. Seven and a half years into her marriage to the Reverend Barnes, there was not only no marriage but no pretense of one. Rankin lived in the rectory; Pancho lived in the big house. There was no formal, legal separation, but they never lived together again.

There was also no animosity. Pancho liked Rankin, and he was fond of her. In small doses, they actually enjoyed each other's company. But the nonmarriage marriage suited them both. Rankin had a wife whom he did not have to support or service. He was free to pursue his ambitions in the church, wherever they took him. Even if he allowed himself to dream of a more suitable wife, a helpmate who would entertain church officials and play hostess at teas for the ladies, he knew that the drawbacks of realizing such a dream outweighed the benefits. He was moving up in the church hierarchy now, becoming noticed on the national level. Divorce and remarriage would jeopardize everything he had worked for.

"Dearest sweetheart," he wrote to her when he traveled that year. He was away from California during much of 1928, traveling on church business to the East, on family business to the Midwest. His letters were kind and chatty, affectionate without being intimate, a friend writing a friend. He kept in touch, told her where he was going and what he was doing, and inquired after Billy, but he never said he missed her. She responded in kind, fondly but with little emotion.

Like Rankin, Pancho didn't think much of divorce. Marriage was, as far as she could tell, a confining institution with few benefits to confer on an independent woman of means. She had no desire to be married to anyone, but the current situation was quite tolerable. She had a husband she didn't have to make a home for or share her life with. She had no responsibilities as either wife or mother. But, if she needed to, if society forced her to, she could fall back on the respectability of her status as a married woman.

Now she was consumed by only one thing: She wanted to solo in her plane. Soloing—flying alone and in complete control—would mean she was a real pilot. But her teacher didn't think she was ready, after less than six hours in the air. The situation was further complicated when Ben and the other pilots flying out of Arcadia were kicked off the airfield after one crash too many. While Ben looked around for another venue, Pancho moved her plane to an airfield at Baldwin Park, a few miles southeast of Arcadia. Instead of a eucalyptus tree hazard, this one had a big red barn sitting on the path for takeoffs.

Pancho and her cousin Dean visited Ben's house several times a week to play poker and nag him about allowing Pancho to solo. They let him win at cards, but the strategy didn't work. Increasingly impatient and characteristically overconfident, Pancho took matters into her own hands. She and Dean hooked up with a friend who claimed to have flown solo once. The three kidnapped Pancho's plane, with Dale, the young friend, at the controls and Pancho and Dean squeezed together in the passenger cockpit. Dale managed to take off, narrowly missing the red barn, and fly south to San Diego, but he had great trouble landing. Pancho counted the passes he made over the field—two, three, six, eight, and still he couldn't land. Eventually, they got down in one piece, and Pancho immediately ran over to the resident field instructor, asking to solo. He refused. They took off again, in search of a more agreeable instructor. At Santa Ana airport, their next stop, Pancho tried again, and again was refused. Now it was dusk, and the weather was turning bad. With Dale at the controls, they set off in the rain to try to find their way to Culver City. The fog rolled in, and they had to fly low to get their bearings. Pancho had never been scared in an airplane before, but she was worried now. They were lost. It was dark, and fuel might soon be a problem. Dale, whether he had actually soloed before or not, was flying way beyond his abilities. Pancho also realized that, despite her earlier bravado, she was not skilled enough to pilot the plane either. It was only luck that they happened on an airfield in Compton, many miles from their destination. Shaken, they left the plane there and caught a ride back home.

Ben was furious when he learned of the escapade and refused to give Pancho any more lessons, let alone authorize her to fly solo. It took her most of the rest of the summer to get back into his good graces. When he finally agreed to take her on as a student again, he told her that she would have to make six perfect landings in a row before he allowed her to take the ship up alone. Day after day, she drove out to Baldwin Park to practice her three-point landings. The airfield there was a little longer than Arcadia's, with fewer hazards and less crosswind. That made landing easier, but it was still the hardest part of learning to fly. She kept at it. Finally, one afternoon in early September, she taxied back to the hangar after her sixth perfect landing. Ben climbed out of the ship and told her to take it up by herself.

She opened the throttle and roared down the field before he could change his mind. The little plane lifted into the air so quickly that it surprised her. Without Ben's weight, the plane soared. She sat in the open cockpit, caught in the moment, completely focused, almost breathless with joy. She scanned the horizon. She looked earthward. She checked the key chain hanging from the controls. She pulled back slightly on the stick. Then she stopped thinking and started flying. She climbed to a thousand feet and circled the field a few times, then brought it in for a good landing. She had been airborne, alone, for five minutes. She was a pilot.

Ben barely had time to congratulate her before she took off again, this time with her first passenger, a childhood friend named Nelse Griffith. The excitement of being up with a new pilot was not enough for him. They were all daredevils. They were all invincible.

"Hey, let's show them something," he yelled at Pancho when they had flown around for a few minutes. "I'll wing walk. You bring it across the field low." Nelse inched out of the passenger cockpit and stepped out onto the wing, crouching, holding the flying wires with both hands. Pancho, grinning, flew the plane fifty feet above the field, made a pass, then zoomed up and came around again with Nelse still clutching the wires. When she'd unloaded Nelse, it was Dean's turn for a run. Pancho didn't want the afternoon to end. Up above the earth, in the pilot's seat, she was herself, with no apologies, no compromises, no holding back. This was an adventure of her own making, and she could have it any day she wanted. The German flier Thea Rasche, a contemporary of Pancho's, said that flying was "more thrilling than love for a man and far less dangerous." For Pancho the thrill was more visceral. "Flying," she told her friends, "makes me feel like a sex maniac in a whorehouse."

6

One of the Boys

fter her solo flight, Pancho was at the airfield every day, practicing
figure eights and landings, learning to read the terrain, becoming
increasingly confident at the controls. Just a month after soloing, she
took her first long-distance flight, a 150-mile jaunt up to Santa Barbara
and back, flying with a map opened on her lap, following roads and railroad tracks when she could find them. If she got lost, she would swoop
down low over a town and try to catch the sign on the railway depot. If
she needed to know which way the wind was blowing or how hard, she
would fly low and look at laundry flapping on a line. There were no instruments to guide her, no beacons, no radio, only faith in her own instincts and a great sense of adventure. A few weeks later, her second
long-distance trip, this one to San Francisco, was a little more adventurous than even she wanted, when her engine developed problems,
misfiring, backfiring, quitting in midair and forcing her to make eight
separate emergency landings. At each stop, she'd clean the fouled spark
plugs and take off again. Flying home late on the final leg of the return
trip, she saw fire coming out of the exhaust and lighting up the sky. She
got down quickly. Three days later, she traded her old plane plus
$2,500 in cash for a Travel Air Speedwing biplane previously owned by

the Hollywood director Howard Hawks. The Speedwing was a faster, more responsive plane. Pancho called it "the sweetest ship that ever lived." Her cousin Dean, seeing himself outclassed, immediately went out and spent $25,000 on a new cabin plane for himself.

Pancho spent most of the winter of 1928 and into the spring of 1929 hopping from airport to airport in her Speedwing. There were now more than fifty airfields in the Los Angeles basin, each with its own personality, each with its own cast of characters, and she came to know most of them. She came to be known, too, among the local flying fraternity. It was not just that she was one of the very few female pilots. It was that most of the men had never before encountered a woman like Pancho. In her dungarees or a pair of old jodhpurs and blue cotton work shirt, she lugged her own gear, serviced her own plane, and asked for no favors. She bummed cigarettes, ate raw hamburgers—"cannibal sandwiches," she called them—and told stories and off-color jokes with the best of them. Many who saw her from a distance didn't even realize she was a woman. Even those who knew her well didn't know she was wealthy.

One of Pancho's favorite jaunts in those days was the flight between Baldwin Park and Carpinteria, a hundred miles up the coast just south of Santa Barbara. It was here that Ben Caitlin had taken a job managing the local airport. A new clan gathered around him, and Pancho wanted to be part of it. She would fly up there, sometimes by herself, sometimes with Dean, socialize all afternoon, and then fly back home. As she spent more and more time with Ben and the gang, she left for home later and later in the day. Soon she was making the entire return trip after dark, jumping the trees at the end of the Carpinteria airport and teaching herself to night-fly as she went. The highways had barely enough traffic to make them visible, but most of the towns were lighted. She could identify Baldwin Park all right, but had a terrible time finding the airfield because it was completely without illumination. She would drop down and circle near where she thought the airfield might be, waiting for a car to come by. If she was lucky, the headlights would catch the old hamburger stand that stood at the corner of the field. She'd get her bearings and make her approach. Few pilots risked the hazards of night flying in those days, but Pancho got so proficient on these Carpinteria–to–Baldwin Park runs and grew to be such an exponent of night flying that she began carrying paying passengers over the city to see the lights.

At Carpinteria she met a strikingly handsome man named Bob Short, a cocky pilot with a bad reputation whose disregard for rules had gotten him banned from more than one airfield. He was known to have a mean streak, but he was also a great talker who was fun to be around. Pancho was taken with his looks and his brashness, and when one day he asked her for a ride back to Los Angeles, she understood the subtext of the request and quickly and eagerly agreed. It was one of her after-dark flights, and when they arrived at Baldwin Park, they pushed the airplane into a hangar and without discussion, took Pancho's car, which was parked at the airfield, back to San Marino. That night, they made love on her big canopied bed, but over the next few weeks, during their short, intense affair, they moved from room to room in the mansion, acting out mutual fantasies on top of the grand piano, under the library table, and on the white bearskin rug in front of the fireplace. Pancho got that idea from a movie she saw, *The Merry Widow*, made by her friend Erich von Stroheim.

Pancho's attitude toward sex was uncomplicated: She enjoyed it. She enjoyed it in a way women were not supposed to enjoy it— enthusiastically, unapologetically, for the physical excitement, the jolt, the charge. Others might long for deep companionship, emotional sustenance, and life commitment. Pancho just wanted to have fun. That, she and Bob Short had, until one day he made the mistake of taking Pancho's plane without permission and flying it hard. She was so angry that she threw him out, abruptly ending the affair.

At the Baldwin Park field, she met a parachutist, a tall, rawboned young man named Slim Zaunmiller. Together, they flew to local airfields on Sundays to put on shows and pass the hat. Pancho began with aerobatics: spirals, sideslips, inside loops, outside loops, split S turns, barrel rolls. Then came one of her favorite tricks, a maneuver she and her hangar friends had developed for their own entertainment. She would drop a roll of toilet paper out of the plane, holding on to one end. As the roll unwound, she zipped the plane back and forth, cutting the unspooling paper with the wing of the plane as she descended. After that, it was Slim's turn. Pancho took the plane up to a thousand feet and dropped Slim over the field where he would land, with precision, within a few feet of the appreciative crowd. After a few jumps, when the onlookers were no longer wowed, Slim would go out into the crowd and find a pretty young girl to flirt with, sweet-talking her into taking a ride. He would harness her into a spare parachute and then, at a thousand feet, Pancho would dip the wing of the plane and Slim would give the girl a push while pulling her ripcord. Pancho perfected the technique of kicking the plane's tail out of the way so the 'chute could open safely. Then she would put the plane down as quickly as she could, trying to beat the crowd to the site where the girl had landed. Miraculously, none of the girls were hurt. After a big kiss from Slim and applause from the audience, a few even managed to smile. Pancho and Slim called their act the Pancho Barnes Flying Mystery Circus of the Air, and they made decent money on those Sunday outings. Slim did it for the bucks. Pancho did it for the fun.

What with the barnstorming, airfield hopping, and occasional longer trips, Pancho accumulated more than sixty hours of flying during the six months after her solo. Now she ventured down to Mexico, with her cousin Dean, looking for new adventures. They flew south to Ensenada, where the rumrunning ships were harbored. On payday, the money flowed, and Pancho would charge ten dollars a head for joyrides. Back at the hangars at Baldwin Park, Carpinteria, Metropolitan, March, Ross, Mission—all the airfields she hopped in and out of—she entertained fellow pilots with stories of her Ensenada adventures, of squeezing seven passengers onto a single flight, of impersonating a Mexican official, of buzzing the village streets so low that barbers nearly slit the throats of their customers. She loved the camaraderie in the hangars, the long evenings of talking and drinking and smoking. The planes were so unstable, the airfields so full of hazards, the flying conditions so primitive that when pilots shared their experiences, even if they were half-bragging, they were also sharing valuable information. "Hangar flying," as pilots called these long bull sessions, alerted them to everything from problems with aircraft to the best local mechanics to the prevailing winds at remote airstrips. The long days of risky flying followed by the long evenings of talk wove them into a tight-knit club, of which Pancho was the only female member. They called themselves the Short Snorts, and their formal membership card was a dollar bill autographed by all the other pilots in the group.

Hangar flying was a social event, too. Fun was almost always on the agenda, and Pancho was almost always at its center. She concocted a scheme to amuse her buddies while deflating the egos of some of the new hotshot pilots she saw hopping from airstrip to airstrip. The hangar fliers would single out some young man who had just flown a good race or broken a record or somehow had developed what they considered an overly high opinion of himself. Pancho would saunter up to him and tell him that a very exclusive pilots' club was being organized and that his name had been proposed for membership. He would recognize her right away—Pancho was becoming a local legend and was perhaps the most recognizable pilot in Southern California—and, knowing of the more experienced pilots who hung around together, was invariably flattered to be invited into their midst. Pancho would demand a membership fee on the spot, payable in cash. The fee might be five dollars or it might be fifty—the hangar fliers would have decided in advance just how much they could get away with charging the new recruit. Once Pancho had the money in hand, the game was revealed.

"Listen, sucker," she would tell the pilot as she walked away, "that's all there is. Now go out and try it on someone yourself." Then she and her friends would use the money to throw themselves a party.

Another favorite trick was for one of the members to call for everyone to show his card, the autographed dollar bill, while out carousing at a bar. The unlucky pilot who was not carrying the signed bill in his wallet that night was stuck with the bar tab.

Before long, the group's parties moved from the airplane hangars and bars to Pancho's San Marino mansion. The location was near many of the little airstrips, especially the field at Alhambra, about a mile away, where pilots arrived nightly with bootleg liquor from Mexico. One plane landed every day with a hundred ten-gallon cans of red-cap pure grain alcohol, a can of which often made its way over to Pancho's, where she and her friends made bathtub gin. She could also afford the good stuff, branded whisky in bottles from Scotland. The parties were soon legendary, attracting all the famous fliers of the day, from Jimmy Doolittle, who had flown cross-continent in 1922 and had since set a number of airspeed records, to Roscoe Turner, one of the era's most flamboyant flying showmen. The parties might last an evening or a weekend, or even longer. Sometimes Pancho would go away while a party was in full swing and return several days later to find her guests still drinking her liquor, loudly entertaining one another with tall tales, and using her upstairs bedrooms for their own purposes. "Everybody here," she wrote to one of her friends, "is busy talking about breaking new records, getting drunk and keeping up with their horizontal exercise."

Meanwhile, she was also continuing to entertain lavishly at her Laguna Beach house, perched on a two-hundred-foot bluff jutting out into Emerald Bay and the Pacific Ocean. The house was originally built just a few hundred yards from Grandmother Dobbins's more elaborate Newport, Rhode Island–style mansion. Caroline Dobbins was a stern woman, then in her late eighties, and the undisputed matriarch of the family. She was an astute businesswoman who had, through smart investments and real estate purchases, parlayed her husband's money into an even greater fortune. She held others to her own exacting standards, expecting decorous behavior, high moral character, and conservative spending. Horace Dobbins, one of her grandsons and the mayor of Pasadena, was a model of this behavior. So was the Reverend Barnes. But her granddaughter Florence—Caroline Dobbins would never have dreamed of calling her Pancho—was another matter. She disapproved of everything about her granddaughter, from her lack of maternal instinct to her lack of financial restraint, from her flying to her mannish dress. As Pancho's parties grew bigger, louder, and more frequent, Caroline, who had a ringside seat, began complaining to her granddaughter. Others in the family deferred to the matriarch. Not Pancho. "If you don't like it, Nana, then you can just move the house," she told her grandmother.

That was just what Caroline did. She hired a top Los Angeles architect to take apart and then reconstruct Pancho's house farther away from hers on the twenty-acre property. While he was at it, he remodeled, adding a number of new guest rooms and a swimming pool, one of whose sides was the basement wall of the house. Through portholes in the wall, guests in the basement bar had an underwater view of the swimmers. Pancho used the house many weekends and almost all summer. In San Marino, she hosted her hangar buddies. Here at the beach, it was the Hollywood crowd.

Ramon Novarro, one of Hollywood's biggest stars, was still a frequent guest. Novarro was warm and attentive, and Pancho was initially attracted to him. But she soon discovered that his romantic attentions were reserved for men. The two became close friends and constant companions, partying at Laguna, barhopping in Los Angeles, and zooming around Hollywood in one of Pancho's high-powered automobiles. Ramon had a special flying outfit custom-made for Pancho, with powder-blue suede pants and jacket, a blue silk scarf, and soft Brazilian leather boots.

Her old friend Erich von Stroheim was also a fixture at the Laguna Beach house. The two were more than friends. Pancho worked as a scriptwriter for Von Stroheim on and off for almost six years. He put her on a $75-a-week retainer and called her when he needed her, sometimes not giving her work for months, sometimes demanding that she work twenty hours straight rewriting a screenplay. Theirs was a tempestuous relationship. Von Stroheim habitually engineered fights with all his writers and actors, believing that if they were emotionally charged they would perform better. One evening at the beach house, where he and Pancho often did their work, Von Stroheim started taunting her.

"All these stories about you posing as a man down in Mexico . . . that never happened, did it?" He was teasing, but there was an edge. With Von Stroheim there was always an edge.

Yes, it did happen, Pancho told him. You know it did.

They argued back and forth, Von Stroheim purposely escalating the exchange, Pancho taking the bait. Finally, she couldn't stand it anymore.

"Well, I'll show you what kind of a man I can be," she told him. Then she hit him hard on the jaw. He reeled and fell backward. In a rage, he ran to his upstairs guest room, grabbed a pistol, and came down threatening to shoot her. The little drama ended as quickly as it had begun, and they went back to being friends until the next orchestrated blowup.

The actress Ruth Chatterton and her mother, Tillie, were Laguna habitués, as were new acquaintances Gigi Parrish, a minor actress, and her husband, Dillwyn, a cousin of the famous artist Maxfield Parrish. Another regular was George Hurrell, a photographer whose dramatic portrait style Pancho loved. Hurrell, who was then barely making a living taking photographs of artists and their work, worked magic when he photographed Pancho. With artful poses, careful makeup, and soft lighting he changed her from a plain, fleshy-faced woman into an exotic. Pancho was anything but vain about her looks, but she loved the Hurrell photographs. They made her look like a star. She introduced Hurrell to Ramon Novarro, who sat for a series of portraits and was so impressed by the results that he showed them to a friend, the actress Norma Shearer. Shearer, in turn, was so impressed that she showed them to her husband, who happened to be Irving Thalberg, the vice president of M-G-M. So began Hurrell's sixty-year career as M-G-M's chief still photographer.

But Pancho's Laguna Beach parties were more bacchanals than opportunities for industry networking. Lubricated by liquor—Pancho's bar was reputed to be the best stocked in Southern California—Pancho and her friends danced, swam naked in the pool, and rode horses by moonlight on the beach below the cliffs. One night, a Mexican army officer she'd met on earlier adventures ate the lace underwear off a Hollywood starlet, creating a mild sensation.

As Pancho used the beach house more and more, she began to consider building her own small airstrip on the property. She imagined not just herself but her Hollywood friends—many of whom were enamored of aviation—and her flying buddies the Short Snorts ferrying guests in and out of Laguna Beach for parties that would last almost without interruption all summer. She contacted Southern California Edison to arrange for electrical poles and power lines to be moved, running afoul of her grandmother, who called on her trusted grandson Horace to handle this latest problem. Pancho attempted to finesse her grandmother's objections by writing several letters to the mayor of Laguna Beach and the president of the local chamber of commerce, touting the proposed airstrip as "a decided asset to Laguna Beach from a publicity standpoint."

The officials seemed to share her enthusiasm. But when she graded a seven-hundred-foot dirt airstrip on the property and started using it, local residents complained of the noise, the dust, and the danger. The extremely short runway was dangerous enough. But the wind coming in off the ocean and sweeping up the cliffs made landings even more treacherous. The city council, in a bind because Laguna Beach officials had already expressed support for the airfield, referred the complaints to the city attorney, who reached an agreement with Pancho to be "more conservative" when flying. A year later, Dick Dodds, a wealthy sportsman and aviation enthusiast, was attempting to land on Pancho's airstrip when he came in too fast. Realizing his mistake, he climbed and turned, but was caught in an air pocket and lost control. He died when his plane crashed into the cliffs below Pancho's house. After that, no one, including Pancho, used the strip.

The wild parties at Laguna Beach and San Marino were part of a classic Roaring Twenties lifestyle that Pancho was supporting with her inheritance. She was keeping up two large houses, each with its own staff of cooks, housekeepers, gardeners, and stable hands. She had a full-time nanny-nursemaid for Billy and a part-time private secretary for herself. She wore a white fox fur and gave herself a new Chrysler Imperial convertible for Christmas.

Pancho's attitude toward money was simple: She had it, so she spent it. She knew nothing about finances and cared less. No one had taught her, or even talked to her, about keeping track of expenses, about budgeting, about making thoughtful decisions before she spent. Now, on top of her prodigious household and entertainment expenses, she also bore the costs of buying, maintaining, and flying airplanes. But ever since the days when she'd earned a few extra dollars from film work, she prided herself on being able to bring money in. Many well-known pilots helped support their flying by signing contracts with oil companies. They painted the sides of their planes with a company's insignia and went from airport to airport promoting its products. When the pilots participated in air races, their painted planes served as flying advertisements. They were also called on to haul company executives when needed. In 1929, Pancho signed a three-year contract with the Union Oil company for all these purposes.

She also earned money as a test pilot for Bach, Lockheed, and Beechcraft, flying their ships eighty-seven times, by her count, in a single year. A new plane had to be field-tested for speed, stability, maneuverability, maximum load capacity, and anything else the engineers needed to know before it went into production. Pancho was asked to do some of this work not just because she was one of a handful of skilled pilots but because she was a woman. The aircraft companies figured it was wonderful publicity to have a woman test the planes. It showed how *easy* the ship was to fly. If a woman could fly it, then anyone could. Pancho understood the companies' motives well, but always jumped at the chance to fly something new.

Lockheed hired her to test the maximum load capacity of their Vega.

Long-distance flying meant outfitting planes with enormous gas tanks, which added significant weight. How much could the plane hold and still be airworthy? This is what Pancho was helping Lockheed to find out. On the first two tests, she couldn't get the plane off the ground. She got airborne on the third attempt, but when she landed at Burbank airport with two thousand pounds of fuel on the plane, both shock cords on the landing gear broke, and Pancho struggled to keep the plane on the runway. She was unhurt, but the near accident caused Lockheed to move the tests to a more remote location.

Sixty air miles north of Los Angeles, just over the San Gabriel Mountains, lay the vast, flat Mojave Desert. There were almost no people out there, few towns, little development, no trees. The weather was clear and dry. The desert was dotted with dry lakes, several of them so expansive that their flat, hard surfaces, miles long, made natural landing strips. Out in the Mojave, the world was almost all sky, an enormous bowl inverted over a big, empty platter. It was a pilot's paradise, and a test pilot's haven. Pancho began landing the Vega on a lake named Muroc after a tiny settlement near its parched shores. If she got into trouble here, there were no obstacles to contend with, no other aircraft, no changeable weather, just miles and miles of safe landing surface.

It was while flying the Vega over the Mojave that she first saw a little ranch, almost equidistant between Muroc and another huge dry lake, Rosamond. It was out there all by itself, a rectangle of deep green against the tawny plain of the desert. She flew low to take a look. The deep green was alfalfa, acres and acres of it, the irrigation ditches miraculously full of water. But it was the location that interested her most. What if you had an airport between those two dry lakes, she thought, an airport next to that alfalfa ranch? You could fly *anything* in and out of that airport. There would always be a safe place to land, always a vast expanse of cloudless sky to explore. She circled the ranch again, then forced her mind back to the Vega and the test flight. A few minutes later, she landed safely on Muroc Dry Lake.

━━ ⋈⧫⋈ ━━

The real glory of flying planes in those days lay not in testing them but in racing them, and in breaking records—speed, altitude, endurance, anything that could be measured. Pancho threw herself into that as well. On February 22, 1929, she flew in what was billed as the first women's air race in the world, a two-lap, forty-mile course between Grand Central Airport in Glendale and Metropolitan Airport in Van Nuys. The occasion was the gala opening of a $3 million expansion of Grand Central, including a terminal building with a posh restaurant, and the first paved runways on the West Coast. Only six years before, the airport had been carved out of forty-five acres of orange groves. Now a crowd of a hundred thousand, including Jean Harlow, Wallace Beery, Gary Cooper, the governor of California, and the mayor of Los Angeles, gathered to celebrate aviation's coming of age. They listened to dedication speeches and watched flying exhibitions, from dogfights to stunting to parachuting, culminating in the two-lap race.

The race had been Bobbi Trout's idea. Pancho had met Bobbi a month before at the airstrip in Carpinteria, and they liked each other immediately. Bobbi was a tough, no-nonsense flier who had just set the women's solo endurance record, staying aloft first for twelve hours and eleven minutes, then quickly breaking her own time to remain airborne for almost seventeen and a half hours. Like Pancho, she was always ready for a challenge, and like most of the handful of female fliers of the day, she was particularly interested in promoting women in aviation. Bobbi instigated the race by issuing a public challenge to all local female fliers in the pages of the *Los Angeles Times.* Two answered: Pancho and the Beverly Hills flier Margaret Perry, the first woman to own and operate a Southern California airport.

Amid much fanfare, the three walked out on the slick, paved runway, Margaret Perry to her Sparton, Bobbi Trout to her Golden Eagle monoplane, and Pancho to her Travel Air. It was the first time most of the thousands of onlookers had ever seen women fly. Pancho, in her trousers and leather jacket, a beret pulled down tight over her head, took the lead immediately and kept it. She not only won the race in 24.6 minutes, beating Margaret by almost 6 minutes and Bobbi by almost 8, she lapped both of them. It was no surprise. Their 115- and 60-horsepower machines were no match for her 225-horsepower Travel Air.

In another publicity-driven race, Pancho matched skills with the mustachioed Roscoe Turner. In his powder-blue military jacket adorned with diamond-studded epaulets, his thick leather belt with its huge silver buckle, his gold and crimson helmet and goggles, his knee-high boots polished to a mirror shine—and his pet lion cub, Gilmore, who accompanied him on all flights—Roscoe Turner was the most glamorous, most ardently self-promoting aviator of his day. He and Pancho were set to race from San Francisco to Los Angeles, both of them carrying undeveloped film taken at a Stanford football game that afternoon. Roscoe's film was headed for the *Los Angeles Examiner.* Pancho was carrying hers for the *Times.* She had no baggage compartment in the plane, so she flew the entire distance with the negatives tucked under her arm. Roscoe was famous for saying that he could never see any other reason for an airplane than to go fast. That day, Pancho went faster. She beat him back to Los Angeles by twenty minutes and unchivalrously rubbed his nose in it at the victory banquet that night.

7

Flying Faster

Of the 4,690 licensed pilots in America in the summer of 1929, only 34 were women. When a woman showed up at an airfield, test-piloted a plane, or flew in a race, she—along with the airfield, the plane, and the race—was assured publicity. Female fliers were so much of a novelty that they were almost a sideshow. They were also the most dramatic, most visible symbol of women breaking with their Victorian pasts, defying convention as they defied gravity. It was a new age, when young women of a certain class used their privilege not to shield themselves from experience but rather to lunge at it, and no one lunged harder than Pancho and her cohorts. The newspapers ate it up.

That was why, when plans were announced for the first National Air Races to be held in Cleveland that summer, they were quickly followed by plans for an all-female cross-country air derby, the first in the world. It would be an endurance marathon as much as a race, with the women flying sunup to sundown every day as they covered the 2,800 miles from Santa Monica, California, to Cleveland, Ohio. Each night they would stop at a different sponsoring city to be fed, photographed, and fêted. Then, after more than a week of flying, with much hoopla, the racers would land in front of the main grandstand at Cleveland Municipal Airport, in the midst of the ten-day national event. It was a publicity man's dream.

When the race was first proposed, officials considered making a rule that each pilot be accompanied by a male mechanic to take care of forced landings and handle the hazards of the trip over mountains and across deserts. Quick to see the possibilities of this arrangement, Hollywood studios flooded the race office with entrants, young women who turned out to be actresses and starlets rather than fliers. The accompanying "male mechanic" was the flier. Meanwhile, the local press raged against the race. WOMEN'S DERBY SHOULD BE TERMINATED, read the headline in one Los Angeles newspaper. "Women have been dependent on men for guidance for so long that when they are put on their own resources they are handicapped," the story went.

The bona fide women pilots who had registered for the race were outraged. To them, the derby was a critical challenge, a way to showcase their talents publicly, to show the country that in the sky women were as skillful and as brave as men. The race, said altitude and endurance record holder Louise Thaden, was "more important than life or death." The women objected long and loud, insisting that the event go forward and that all competitors be fully licensed pilots who would fly solo. With Amelia Earhart leading the fight, the women managed to talk the promoters into a real race.

It was not an easy course. For eight days, ten to twelve hours a day, the women would fly by dead reckoning, hopscotching across the Southwest and Midwest, guided only by compasses, sectional charts, and Rand McNally road maps. Each would carry a gallon of drinking water and a three-day supply of malted milk tablets and beef jerky in case of a crash in desolate terrain. The pilots could stop en route only for fuel, rest, and food, with seventeen scheduled checkpoints, and overnight stops in San Bernardino, Phoenix, El Paso, Fort Worth, Wichita, St. Louis, and Columbus.

The requirements for entry were a pilot's license and a minimum of one hundred hours solo flying time. AE estimated that perhaps thirty women in the nation, including Pancho, were qualified. Twenty-three registered for the race, and on August 18, nineteen took off from

Clover Field in Santa Monica. Along with Pancho and AE, there were Bobbi Trout and Margaret Perry, skydiver and flying-school owner Phoebe Omlie, commercial Alaska pilot Marvel Crosson, closed-course racer Gladys O'Donnell, long-distance flier Ruth Elder, triple record-holder Louise Thaden, seaplane pilot Ruth Nichols, wing walker Vera Dawn Walker, and entrants from Germany and Australia.

On the dirt field that August afternoon, the airplanes were strung out in two long lines as a crowd estimated between 100,000 and a quarter of a million waited in the dust and searing heat for the radio-relayed pistol shot from Cleveland to cue the starter on the field. One of the largest aggregations of newspaper reporters, photographers, and newsreelers ever to assemble on the West Coast was there. Movie and stage comedian Will Rogers, an aviation enthusiast, presided over the ceremonies, entertaining the crowd—but not the leather-jacketed fliers—by referring to the entrants as "flying flappers," "petticoat pilots," "sweethearts of the air," and "winged beauties." He dubbed the air race a "powder puff derby." In the press tent, a reporter turned to his colleagues. "I don't care what you guys write about their bravery, their skill, their sportsmanship or their adaptability to goddamn aeroplanes," he said. "What I'm gonna say is, 'Them women don't look good in pants.'"

At precisely two P.M., the pistol shot in Cleveland sounded over the loudspeaker in Santa Monica, and at one-minute intervals, the contestants took off at the wave of the starter's flag. The first afternoon's flying was a sixty-mile, get-the-bugs-out hop to San Bernardino. Louise Thaden landed first, twenty-seven minutes after takeoff. Marvel Crosson was second. Pancho clocked in with the third-fastest time.

Pancho was confident as she flew over the familiar Southern California turf that first day. She had spent several weeks in June flying the entire course, all the way to Cleveland, so she knew well what lay ahead and felt prepared for it. She had not done as much cross-country flying as some of the other women, but what she had done, she had loved. She loved the challenge to wits and stamina, the feeling that she was alone and in charge.

That night, the pilots were fêted at a much-publicized banquet and then sat through a lengthy briefing on the next day's flight. It was not until after midnight that they were able to go to their rooms and go to sleep. Fatigue, it would turn out, was almost as great a hazard as the flying itself. They were up at four A.M. and in the air by six.

By mid-morning of the second day, flying across the desert toward a refueling stop in Yuma, Arizona, the women, sitting in open cockpits, wearing leather jackets, and flying east into the sun, began to feel woozy as the temperature soared to the triple digits. Landing at Yuma, AE ran into a sandbank and damaged her propeller. Flying over the Gila River country of southern Arizona, Marvel Crosson was overcome by the heat and the turbulence. She suffered a severe bout of airsickness and parachuted out—too late and too low. Her body was found two hundred yards from the wreckage of her plane.

The other pilots heard about Marvel's death at their scheduled stop in Phoenix that night. Pancho had flown the fastest leg and now led the field in elapsed time, followed by Louise Thaden, Gladys O'Donnell, and then AE. Stunned by the news, the women nonetheless wanted to carry on. Flying was risky. The women knew and accepted that. But the American public was apparently less ready to. Race organizers were immediately pressured to end the event. "Women have conclusively proven that they cannot fly," one newspaper editorialized the next day when it reported on Crosson's death. The women held firm. "It is now all the more necessary that we keep flying," AE told the press. "We all feel terrible about Marvel's death but we know now that we have to finish."

The next day, again battling the desert heat, there were more mishaps. Claire Fahy damaged her biplane in a forced landing. The Australian "Chubbie" Miller ran out of fuel in flight and struggled to bring her plane down safely. Blanche Noyes discovered a fire in the baggage compartment of her plane, landed quickly on a mesquite-covered ridge, put out the fire by throwing sand on it, and took off again. Ruth Elder, gripping the controls with both hands during a patch of turbulence, watched all her maps blow out of the cockpit and was forced to land to get directions. On the leg to Pecos, Texas, Pancho made an unscheduled landing near a small town, where she discovered to her chagrin that she had drifted off course into Mexico. She managed to get airborne again before the authorities had a chance to detain her. But later that day, her luck ran out.

She was flying into Pecos just seconds from touching down at the airfield when she hit something, she had no idea what. The airfield had looked clear to her. The approach was smooth. The landing seemed to be routine. But within a few feet of touching down, she heard a crash and a grinding noise as her landing wheels hit and then caught on something. She had no time to react. Her right wing hit whatever was out there, spinning the plane around. Then her left wing hit. It was only after she jumped from the cockpit and got clear of the plane that she saw what had happened.

The speed cowling on her Travel Air was so bulky that it created a blind spot in front of the plane as it nosed down. What she hadn't been able to see, directly in front of her on the runway, was an automobile crossing the field. It hadn't been there when she scanned the field on her approach, and it shouldn't have been there at all. She and the driver were both shaken up but unhurt. The Travel Air, however, was a mess. The right wing was demolished, and the supports on the left wing were broken. The plane could not be repaired on the field. It would have to be loaded on a train and shipped to the Travel Air company in Wichita for extensive work. For Pancho, the 1929 derby was over.

She took the bad luck gamely. "I've flown that plane for two hundred hours," she told a Wichita *Eagle* reporter when she arrived in that city two days later to arrange for the repairs. "I have flown coast to coast and from one border to another. Never before have I damaged it and, of course, my first accident would have to come on an occasion of this kind." She caught a flight to Cleveland the next day with a Travel Air representative, determined to enjoy the rest of the National Air Races.

Meanwhile, the seventeen remaining pilots flew on. In Fort Worth, the third stop after Pecos, twenty thousand spectators broke through police lines to swarm the airfield when the women landed. Many in the crowd were women themselves, curious to see firsthand these aviatrixes they were reading so much about. The women were so curious about the aircraft that AE complained that they poked umbrellas through the fabric of the wings. In Fort Worth, Margaret Perry, who had raced against Pancho and Bobbi earlier that year, took sick with typhoid fever. That left sixteen still in the race. At the overnight stop in Wichita, they sat through yet another banquet in their honor. In Kansas City, they stopped for a formal luncheon set up in the hangar of a flying school; in St. Louis, another banquet.

By late afternoon of the seventh day the women reached their final overnight stop, Columbus, Ohio. It was now just a 125-mile dash to the finish line. Louise Thaden was leading the field in elapsed time, with AE and Ruth Nichols neck and neck behind her. The next morning, Ruth's plane, taking off just ahead of AE's, suddenly dipped its wing, crashed into a tractor parked at the end of the runway, and flipped over. Instead of taking her turn, AE climbed out of the cockpit of her Vega and ran over to help her rival out of the plane. Ruth was unhurt. AE lost time she could not hope to make up on the short hop to Cleveland.

Meanwhile, Louise Thaden flew on, holding what should have felt like a comfortable lead. But she wasn't comfortable. There had been so many mechanical failures during the race, so many forced landings. Thaden knew that if she had engine trouble on this final leg and was forced to land, she would lose it all. She told herself to baby the engine, take it easy, cruise in. She made up her mind to cut her speed, pull back the engine by one hundred revolutions. But when she sighted Lake Erie, she couldn't help herself: She opened the throttle and powered in. Tens of thousands of spectators cheered as she crossed the finish line at Cleveland Municipal Airport. An hour later, Gladys O'Donnell flew across, then AE, two hours behind the winner.

In the end, fifteen of the twenty-three entrants finished the race, the highest percentage of finishers, female or male, in any cross-country race up to that time. They had battled tough weather, primitive airfields, overzealous crowds, and seven nights of chicken-dinner banquets. The newspapers might continue to call them "winged beauties" and "sweethearts of the air" rather than what they preferred to be called—pilots—but they had proven themselves brave, resourceful, and skilled aviators.

That night, Pancho and the other women pilots put on evening gowns to attend a black-tie banquet in their honor at the Hotel Statler. The next day they joined the crowds—more than a half-million spectators attended the National Air Races—to watch the other events. Pancho watched as Travel Air planes dominated the races. She was already a Travel Air enthusiast and owner, but at the Nationals she saw a new Travel Air, a wonderful, sleek, fast plane unlike any other ship in the air.

She saw it on Labor Day, in the biggest race of the entire Cleveland event, a fifty-mile free-for-all. It was a low-wing, snub-nosed monoplane, painted a flashy scarlet and streamlined down to the hand-formed aluminum-alloy coverings for the nonretractable landing gear. At first, an Army plane moved out ahead in the race. Military planes had traditionally won these speed events. But the "scarlet marvel" soon took over, and it stayed in the lead through the ten laps around the pylons. Going full throttle, it lapped Roscoe Turner's Lockheed Vega, taking fourteen minutes to complete the race and clocking 194.96 miles per hour, the fastest speed ever recorded for any commercial airplane.

Technically called the Travel Air Model R, it was dubbed, Pancho learned, the Travel Air Mystery Ship, because the company had kept its development under wraps for more than a year. At the Wichita factory, founded by a partnership of three of the greatest names in the industry—Beech, Stearman, and Cessna—the glass windows of the production shop were ordered frosted, no one but the engineers working on the project knew about it, and all leaks to the newspapers were plugged. The secrecy paid off. The Mystery Ship was the hit of the National Air Races. It was, aviation enthusiasts raved, "pure speed, grace and performance." With its top speed of more than two hundred miles per hour it was, as one observer quipped, "so fast that it takes three men to see it."

For Pancho, it was love at first sight. When she learned, some months later, that a second Mystery Ship was available, she jumped at the chance to buy it. It cost her $12,500 plus $650 for additional equipment, but the money didn't matter. Now Pancho was the only woman owner of the fastest sport plane in the nation, one of just four constructed. She was the envy of every pilot, the talk of every hangar. She had the ship painted scarlet with deep yellow scallops on the wings, like the Mystery Ship she saw at the races. Then she went out to see just what it would do.

⚊•⚊ ▰◈▰ ⚊•⚊

AE held the women's speed record, 184.6 miles per hour. Pancho knew she and her Mystery Ship could beat that. On August 1, 1930, she took off from Metropolitan Airport in Van Nuys. A measured mile course had been set up. Racing officials were present. The press had been alerted, and newspaper reporters were gathered on the field. Pancho took the ship up, leveled off, and flew full throttle. She was fast, she knew, but how fast?

Not fast enough: 184.1 miles per hour, five-tenths of a mile slower than the record. Three days later, she was out at Metropolitan again, roaring over the measured course only 164 feet above the ground. She finished the first mile in less than eighteen seconds. Officials clocked her at 197.26 miles per hour. She flew two more laps, the scarlet Mystery Ship streaking through the air. When it was over less than a minute later, she had averaged 196.19 miles per hour and had taken the record. The press proclaimed her victory. Fans wrote to her in San Marino asking for her autograph. Union Oil, the company she flew for, designed a full-page magazine advertisement around her, showing the Mystery Ship sweeping across the sky, bending the boughs of the trees it passed. Pancho's victory was "a combination of sheer nerve, skillful piloting, faultless motor and ship, and perfect aviation fuel," read the copy. At least for the moment, Pancho Barnes was the fastest woman on earth.

8

Much Here Revolves Around Me

More than anything, Pancho loved to fly fast. No other thrill matched it. But once she had set the women's speed record, she had little interest in closed-course racing. Flying measured miles or circling around pylons in a field was not her idea of fun. It was technically challenging, but it was also repetitive and predictable. For Pancho, the adventure of flying lay in setting off on long cross-country trips where anything could happen—engine trouble, storms, fog, mountains appearing where they shouldn't be, hazards on landing strips—where you might have to make an emergency landing or find your way across new terrain, where wits and courage and luck kept you in the air.

She got an opportunity to do the kind of flying she loved best when Pickwick Airlines asked her to fly from Los Angeles to Mexico City to open up a new passenger route. She would be the first woman ever to navigate over the interior of Mexico. She knew Pickwick had asked her as a publicity stunt: If a *woman* could fly the route, it must be safe and easy and could be advertised as such. But she said yes anyway. In fact, the route was quite challenging—just her kind of challenge—and it would be a wonderful excuse to get down to Mexico City again, where she and Roger Chute had such exciting times a few years before.

Pancho took off from Metropolitan Airport in her Travel Air Speedwing biplane. She had painted "Mexico or Bust" on the side, next to a picture of a foaming beer mug. The trip took her five leisurely days, flying no more than three or four hours a day, with stops in Tucson, Nogales, Mazatlán, and Guadalajara. When she landed in Mexico City, she was met by officials and dignitaries, presented with an honorary Mexican pilot's license, and whisked away for three days of nonstop parties and cantina-hopping with her old friends and a phalanx of new admirers. She was the center of attention, and she loved every minute of it. A few months later, she was back in Mexico City, one of two women among twenty fliers in a four-day international race to Kansas City. She finished but did not place. Then she was off again, flying from Los Angeles to Chicago and back, then from Los Angeles to South Carolina, a terrible trip including one harrowing nine-hour stretch in the air dodging storms across Arizona, New Mexico, and Texas. Weather forced her down three times in the next three days, but she made it across the continent safely. By the end of 1930, Pancho had flown alone across America ten times.

She still had a contract with Union Oil, which helped subsidize some of her trips. The company sponsored a tour of the major cities of the West Coast, with Pancho flying the president of the Association of Pacific Advertising Clubs on hops from Los Angeles to Vancouver, British Columbia. For Bock Aircraft, she flew potential buyers of planes on jaunts to Palm Springs for lunch or overnight to San Francisco. She still occasionally worked for Lockheed testing planes, and later secured a sponsorship deal with Gilmore Oil, Roscoe Turner's old company.

Like a number of Southern California pilots, Pancho also made money stunt-flying in motion pictures. Hollywood, like the rest of the country, had gone plane crazy after World War I. The flamboyant director Cecil B. DeMille learned to fly in 1917 and operated several airstrips in the Los Angeles area just after the war. He founded both a local aviation company and an airline. Syd Chaplin, Charlie's half-brother, owned an airfield across from DeMille's. Jack Pickford,

Mary's brother, was an aviation enthusiast. William Wellman, a wartime pilot, went on to direct a number of aviation movies, including *Wings,* winner of the first Academy Award for Best Picture. Wallace Beery owned his own airplane. So did the western stars Hoot Gibson and Gene Autry. Hollywood understood America's fascination with airplanes because Hollywood shared it. By the early 1920s, the major studios had all produced box office attractions in which flying and airplanes were a major part of the action. By the early 1930s, Hollywood had produced more than 250 feature films and 25 serials using stunt pilots.

The aerial performers in these new movies were men hired from among the ranks of the barnstormers who hung around a little airfield in Venice, an erstwhile barley field on the edge of Santa Monica Bay. Many were World War I flying aces who found it impossible to settle into peacetime occupations. Some had crisscrossed America as Flying Vagabonds, Winged Gypsies, and Aerial Nomads, appearing at fairs and carnivals and circuses, paid as much as $1,000 by local businesses to perform for special events. By the late 1920s, they were regulars in Hollywood.

The money was good before the Depression. The pilots, by a gentlemen's agreement, adhered to a rate scale established a decade earlier by a fraternity of newsreel stuntmen called the Thirteen Black Cats. Upside-down flying would bring a $100 paycheck. Putting a plane into a dizzying earthbound spin was worth $50. Crashing an airplane into a tree, whether the pilot walked away or not, was, at $1,200, thought to be worth the risk. Stunt pilots also earned good money for performing rolls and loops, for formation flying, for precision takeoffs and landings. In the heyday before the Depression, top stunt pilots were making as much as $50 a day even when they didn't perform dangerous stunts.

When the workday was over and it was time for some serious, alcohol-fueled, yarn-spinning hangar flying, the stunt pilots headed over to Pancho's San Marino mansion, where there was a twenty-four-hour-a-day open-door, open-bar policy. They drank and talked. They entertained themselves by riding Pancho's horses through the city streets and, on some particularly wild nights, into the Spanish-tiled entry of her home. Her place was their unofficial headquarters, just as it was for the everyday pilots she met when she hopped from airfield to airfield. They could party for days, sleep it off in one of the upstairs bedrooms—with or without Pancho, depending on whim and availability—and then come down for more. The guest list was a Who's Who of Hollywood stunt pilots, men like Frank Clarke, Leo Nomis, and Ira Reed. Clarke was the best-known, most sought-after stunt pilot in town, a crazy, daring man called Spook because he seemed to have an almost hypnotic power over people. Pancho thought he was one of the greatest characters who'd ever lived. She adored him. She was his shadow. He was the most exciting man in her life. They were not intimate, although Pancho may have wanted them to be. They were close, good-time buddies.

Reed was another of her favorites, a full-blooded Pawnee from Oklahoma who used to entertain air-show audiences by hanging by his braids from the axle of a low-flying plane. He had designs on Pancho. After he had made several insistent attempts to get her upstairs to one of the bedrooms, she made him a bet. She sent him on an errand to Bakersfield, a hundred miles away, in his old, ailing automobile. If he got back to her house by nine that night, she would sleep with him. She had no objection to sleeping with him, but she figured the car would never make it. Ira burst in the door that evening with minutes to spare, and the two began an on-again, off-again affair that complemented their friendship.

In that grand time before the Depression changed everything, the stunt pilots lived the most enviable of lives: thrilling, unpredictable, and lucrative. Working on Howard Hughes's *Hell's Angels* was one of the most exciting flying opportunities of the time. Hughes had taken up flying in 1925, when he was twenty years old, and had become an immediate, obsessive enthusiast. By the late 1920s, he had produced a few movies, but Hollywood didn't take him seriously. The scriptwriter Ben

Hecht called him "that sucker with money." But Hughes had a plan. He would produce and direct an epic film about World War I flying aces that would combine his love of flying with his love of movies and establish his reputation.

In the spring and summer of 1927, Hughes's scouts scoured the United States and Europe, spending his money freely, buying or leasing eighty-seven vintage planes for a total of more than half a million dollars. Back in Southern California, Hughes was busy turning a San Fernando Valley alfalfa farm, a patch of land surrounded by asparagus fields and chicken ranches, into a self-contained airport he named Caddo Field. There he built the sheds, hangars, and repair shops necessary to house and maintain the fleet of planes, and there he started filming his aerial epic, hiring more than seventy stunt pilots with Frank Clarke as their chief. At first, he took novice pilots at $10 a day, but when they cracked up three planes in quick succession, he changed his strategy and hired experienced professionals—the men who partied at Pancho's—for $200 a week.

By 1928 Hughes had spent more than $1 million on flying sequences alone. In one dogfight sequence, thirty planes were in the sky and in the frame at once, dodging, darting, looping, spinning, sideslipping, performing an orchestrated aerial ballet. In another, a spectacular attack scene, World War I fighter planes gunned down a German dirigible. At one point, Hughes moved the entire filming operation from Los Angeles to Oakland in search of just the right kind of fluffy clouds. Six months, four fatal accidents, and $250,000 later, he moved everyone back to Caddo Field. Finally, after more than two years in production, *Hell's Angels* was ready.

Hughes released it for preview, but it was a silent film, and that era was passing. *The Jazz Singer* had opened in late 1927, and audiences were becoming increasingly accustomed to talkies. *Hell's Angels* would not succeed as a silent movie. Other filmmakers caught in the same historical moment solved the problem by dubbing in sound. Hughes went back and at considerable expense refilmed all the close-up shots on a soundstage. Then he rehired a crew of stunt pilots to go back in the air so he could record engine sounds for all the flying sequences. Through her friendship with Frank Clarke and her reputation among the stunt fliers, Pancho was hired to do some of the aerial sound work. She was the only woman flier on the set.

Pancho spent whole days flying her Travel Air Speedwing in the skies above Caddo Field and out in the Mojave above the dry lakes. She buzzed a red balloon tethered at a thousand feet above the field with a sound recorder hung underneath, diving, spinning, and creating engine sounds for every maneuver Hughes had caught on film. *Hell's Angels,* which ended up costing Hughes $3.8 million of his personal fortune, premiered in Hollywood on May 27, 1930. It was the gaudiest, splashiest affair that gaudy, splashy town had ever seen. Hollywood Boulevard was blocked off for half a mile, and streetcars were detoured as a crowd of more than a million packed the area. Thirty planes flew overhead, caught by the beams of 250 searchlights that scanned the skies. The picture broke all attendance records wherever it opened—Los Angeles, New York, Boston, London. It was hailed as "the best spectacle that has ever been produced in motion pictures" and "the greatest masterpiece the screen has ever known." To Pancho and Frank Clarke and the other stunt pilots who worked on the movie, the film's success meant good money and greater opportunities as Hollywood intensified its love affair with the aerial movie.

During the filming and refilming of *Hell's Angels,* Pancho found work as a pilot on *The Aviator, Young Eagles,* and *Air Mail Pilot,* all long on airborne action and short on plot. She worked on *The Lost Squadron* with her friend Erich von Stroheim, who had a part parodying himself as an imperious director. She worked on *The Flying Fleet* with Ramon Novarro. She flew in *The Dawn Patrol,* a Howard Hawks movie starring Douglas Fairbanks, Jr. For *The Flying Fool,* a Pathé Pictures movie starring William Boyd (who later endeared himself to children as Hopalong Cassidy), she was hired as technical director. It was her job to pick the stunt pilots for the movie, oversee their work, and orchestrate the flight scenes. Pancho convinced Pathé to pay her three pilots, including top professionals Frank Clarke and Leo Nomis, $100 a day for guaranteed work. "I know all the tricks the pilots use to make money," she told her studio bosses. "I'll make sure they give me a real day's work."

Howard Hughes was enraged. This was during the seemingly interminable filming of *Hell's Angels,* and he was paying his pilots—including Clarke—$40 a day for completing the final scenes. Not only was Pancho showing him up by paying her pilots considerably more, she was also stealing Frank Clarke away from the film. Hughes insisted that Clarke return to Caddo Field. Pancho stood her ground. Frank had signed a contract with her. Hughes wasted no more time arguing. He went directly to the studio head at Pathé and got him to release Clarke from his contract—but not before Pancho had extracted a promise that her friend receive $125 a day for his remaining work on *Hell's Angels.*

When Hughes's aerial epic finally opened, along with Hawks's *The Dawn Patrol,* stunt pilots, already well known in aviation and motion-picture circles, came to the attention of the general public through newspaper stories, newsreels, and fan magazines. They were decreed the real leading men of the popular aviation pictures, the new heroes of the day, dashing, daring, death-defying. Pancho didn't have a high-profile stunt-flying career like some of her male friends, but she was the only woman who was part of their world, and she loved it. She also worked in Hollywood in ways they didn't.

Ever since she had started doctoring scripts for Erich von Stroheim, she had fancied herself a woman of untapped literary talent. She was a marvelous storyteller. She knew that; all her friends told her so. In the hangar after a day of flying, in the basement barroom of her Laguna Beach house, around the dining table in San Marino, she was the consummate yarn-spinner, the raconteur who knew how to stretch a story for dramatic tension, how to deliver a punch line, how to tease and joke and curse and keep everyone listening not out of politeness because it was her liquor they were drinking, but out of fascination with the tale and the way she told it. Now, in rare moments away from the airfield and on the ground, when she forced herself to sit quietly, she started to write. First, she tried screenplays. She wrote a script called *Air Male* in 1931 and placed it with an agent who was optimistic about selling it. But nothing happened. John Ford's movie *Airmail* was already in production. She and a flying buddy had more success with a script called *Test Pilot,* based on a Frank "Spig" Wead story. The movie was later made with an all-star cast, including Spencer Tracy, Clark Gable, Myrna Loy, and Lionel Barrymore.

Pancho tried her hand at short-story writing too, producing a yarn about a pilot who races for fame and fortune and dies in a fiery crash. She began a book, "O.K. Death," about an airline pilot and his flying career. She explored the other subject she knew well, horses, beginning a manuscript called "Knee Deep in Clover," about a girl named Jo-Jo, who wants to be a jockey, and her horse, Golden West. She began to write a bodice-ripper based on a Von Stroheim script called "Wedding March," set in Vienna. Her typing was hunt-and-peck, her spelling was marginal, but she understood the genre: "Mitzi clung to him with all her strength. He turned to her brutally; her eyes implored him and she managed to whisper hoarsely between her choking sobs: Don't . . . don't . . . PLEASE don't! I'll marry you," read one overheated passage. She even attempted verse, writing about her male alter ego in "A Sailor's Senorita":

> *To old Laguna, land of manana*
> *There came a sailor, brave and strong was he*
> *In search of treasure of boundless measure*
> *Many years he'd sailed the salty sea*

All the manuscripts were equal parts action and cliché. None were complete. None were edited. All were written hastily, as the mood hit, in between flying and partying. Then they were forgotten. Pancho relished the idea of being a writer but not the part where she had to apply the seat of the pants to the seat of the chair. As she told Rankin, who was off traveling on church business, "Aviation is my real calling. . . . I think I will stick pretty close to the airplanes."

Through 1930 and 1931, she began combining her skills in speed racing and cross-country flying. In August 1930, she flew through thick fog to win the first Tom Thumb aerial derby, a 225-mile mini-race from Long Beach to Santa Paula and back. The next summer, leading her fourteen opponents all the way, she won the event again. She set the speed record from Los Angeles to San Francisco and another from Los Angeles to Sacramento. When she landed in Los Angeles after the record-setting two-hour-and-thirteen-minute flight from the state capital, twenty thousand spectators cheered her on the field, and the governor of California presented her with a trophy engraved AMERICA'S FASTEST WOMAN FLYER.

But in the big national races, the 1930 and 1931 cross-country derbies, she failed to live up to the honor. In 1930, she was set to race accompanied by her pet Chihuahua, Chito, who was harnessed into a tiny parachute. But she was disqualified at the last moment when officials discovered that her Mystery Ship lacked necessary certification from the U.S. Department of Commerce. In the 1931 derby, flying with a Japanese good-luck charm hanging from her instrument board, she placed third coming into the first stop in Calexico, fell to fifth at Tucson the next day, and placed sixth for the next several days. She still hoped to make up time and finish in the money, but a storm grounded her on the sixth day. By the time she finally made it to Cleveland after waiting out the weather, she was not even in the top ten. "I haven't done anything particularly to cover myself with glory," she wrote to Rankin after the 1931 derby disappointment. "But," she added, "you would be surprised how much here revolves around me."

Pancho wrote to her husband regularly, whether it was she who was traveling the country or he on one of his increasingly frequent business trips. Their already amiable relationship seemed to grow closer the farther apart they were. She wrote to him when he traveled to Minneapolis, Chicago, and Cincinnati, to Mexico City, to Switzerland, Austria, Scotland, and England. He sent congratulatory telegrams when she won races, little notes on her birthdays. They had not lived together since 1928, but when they weren't on the road or in the skies, they lived

within a few miles of each other and, to some degree, still shared a social circle. That changed in the spring of 1931, when Rankin assumed
the position of executive secretary of the National Council of the Episcopal Church and moved to New York City, taking up residency in the
Gramercy Park Hotel. "You're a swell guy and they better appreciate
you—OR I WANT TO KNOW WHY," Pancho wrote to him. "I feel
you are much too good for anybody and that they ought to make you
pope of the outfit."

She was happy for Rankin, delighted that his career was flourishing.
She was unfazed when he took nine-year-old Billy along and enrolled
the boy in a boarding school in New Jersey. Pancho had shown only
limited interest in her son since he was born. That first year he was
away, she even neglected to send him a card on his birthday. "I was
away on a trip at the time," she wrote him later. "I could not get word
to you because I did not know your address."

Privately, Rankin's move to the East Coast made very little difference to Pancho. But publicly, she still maintained the fiction of their
marriage, at least to some people. It was easier than explaining the reality. Announcing to an acquaintance the news of her husband's reloca-
tion, she wrote: "I will remain here in California, primarily because
transplanting me into another environment than the one I so dearly
love would cause me the greatest unhappiness and secondly, because all
my business interests are here."

As their separation grew longer, their letters grew warmer. "Dearest
lover," Rankin addressed her in a letter from Niagara Falls, where he
was attending a social-work conference. "I love you, dear," she answered the next week. "Because I haven't written lately is no sign that
I am not thinking of you." She signed her letters "your grass widow."
"With a world of love to you," he answered. They never saw each
other.

This odd long-distance relationship, with its combination of tender-
ness and detachment, warmth and estrangement, was evident when
Pancho took seriously ill during one of her flying tours of California.
Alone, more than five hundred miles from home, she was rushed from

an airfield in Redding to the local hospital. The pain in her right side below the abdomen was unbearable. It was her appendix, the doctor thought. But during the operation, he discovered a tumor on her right ovary. He took it out, as well as the ovary and everything else. A month before her thirtieth birthday, Pancho had a total hysterectomy. She wrote to Rankin that she was "having pain" and "under opiates." He didn't come west to see her. Instead, he sent a cheery note. "Just take it easy now, sweetheart," he wrote.

Pancho did not mourn the loss of her reproductive capacity. She had no desire whatsoever to have another child. In fact, the hysterectomy had definite benefits: It would make her active sex life more convenient. But she did mourn the loss of the $1,000 the operation cost her. By the early 1930s, California, like the rest of the nation, was going through the worst years of the Great Depression, and Pancho was not immune. She had been spending down her inheritance for almost a decade, using it as if it were a renewable resource. But it wasn't. Most of her wealth was in real estate, in houses that generated no income and were enormously expensive to keep up, and in other property on which she was still paying mortgages. She had holdings in the company that owned her late grandfather's hotel in Philadelphia, but few could afford the luxury of staying in first-class accommodations in the midst of the Depression.

Suddenly, money became a problem. Oil companies stopped sponsoring front-page fliers, cutting their stipends as airborne publicists and withdrawing financial support for races. There was no more easy money to be made by ferrying executive passengers around the state. Hollywood wages plummeted, not for stars, but for workers like Pancho. Horse fanciers could no longer afford to buy the Thoroughbred stallions she kept in her stables. She sold one extraordinary horse for only $150, and was glad to get it.

But she would not stop spending. In a single month in 1932, she spent almost $3,000, three times the average *yearly* income of a Depression-era worker, paying for the upkeep on the Laguna Beach and San Marino homes and on her cars and planes, and for the salaries of her servants and other workers. Since 1923, when she came into her own money, she had spent both lavishly and carelessly. Now circumstances forced her to care. "I am anxious to get my finances straightened out," she wrote to Rankin. She did not know how much she spent or where it went. She just knew it was going, and fast. For a few months, she dutifully tallied her expenses: $2,350 spent in July, $2,998 in August, $1,289 in September. But she was not organized enough to continue keeping detailed ledgers. Still, she tried to rein herself in. "I am cutting down as much as possible on everything," she wrote to Rankin.

The parties at San Marino were now potluck. No more pounds of prawns piled high on shaved ice. But it was still her liquor that everyone guzzled. She dispensed with the services of her gardener, letting the grounds of both homes go untended. With great regret, she fired the man who had been in charge of her stables for many years. "I have been trying for some time to sell the horses but have met with little success," she wrote him. "Things have come to such a point that I can no longer afford to maintain the stable." She started selling off some of her real estate holdings at prices far below their worth of a few years earlier. Her finances were in such disarray that she decided she had to part with her most prized possession, her beautiful, sleek $12,000 Travel Air Mystery Ship, the plane that made her the envy of the Southern California aviation world. Maintenance, gas, and hangar fees were just too much. The plane was too valuable an asset to hold on to when she needed money for daily expenses. But Pancho, who had a hard time being practical about anything, was least practical about airplanes. She knew she should sell the Mystery Ship, but for a while she considered trading it for another plane. Howard Hughes owned a Boeing P-12, the last of the fighter biplanes the Army had commissioned, a stallion of a ship with a huge engine. "I would give my soul for that ship," she wrote to a friend. For more than a year, she tried to work the trade, but Hughes remained uninterested. Finally, grieving for the loss of her Scarlet Streak, her low-winged beauty, she authorized a local flying service to try to find a buyer.

Times were tough for the stunt pilots, too. Just as their collective star was rising with the release of *Hell's Angels,* Southern California began to reel from the Depression. Fliers who had never worked on a picture before, student pilots, amateurs desperate for work, began to compete with and underbid the experienced men. These novice fliers often worked for a loss just to get started. They performed dangerous stunts for a few dollars—anything to be employed, anything to make enough money for food and rent. Meanwhile, the professionals, Pancho and her gang, the smiling heroes of the fan magazines, were out of work.

Howard Hughes was filming two aviation cheapies, *Cock of the Air* and *Sky Devils,* using outtakes from *Hell's Angels* and the work of inexperienced pilots willing to do stunts for five dollars a day. "Howard Hughes is a two-for-a-nickel son of a bitch," Pancho told her flying friends as they sat drinking around the dining room table in San Marino. She had not forgiven him for stealing Frank Clarke away from her Pathé picture. The group that gathered most nights and every weekend at Pancho's spent long, boozy hours complaining about the interlopers who were undercutting them, and about the directors who were hiring the interlopers.

It was Pancho's idea to do something about it, to organize, to form a union of motion-picture pilots who could band together to demand fair wages. She called the American Federation of Labor local that represented the motion-picture cameramen and asked for support and advice. She talked to David Behncke, who was working with the local airline pilots on attempts to unionize them. She talked up the idea at her home and in the hangars of the local airports. On January 5, 1932, the Association of Motion Picture Pilots (AMPP) was officially chartered with twenty members, including all the top stunt pilots who had been working in Hollywood for more than a decade. Pancho, the only woman in the group, was elected secretary-treasurer. The veteran stunt pilot Leo Nomis was unanimously elected president. Pancho had once asked Nomis how he managed to spin his plane so close to the ground.

She marveled at both his skill and his courage. "I spin until I know it's time to pull out," he told her. "Then I spin one more time." Less than a month after his election, Leo Nomis was killed trying to come out of a thousand-foot spin while working on Paramount's *Sky Brides*. Frank Clarke, who had been elected vice president, took over.

During its first few months, the AMPP set wages for daily stunt work, established a pay schedule for specific stunts, as in the pre-Depression years, and adopted safety rules that governed all types of motion-picture flying services. But the new union seemed powerless to prevent the hiring of inexperienced pilots. It wasn't until May 1932, when Paramount began shooting on location in Bishop, California, just south of Yosemite, with a crew of nonunion pilots, that the AFL provided the necessary muscle. Four officers, three from the motion-picture industry and one from the California State Federation of Labor, "descended in wrath," as Pancho reported to the membership, stopping the Paramount production. Negotiations followed, and filming resumed with members of the AMPP.

As the union grew in strength and numbers, and as the Depression deepened, the pilots stuck together in ways that far exceeded their chartered mission. They flew each other to distant locations. They shared what work was available, ceding jobs to those men who had been unlucky in getting work or who had families to support. They came together all too frequently to mourn one of their kind, the funerals often turning into impromptu air shows followed by drunken wakes that lasted for days. By the end of 1932, Hollywood filmmakers recognized the AMPP as the only accredited organization in town whose members were masters of their trade, qualified to fly everything from single-engine planes to transports and bombers, able to perform any stunt a script might call for. Occasionally a wildcat pilot would still undercut the union, but more and more the major studios were looking to hire dependability and experience—and to avoid run-ins with the AFL. The studios also depended on the AMPP for technical advice, hiring union pilots to coordinate stunts and direct aerial sequences. In the depths of the Depression, the union helped the pilots make a living.

But unionization also meant that many others were shut out, not just the amateurs who had been trying to undercut the experienced fliers, but men like Paul Mantz, a daring and skilled pilot who had never flown in pictures. With his slick black hair, Clark Gable mustache, and lean face, Mantz was made for the movies. But he was stuck: He couldn't get work unless he had a union card, and he couldn't join the union until he had screen credits. He went to the flamboyant showman Roscoe Turner for help, asking how he could get into the AMPP.

"Go see Pancho," Roscoe told him. "She organized it."

"Who's Pancho?" Paul asked.

"Once you meet her," Turner said, "you'll never have to ask again."

Like most people who met Pancho for the first time, Paul was taken aback by her rough clothes and rougher language, but the two took an instant liking to each other. Paul was brash, self-assured, and notably handsome, just Pancho's kind of guy, and that made her enjoy her sense of power even more. He needed her help. He came to her for help. She loved it.

"Paul," she told him, "there's some work around here that the boys won't touch. Find it."

He did. He bid $100 on a stunt no one wanted to do—flying through a Hollywood Hills canyon with a wing walker in *The Galloping Ghost*— and went back to the AMPP to get his card. Frank Clarke, then the undisputed king of Hollywood stunt pilots, may have guessed that he was meeting his match when he met Paul Mantz. The two, in fact, would become rivals for the top spot, with Mantz taking over by the late thirties. But on that first day, Frank Clarke was clearly in charge. After quizzing Mantz about his bid for the stunt, Frank informed him that the union's initiation fee was $100, his entire first paycheck.

Paul was furious. He knew that the other pilots had paid $10 for their union cards. He went fuming to Pancho. She laughed at Frank Clarke's none-too-subtle manipulations and told Paul to pay up.

"It's the best deal you'll ever get," she said.

Paul Mantz and Frank Clarke and a handful of other stunt pilots went on to lucrative careers, thanks to Hollywood's continued affinity for flying pictures, the AMPP, and, of course, their own considerable skill and courage. Stunting was even more a male domain than racing, record breaking, or cross-country flying. Pancho was always the only woman. She had not flown the big stunts. She didn't have the skill, and she didn't have the patience to acquire it. But she had made a big difference. The union boys would continue to meet at her San Marino house to drink her liquor and share their harrowing tales. Pancho loved being in the thick of it, but she was also ready, once again, for something new.

9

Love and Politics

Pancho unexpectedly decided to try her hand at politics. She had strong opinions about everything, no doubt including the way Los Angeles was run, and she was buoyed by the experience of organizing the AMPP. But she had never taken a public stand on a municipal issue or worked for a candidate or shown much interest in the political process. She was, moreover, the antithesis of a political animal. Her moves were as uncalculated as a child's. Her decisions came from the heart, not the head. But Pancho loved being connected, being in the know, being the one to whom others turned for important favors. Most of all, she loved being the center of attention.

In the spring of 1932, the elected supervisor for Los Angeles County's Third District died in office, and one of Pancho's good friends, Buron Fitts, a candidate for L.A. district attorney, encouraged her to make a bid for the open seat. Supervisors were the top legislative officials in the county, so the post was an important and powerful one. Although Pancho didn't live in the Third District, which primarily encompassed Hollywood, she did own an apartment building on Sunset Boulevard, which arguably qualified her to hold the office.

In May, Pancho was city-hopping from Los Angeles to Vancouver,

British Columbia, as part of an airborne goodwill tour to promote the
1932 Olympics, scheduled for Los Angeles that summer. As the only
woman in the nineteen-pilot contingent, she was given the honor of
heading the flight. At the stop in Sacramento, Pancho went to see Governor James Rolph, Jr., the man who had honored her with a trophy a
year before, to ask him to appoint her to the open supervisor's seat. But
it wasn't going to be that easy. Rolph told her she would have to run for
the office in the upcoming August election.

Back from the goodwill tour, Pancho announced her candidacy and
successfully fought off a residency challenge that would have kept her
name off the ballot. Then she threw herself, full force, into the race.
She opened three campaign offices; gathered an impressive list of endorsers that included Amelia Earhart, Jimmy Doolittle, Ramon Novarro, Frank Clarke, and a number of union locals; drafted a vague but
powerfully worded platform statement; and printed up thousands of
brochures. For the cover, she selected a Hurrell photograph. It showed
a handsome woman dressed in a crisp white shirt under a tailored
leather aviator jacket, her body tilted forward, her head slightly cocked,
as if she were just about to reach out and shake a hand. This woman's
face is carefully composed and enhanced by makeup. Her smile is controlled and self-assured. The caption under the photograph reads
"Florence Lowe Barnes." Her nickname appears nowhere in the pamphlet.

Like most inexperienced candidates, Pancho played on her outsider
status. She called the county's elected officials "shrewd men . . . who
have no scruples or conscience, but who are political profiteers." These
men, she wrote in her campaign brochure, "hoodwink the people into
voting for them, and then proceed to bleed the public thru' devious
methods . . . much handshaking and valueless promises." Pancho
made no promises other than to get things moving. "Never before has
there been such a need for action," she wrote, without specifying just
what action. "I do not represent any interest, clique or group of individuals and am dictated in my actions only by my own judgment and
conscience."

Florence Lowe Barnes billed herself as a native daughter of California and mentioned pointedly that she was the granddaughter of T.S.C. Lowe, the wife of the Reverend Rankin Barnes, and the mother of an eleven-year-old boy, the latter circumstance conferring on her "an understanding and sympathy for other women, and especially for children's welfare." Elsewhere, she called herself a "staunch fighter for the rights of people." AE, quoted prominently in the brochure, offered a most generous endorsement: "You are doing a splendid thing by running. As a sister pilot and my friend I wish you every success."

During early August, Pancho spread the word as only she could, by dropping leaflets from her plane. Then she rigged a smoke pot to her Travel Air exhaust pipe and advertised her candidacy every afternoon by writing VOTE FOR FLORENCE LOWE BARNES in the skies above Los Angeles. Among those who were impressed by Pancho's dramatic flair was Sid Grauman, owner of Grauman's Chinese Theatre. "The writing in the sky was 100 percent," he cabled her in mid-August. "As one showman to another, please accept my congratulations for an artistic achievement." But the artistic achievement did not translate into a political one. When the votes were counted on August 30, 1932, Pancho came in fifth in a field of thirteen candidates. It was not a bad showing for a political novice, and with her endorsements and the increasing familiarity of her name, it could have been a prelude to another run for office. She had had fun that summer moving in political circles, banqueting, glad-handing, occasionally speechifying, and looping through the summer skies to write her name for thousands to see. But Pancho rarely did the same thing twice. She had given politics her best—and only—shot.

If she was disappointed, she didn't show it. She didn't have time. Hours after the election results were announced, her friend Buron Fitts, who had won his race for Los Angeles D.A., called Pancho to arrange a flight to Mexico. During the campaign they had joked about taking such a trip, half vacation, half adventure. Now Buron was on the phone asking Pancho to be at the airfield in an hour. That was impossible, she told him. Make it two. She needed at least an hour to remove all the skywriting equipment.

They took off in her open-cockpit plane near sundown. Pancho knew this was no time to start for anywhere, especially no time to embark on a flight of several thousand miles, but Buron was insistent. The race had been hard on him. He had political enemies and was often accompanied by bodyguards. He couldn't wait to get away.

They left that evening just to get a few miles under their belts, stopping in Phoenix for the night. There Pancho partied with several pilots and Union Oil company friends who happened to be staying at the same hotel, while Buron spent a few hours working on an ongoing case. The next evening they made it to El Paso, where Buron encouraged her to cross into Mexico right away. Pancho proceeded to educate him in the niceties of international relations. There was a certain established protocol to clearing the border, she said, which she had learned through vast experience. It consisted mainly of playing checkers with the Mexican immigration officials. After a few games, it was acceptable to broach the subject of border crossing. But the subject had better be broached indirectly. Pancho would say that her boss—a fiction; there was no boss—was going to make a lot of difficulty for her if she didn't get her papers in order that night. But she guessed she'd just have to take his guff, because this boss simply didn't understand how difficult and complicated crossing the border was. Nodding sympathetically, her checkers-playing friends would stamp and sign her documents, and within fifteen minutes, the paperwork would be done. Then they all relaxed for a few more games and a beer or two. Pancho had found that border officials were in a much better mood after a sociable evening than they were if awoken at dawn by a gringa pilot in a hurry to get going.

Following the Pancho system, they took off at sunrise without incident, only to fly directly into a tropical storm that buffeted them with high winds and soaked them with sheeting rain. Visibility was so poor that Pancho had to fly low, navigating along a set of railroad tracks to Chihuahua. The airport there looked like a lake. She had no idea whether the water on the runway was two inches or two feet deep, but she had to land somehow. The safest move, she thought, would be to come in tail low, nose up, dragging the plane's tail in the water to keep from flipping over when the front wheels hit. It was a spectacular landing. The water, it turned out, was six inches deep, and when the ship touched down, the spray fanned out in all directions. Even as she gripped the wheel, she was enjoying the wild ride.

They took off the next morning, bad weather dogging them all day. Stiff headwinds forced Pancho to make an unscheduled landing at a deserted airfield where they waited most of the afternoon for a man on a burro to ride out to the nearest town and bring them back a can of gasoline. That night, still flying in heavy rain, they came into Mexico City drenched and shivering. But from then on, the trip was one long, uninterrupted party.

Pancho made friends with a number of Mexican air force officers and hosted a noisy, liquor-fueled party in her hotel room. But when the group took off to a striptease nightclub in search of further entertainment, Pancho found herself left on the curb. The club was men only, the bouncer informed her. The solution was obvious: The next night, with the aid of a quick haircut and a borrowed Mexican air force colonel's uniform, she was back at the club, pushing past the bouncer and ready for fun. That was only the beginning. Pancho, Buron, and their new friends settled into a week of hard carousing, hitting the bars and the cabarets, often joined by women who did not guess that Pancho was one of them. At one cantina, Pancho, in the colonel's uniform, was sitting with a prostitute on her knee when she recognized a fellow patron as the husband of one of her classmates from the Bishop School in La Jolla. The man didn't recognize her, and under the circumstances, she thought it best to not introduce herself. The week ended with an invitation to a formal diplomatic dinner hosted by the president of the country in honor of another pilot on a goodwill tour.

The return trip was harrowing. Pancho took off in a rainstorm. She cleared the mountains outside of Mexico City at nine thousand feet only to find herself flying blind in a thick cloudbank. She took the plane higher and higher, the air increasingly chilly, the clouds still so thick they seemed solid. Still she couldn't get out of it. At twelve thousand feet, she broke out on top, more relieved than she was willing to let her passenger know.

When they at last landed at Mazatlán, Buron was ready to crawl into bed. But Pancho needed to let off some steam. She figured this was their last night in Mexico, and they ought to raise a little more hell before leaving the country. She rounded up a few girls and brought them up to Buron's room to tempt him. When he refused, Pancho took the girls out for a drink and then headed out alone to the beach. The water was absolutely still, the moonlight so bright it cast sharp shadows. Pancho took off all her clothes and went for a long swim.

The next day she put in eighteen hours of flying, the roughest day she'd ever spent in the air. She had outflown the storm, but now the September sun beat down on them in their open cockpits. Pancho had spilled gasoline on her jacket during a short stop to take on fuel, and the fumes nauseated her and made her dizzy. She fought vertigo all afternoon but kept on flying. At nightfall, she discovered that the panel lights in her plane had burned out, and she couldn't see the key chain hanging from the instrument panel, her guide to whether she was flying level. Below her, the landscape was dark, offering no clues to her position. The long day in the hot sun, the monotonous drone of the engine, the gas fumes, the week of almost nonstop revelry . . . She began to lose her sense of the plane, of where it was in the sky, of direction, of up and down. Now, all of a sudden, it seemed to her that the plane was doing a slow roll to the right. Could that be what was happening? She fought the nausea and groped in the dark for the key chain. It was hanging straight down. But how could that be? She still felt the plane rolling. She should land and rest. But there was nowhere to put the ship down. For the first time since she had started flying, she felt truly frightened. She was at the edge, and she knew it.

Then she saw something below—a light, a moving light. It focused her attention, gave her a point of reference. She could feel the plane around her again, feel its position in the sky. She took the plane down to get a better look. It was a train. She followed its lights across Arizona, across the Colorado River, across the southeast corner of California, her confidence restored. At Indio, close to midnight, they stopped for gas and a big steak dinner, one of those extraordinarily hearty meals people eat when they have just cheated death. Pancho called her San Marino house, where there was a contingent of pilots in residence, eating, drinking, and carrying on as usual regardless of the absence of their hostess. She asked about the weather. These fliers were better prognosticators than the weather bureau. The fog was rolling in, they said. "If you hurry, you can make it," a man named Blackie told her.

By the time she hit the Los Angeles Basin, the fog was solid pack clouds and she was flying blind. She flew on top of it, trying to figure out where she was, circling, wasting gas. She hadn't taken on much fuel at Indio, knowing she was so close to home. Then up ahead, on the blanket of fog, she saw a dim circle of light. It took her a minute to realize that it was the beacon from March Field, an Army airstrip she knew well. That's where she would land. She knew exactly where the beacon was and what her approach should be. She gunned the engine, then pulled back on the stick and settled down through the fog, blind. She let the plane sink, then gunned the engine again, stalling, sinking, looking for the ground. She never saw it, even after the landing wheels hit. The fog was that thick. Taxiing toward the hangar, unable to see anything in front of her, she ran into a tent and bent her propeller. A few weeks later, she returned to March with a new propeller. When the plane was repaired, she started taxiing up to the fuel tanks, but the engine quit in a few hundred feet. The tanks were empty. She had landed at March with less than a minute of flying time left. She had almost killed herself and her passenger.

＊＊＊＊＊

By the early 1930s, Pancho had been flying for only a few years, but American women had been airborne for a generation. They had barnstormed, stunted, broken records, flown across the country and across the ocean. Now they were looking for ways to organize, to serve their country in the air as men did. Female fliers had come together after the 1929 derby to form an organization called the Ninety-Nines, after the number of charter members, but that group's mission was more public relations than service. Although Pancho was a member, she was looking for something more. In the spring of 1931, the year before she ran for L.A. county supervisor, she heard about the Betsy Ross Corps, a national organization of female pilots intended to function as an auxiliary of the Army Air Corps, the precursor of the U.S. Air Force. She joined immediately, donning the uniform of khaki jodhpurs and shirt, and meeting with other local women fliers at March Field. But she was soon disappointed by the lack of activities. A few months later, she heard about yet another group, the Women's Aeronautical Air Force, formed in New York. Again, she joined. But whatever the WAAF was doing, it was doing on the East Coast, not the West. It was time for Pancho to step out in front.

In the fall of 1931, with the help of a pilot whose husband was commander of the Army Reserve base at Clover Field, Pancho founded the Women's Air Reserve. It would be a local organization of female fliers, organized along military lines, whose purpose was to aid in disasters where it was impossible to reach people except by plane. Pancho started the WAR so that women pilots would have the opportunity to train, as the men did, and the opportunity to serve, but she had a more immediate, more visceral reason. Women had been barred from that summer's National Air Races in Cleveland. "Women and other amateur pilots," said the event organizers, "tended to rob aviation of its thrills and slow down the speed tournaments." Pancho was livid. Women fliers had already proven their abilities many times over. If they could not fly as fast as the men did, it was because they did not have access to the military planes and the training the men did, not because they were women. Pancho didn't even entertain the thought that women could join the military, but they could form a force of their own. The women pilots of the WAR would show the world, or at least their small part of it, that they were serious, determined fliers with professional skills. Pancho would be their leader, their general. When the official stationery was printed, there she was, at the top, General Pancho Barnes, commander of the troops.

The organization had no military status or official connection, but it was run military-style, from the ranks of the officers to its headquarters in a room at the U.S. Army base in Long Beach to its elaborate uniforms. The women wore Lafayette Escadrille blue jodhpurs with a red stripe down the leg, blue dress shirts, blue suede military jackets criss-crossed with bandolier straps, knee-high black leather boots, and black felt berets set off jauntily to the right. Pancho kept a roll book with the thirty to forty members' names, each name neatly typed, each preceded by a rank—"Captain Bobbi Trout," "Lieutenant Alice Kelly"—each evaluated after every monthly meeting: "Late." "No excuse." "No uniform." The rules were strict. The commander wrote "Efficiency Reports" on all members, grading them on attendance, deportment, interest, discipline, and appearance. Members who wanted out were required to submit written requests to be relieved of duty. Pancho had forms printed to dispense honorable and dishonorable discharges.

On the first Sunday of every month, resplendent in their "horizon blue" uniforms, they landed their planes on the runway at the Long Beach Army base and spent the morning practicing marching drills on the parade grounds. They studied first aid, radio communication, and aircraft mechanics. Some Sundays they convened at Pancho's Laguna Beach property, which was by then vacant and in disrepair because Pancho could no longer afford the upkeep. The grounds were a mess. The pool was empty, the concrete already cracking. The women couldn't believe what was happening to the place, especially Bobbi Trout, who had seen it in its glory days only a year or two before. But this was the Depression. Everyone was suffering. And Pancho didn't seem to care. She shrugged it off. The women skirted the house, hiked down a narrow path along the steep cliffs, and practiced target shooting on the beach below. At a member's house in Santa Barbara, they gathered to practice archery.

Other Sundays they would convene at Mines Field before dawn to receive flying orders from their commanding officer, General Pancho Barnes. Each pilot-navigator team was assigned a special mission: Sometimes they would be ordered to fly to a designated airstrip, circle the field, and return to Mines on a tight schedule. Other times they were assigned to drop bags of flour on X's marked on a distant field, practicing precision skills they might use for emergency parachute drops. The women loved the challenge, and they loved the camaraderie. Whatever else they might be doing the rest of the week—some had families, some had businesses, some had both—on Sundays they were fliers, in uniform. They were skilled professionals, marching in formation, navigating the skies of Southern California, proving their self-sufficiency, proving their competence to the men who would deny them an equal place in aviation and in the military. Also, they were having a lot of fun.

The women of the WAR were never asked to help in the kind of emergency for which they trained, but Pancho did call on them for an emergency of her own. As independent, self-assured, and headstrong as she was, Pancho had a weakness for men, especially dark, exotic, handsome men. She knew she was not a pretty woman, and she didn't care. She couldn't let herself care. She couldn't change her plain round face and her thick neck. She couldn't change her body with its broad shoulders and narrow hips. She was who she was, and she had never let her looks interfere with her love life. Men were attracted to the force of her personality, her enormous energy, her capacity for fun, and her uncomplicated love of sex. She had already made a play for one dark, exotic, handsome man, Ramon Novarro, only to discover that he preferred men. In the early thirties, she made a play for another, also a movie star, a man who called himself Duncan Renaldo. He was an unfortunate choice. Whereas Novarro truly liked Pancho, although he could not love her as she wanted him to, Renaldo was simply a cad, a womanizer and gigolo who saw that Pancho was smitten and took advantage of her generosity by becoming a permanent house guest at San Marino. To him, Pancho was just a rich, ugly woman.

In 1933, he got in trouble with the law for falsifying his passport. He had gone to Africa to make the film *Trader Horn* with Edwina Booth, claiming on his travel documents to be Duncan Renaldo, of American citizenship, born in Camden, New Jersey. But immigration officials said he was really Vasile Dimitri Cughienas, a Romanian who had come to the United States on a freighter and held a sixty-day visa. Renaldo lost the case in court and lost again on appeal. By the summer of 1934 he was being held at McNeil Island Federal Penitentiary in New York, serving a two-year sentence and facing deportation upon release. Pancho thought she could rescue him and, in doing so, win his heart. For the rescue mission she would call up the WAR.

That was not what she told the women or what she told Gilmore Oil when she asked company officials to finance the trip east. She told them a cross-country flight would promote and publicize the Women's Air Reserve, bringing it to national attention while spotlighting women's place in aviation. She did believe all that, and she wanted to do that. But for her, personally, the trip was about Duncan Renaldo. She persuaded the Gilmore Oil Company to pay $500 for gas, oil, and supplies. In return, the women's planes would be painted "Gilmore yellow" and emblazoned with the Gilmore lion insignia. On the morning of August 31, 1934, six fliers in three open-cockpit biplanes took off from Union Air Terminal in Los Angeles bound for New York, with side trips planned for Cleveland, Washington, D.C., and Philadelphia. Pancho, Bobbi Trout, and Mary Charles, the executive officer of the WAR, were the pilots, each carrying her own navigator. They billed themselves as "the first cross-country formation flight of women pilots."

Mary Charles's airplane didn't make it east of Arizona. She miscalculated her fuel at a stop in Kingman and was forced to make an emergency landing, damaging her plane so badly it could not be repaired on the field. She and her partner returned to Los Angeles while Pancho, Bobbi, and their partners continued east, arriving in Cleveland in time to watch the National Air Races. A week later, after a tense night landing on an unlighted field near Washington, D.C., they were met by Phoebe Omlie, a pioneer flier and award-winning racer who was then promoting the cause of women in aviation by serving the U.S. Army as special assistant for air intelligence.

Omlie came with an entourage, so the women rode into town in style, accompanied by motorcycles and flag-draped automobiles. She put them up in her apartment, entertained them, took them on tours of the national monuments. The women spent long evenings trading tales of their flying adventures. Like Pancho, Phoebe was a high-spirited woman who knew how to tell a joke and how to have a good time. She was also politically savvy, well connected in the capital and eager to capitalize on the WAR visit to gain publicity for women fliers. She arranged for Pancho to attend a meeting of the National Advisory Committee for Aeronautics, which was discussing the licensing of female pilots. Familiar with the formality of these governmental meetings as well as with Pancho's frequently off-color language, Phoebe had handed her friend a list of words she was not to use during the discussions. When the meeting began, Pancho gave Phoebe a big grin and then passed the forbidden-word list around the table for the officials to read. It was her idea of an icebreaker, and it worked. In the days that followed, while the other women continued to explore the city, Pancho got serious about the personal motive behind the trip. She spent her afternoons banging on the doors of Army brass, of politicians, of anyone she knew or to whom she could get an introduction, pleading the case of Duncan Renaldo. But she got nowhere. Perhaps she would have better luck in New York.

Pancho and Bobbi put on a show as they approached that city, flying wingtip to wingtip around the Statue of Liberty. When they landed at Floyd Bennett Field, they were surrounded by reporters and escorted to the St. Moritz Hotel, there to rest and prepare for a gala cocktail party in their honor that evening. But when the four fliers showed up in their full-dress WAR uniforms, they were almost refused entry to their own party. A New York ordinance made it illegal for women to wear male attire in public. "You are impersonating a man," one reporter sniffed as Bobbi Trout walked by. After some quick negotiation, the fliers were allowed in.

They stayed in New York almost a month, sight-seeing, taking in Radio City Music Hall productions, catching Gypsy Rose Lee's show in Greenwich Village, marveling at the female impersonators at the Richman Club, riding the Staten Island ferry for five cents. Meanwhile, Pancho continued to work behind the scenes for Duncan Renaldo's release, still having little luck but unwilling to give up. But time—and, more important, money—was running out. The women had been gone for almost two months. The bill at the St. Moritz, they were surprised to discover, took all their money plus the Gilmore Oil money meant to finance their trip home. They were left with nothing but the gasoline in their tanks. They used it to fly back to Washington, D.C., where Pancho made one last attempt to lobby immigration officials. Then, with cash borrowed from Phoebe Omlie, they headed home, sleeping in airplane hangars and eating nothing but cold sandwiches all across the country. When they landed in Los Angeles, Bobbi Trout had seven cents in the flap pocket of her WAR jacket.

The women had had a grand adventure. The East Coast press had been attentive, running stories about their cross-country flight and reporting on their organization's mission. There were respectful interviews. There were photographs of the women standing tall in their impressive uniforms. From a public relations standpoint, the trip had been an enormous success. The WAR had been founded not just to offer a group of Southern California female pilots training and camaraderie, not just to provide emergency services, but to present an image of women fliers as strong and competent. This the trip did.

Pancho was publicly pleased but privately disheartened, thinking she had failed Duncan Renaldo. As it turned out, though, her efforts did make a difference. Renaldo was released from McNeil Island six months early. He arrived back in Los Angeles, jubilant, demanding to know who had intervened in his behalf. When Pancho told him that she had, he rewarded her with a kiss. It was less than she had hoped for, but more than she had ever gotten from him before. He stayed at the San Marino house awaiting his deportation hearing. Pancho had posted the bond assuring that he would appear. But there was no hearing. Five days after the bond was posted, President Franklin Roosevelt pardoned Renaldo. He could stay in the country and rebuild his career. Years later, he became a dashing figure on the small screen, starring as the Cisco Kid in a popular television series, a swashbuckler on horseback, wearing a black, wide-brimmed gaucho hat and a swirling black cape.

His sidekick was named Pancho. The real Pancho never got that far. She had hoped that Renaldo would show his gratitude in some romantic way, that the first kiss was just a prelude. It wasn't.

But unrequited love was not as pressing a problem for Pancho as overdue mortgages. Although she had trimmed some of her expenses by the mid-1930s, Pancho was still living lavishly, still spending first and asking questions later, if at all, still overly generous with her friends. She continued to spend as if she were rich. But by 1935, she was close to being broke. She had used property as collateral to get new loans to buy more property, but now she had no money to make payments and her deals were unraveling. She had used the Laguna Beach house as collateral for a $50,000 loan, which she was now unable to pay back. She sold several lots in Pasadena, raising $3,000. She asked for an extension on a $16,000 mortgage on an Orange County property, delaying payment for another three years. But she could not gain control of her finances. She defaulted on the big loan and lost her beautiful oceanfront estate. There was more: She had no capital to operate the San Marino house. Like many of the erstwhile wealthy hit so hard in the Depression, she simply could not sustain her way of life anymore. It was time to do something, to make a change, to leave that life behind.

As difficult as her financial situation was, the crisis for Pancho was more than economic. By the mid-1930s, she saw that she had gone as far as she would go as a nationally prominent aviatrix. She had not won an important race. Her speed record had just been bested. The male stunt fliers were doing tricks she couldn't do. Amelia Earhart, with the promotional clout of George Putnam behind her, had laid claim to long-distance flying. Louise Thaden, pretty and sweet-tempered, was the perennial race winner. Elinor Smith, only a teenager when she started breaking records, was the new headline grabber. Pancho never had the looks, and she never had the backing. All she'd ever had, besides her exuberance and her love of flying, was her money and her mouth. Now she didn't have her money.

She thought of that green patch of land out in the Mojave, that alfalfa farm between the two dry lakes, the farm she had flown over so many times when testing airplanes. The desert was a good place to fly, and maybe, she thought, a good place to live. It would be cheap, she knew that. But it would be something more: a place unfettered by convention where she could give full vent to her character, a remote outpost sparsely inhabited by quirky people, individualists like her. Pancho had grown up rich in a cloistered, mannered society and had spent enormous energy stripping away the finish of that life. She was, at thirty-four, a woman who loved to tell dirty jokes and hated to take a bath, a woman who challenged men to arm-wrestle and then took them as lovers. The desert might be just the place for her. Like her paternal grandfather, she had always had big dreams. Now she could no longer buy them; she would have to make them. The desert would be her blank slate.

Part Two

Desert Bloom

10

Lady of the Dry Lake

The Mojave Desert alfalfa ranch that Pancho had admired from her cockpit belonged to a man named Ben Hannam, who, like many people and most farmers in the mid-1930s, was struggling. His eighty-acre spread looked better from the air than the ground. Elsewhere in the Antelope Valley, as that piece of the desert was called, there was better land and more water. Elsewhere in the valley, farmers grew top-quality alfalfa, six or seven cuttings a year, the green gold shoulder-high, irrigated by plentiful wells, cut and baled, then sold, before the Depression, for prices that could support a family. But the crop that had once brought $25 or $30 a ton was now going for one-third that, and Hannam was in deep trouble. His eighty acres, seventy of which were planted, did not produce the best hay in the valley, nor was he able to get as many cuttings from the land as some of the other farmers. Just recently, a family, the Grahams, had bought a neighboring homestead, and now, on top of his other problems, Hannam was afraid there wouldn't be enough water in the area for two farms.

Even if Pancho had known any of this—which she didn't—she still would have wanted the ranch. She made her decisions on impulse, not information, and she had fallen in love with the place years ago. She had good memories of helping her father dabble in his agricultural experiments at the Cherry Valley property when she was a child, but her desire to buy Hannam's place had little to do with the ranch or the idea of being a farmer, and much to do with its location. Desert flying was glorious, the bright, clear, dry days, one after another, the uncrowded skies, the miles and miles of hard, flat land, smoother and flatter than any airstrip man or machine could make. Just east of Hannam's spread was Muroc Dry Lake, the largest naturally occurring flat space on earth, forty-four square miles of rock-hard flatness. When the desert got the little rain it did each year, it came down all at once, all four inches of it, and sat on the lake bed. The winds pushed the water back and forth, scouring the land, planing the bed, burnishing the surface sleek, smooth, and seamless. For a flier accustomed to short, pitted dirt airfields where there was always some hazard—a clump of trees, a building, power poles, low-lying fog—the dry lake was the perfect spot in a perfect flying landscape.

Pancho didn't have much left in the mid-1930s, but she did still have an apartment building on Witmer and North Sixth in Los Angeles. This she traded, straight across, in February 1935 for Ben and Kathryn Hannam's eighty acres in a deal that must have renewed the Hannams' belief in the tooth fairy and Santa Claus. Pancho didn't care whether she overpaid for the land. She understood little and cared less about the value of money. What she cared about now was getting out of Los Angeles and starting a new life. She had lost her beautiful Laguna Beach house and could not afford the upkeep on the San Marino mansion. Her parents were dead. Her husband, though they were married in name only, lived in New York. Her friends were all fliers who could just as easily fly out to visit her in the desert as drive over to visit her in the city, and they'd enjoy flying more. There was nothing to hold her in Los Angeles.

She should have tried to find a buyer for the San Marino place, but she was unwilling to let it go yet. There were too many memories there: downstairs parties, upstairs assignations, morning rides along the bridle paths, hangar flying into the night. There was little market for such real estate, anyway, in the depths of the Depression. Instead, she rented the place for the summer to Jack Maddux, an airline owner, and headed for the desert, taking her horses, her dogs, two refrigerators, and her son. Billy had been in his father's charge for years, attending boarding school in New Jersey while Rankin lived in Manhattan and traveled for the church. But now he was a teenager, a boy who dreamed of wide-open spaces, of riding horses, learning how to shoot, maybe even learning how to fly. Ranch life would be good for the boy, Pancho and Rankin agreed. And Pancho could use the help.

She would get help from someone else, too, her new lover, Granny Nourse. Logan "Granny" Nourse, the son of a Missouri farmer, was a pilot and airplane mechanic hired to work on Pancho's plane for the WAR cross-country flight. A small, compact man, not much taller than Pancho, easygoing, with a quiet sense of humor and a gift for story-telling, Granny had been flying since 1927 and had designed and built his own low-wing plane, a precursor to the famous Mystery Ship. He and Pancho met in front of the Lockheed hangar at the Burbank airport in the spring of 1934. Pancho knew a kindred spirit when she saw one. That night, she came home with a bottle of whisky under one arm and Granny under the other. During the months before the WAR trip, the two were inseparable. Pancho may have been pining for Duncan Renaldo, but Granny's was the warm body in her bed. When she left for the East that summer to work for the actor's release, Pancho entrusted Granny with the keys to her Lincoln and the keys to her house. Now, early in 1935, he accompanied her out to the desert.

The Hannam place wasn't much: a small shack by the narrow two-lane highway, a four-room house up a rutted dirt road, and a hay barn. The land was flat and treeless, dusty khaki and dun-colored where the alfalfa wasn't growing. It looked like "the ass end of the moon," one of Pancho's friends said, and it was almost as isolated. The nearest town was more than twenty miles away over bad roads, and it wasn't much of a town anyway, especially compared to the cities Pancho knew, the cities of the Los Angeles Basin. The nearest settlement, Muroc, a few miles north, was little more than a wide place in the road, a whistle-stop on the Santa Fe railroad line. Native Americans had made seasonal stopovers in the area centuries before. Spanish explorers had investigated it in the eighteenth century, and the American frontiersman John C. Frémont had passed through in the early nineteenth century. But it was not until the railroad expanded into the western Mojave in the late 1870s that there were any permanent residents, a few section hands who maintained the track and kept the water tank filled. The first homesteaders had not arrived until 1910, an intrepid couple named Clifford and Effie Corum who were determined to start a farm community in the desert wasteland. They sank wells, planted crops, and, in an effort to attract other settlers, built a combination store and post office. They wanted to name the tiny community after themselves, Corum, but postal authorities objected because California already had a Coram. The couple countered with Muroc, Corum spelled backward, and that's what the settlement came to be called. When Pancho, Granny, and Billy arrived in 1935, Muroc consisted of a gas station, a post office, Charlie Anderson's store, Ma Greene's café, and some shacks for the railroad workers. If you drove through Muroc, you wouldn't see a soul unless you honked your horn.

Muroc was on the west side of Muroc Dry Lake. On the east side, out on the desert hardpan, was a small military encampment known locally as "the Foreign Legion of the Army Air Corps." There was nothing out there but a dozen canvas tents, a flagpole, and seventeen disgruntled men. There was no electricity, no plumbing, no conveniences, no hint of human habitation from horizon to horizon. There was just the scorching desert sun, the bone-cold desert nights, and the wind. When the wind came up, it could whip the dust and sand at a hundred miles per hour, stripping the paint off cars and trucks.

The encampment had been there ever since Lieutenant Colonel Henry "Hap" Arnold selected the area as a training site for his squadron that operated out of March Field near Riverside, California. Like Pancho, he had flown over the desert and seen not desolation, not blistered landscape, not dust and wind, but the dry lakes, natural airfields that could be maintained, he told the Army, at no cost to the tax-payers. Since 1933, groups and squadrons had been flying in from the Army airfield in Riverside to use the area for bombing and gunnery practice. They bivouacked beside their aircraft on Muroc Dry Lake, conducted exercises, and left as soon as they could. The Muroc Range Maintenance Detachment, as the tiny permanent tent encampment was officially called, cleaned up after Hap Arnold's fliers, scouring the desert for spent bombs. The detachment couldn't attract a command-ing officer. Commissioned officers would fly up from Los Angeles, take one look at the place and fly out before their engines cooled. Pancho, like the other area homesteaders, got used to hearing the bombs ex-plode and feeling the ground shake, but she knew little of what went on on the other side of the lake. She would learn. Pancho and her military neighbors were to have a long and interesting relationship.

◆—◆ ⋈◆⋈ ◆—◆

One of the first things she did when she took over Hannam's place was scratch out a dirt airstrip in the desert, hitching up her two new work-horses to a scraper to do the job. They weren't just any workhorses, for Pancho was both an equestrian connoisseur and a sucker for beautiful horseflesh. She had traveled all the way to the Washington State Fair to buy two English shire mares, big, gorgeous horses, half-sisters with premium bloodlines. Belle and Queen would earn their keep pulling the hay baler through the alfalfa fields. But first, they dragged a scraper up and back across the land, leveling a four-hundred-foot-long, fifty-foot-wide airstrip. Now her pilot friends and aviation-minded Holly-wood acquaintances could fly out for visits. Pancho may have moved to the middle of nowhere, but she was not about to live the lonely life of a desert homesteader. Almost immediately, her friends came calling, fly-ing out to ride her horses across the fenceless range, to hunt jackrab-bits, to eat barbecue and bunk on the living room couch or, for those who wanted to rough it, in the barn. Pancho and Granny quickly built a few one-room shacks they euphemistically called guest cabins to han-dle the overflow.

She named the place Rancho Oro Verde, "Green Gold," after the alfalfa, but she was no farmer—although out in the fields, her dungarees dirty, her face and neck already bronzed, her skin already leathery, she certainly looked like one. And, for a short while she got a kick out of hitching up the two mares to the hay baler and working the contraption single-handed, managing both the horses up front and the baler in the rear, jumping from one to another and back again while keeping the thing going straight and steady. The physical challenge appealed to her. It was the antithesis of her Pasadena upbringing, the living, breathing, sweating proof that she was her own woman, that she had escaped her past and started an entirely new life. But the storytelling possibilities appealed to her even more. She had to hire three men to take her place when she quit working the baler. That's what she told her visiting friends, rolling up the sleeves of her shirt to show off the curve of her biceps. The reality was, she tired of the novelty quickly. The work was backbreaking and the rewards minimal.

If Pancho thought she could make a living as an alfalfa farmer, she soon discovered otherwise. An acre yielded two tons of alfalfa. With seventy acres in production, and alfalfa down to nine dollars a ton, the crop did not bring in the kind of money she was used to. It might, with luck and budgeting, support the quiet, frugal life of a homesteader, but that was not Pancho's life. She had an airplane. She had registered horses. She was partial to Lincolns and Cadillacs. She liked to entertain. The first two years were tough. She told a friend that she and her son had to eat jackrabbits to stay alive. Times weren't *that* tough, but it made a damn good story.

For Billy, those first few years were part culture shock, part grand adventure. He had spent his early childhood under the protection of full-time nurses and nannies, growing up privileged as his mother had. His boyhood had so far been divided between his mother's mansion and oceanfront estate and the elite New Jersey boarding school his father had sent him to. There was little to prepare him for the harsh, unpampered life of the desert. Yet those first years were also the best of times. His mother finally paid attention to him, taking an interest in his schooling and athletic activities. She occasionally helped him with homework. She tried to make it to his football games. She spoiled him by buying him his own stallion. Every morning, he would gallop from the barn to the school bus stop and then let the horse loose for a hired man to round up and bring home. The kids on the bus couldn't believe it—not just the gorgeous stallion, the most beautiful horse they'd ever seen, but the fact that Billy was allowed to just drop the reins and forget about him.

During those first few years Pancho was more a part of Billy's life than she had ever been before, but still, he was often left on his own. He spent the time tinkering with airplanes and cars, shadowing the ranch hands, and eating cookies at the kitchen tables of the neighboring homesteaders. He may or may not have come home to a bowl of hot jackrabbit stew.

Pancho, meanwhile, was figuring out another angle. Although there might not be any money in selling alfalfa, she could use the hay to feed a herd of milk cows and then sell the milk. In 1936, she went into the dairy business, fueled by her usual abundance of self-confidence and a loan secured by her land. After all, she reasoned, her father had raised cows, and she had helped him in the summers when she was a child. Later, she had kept a few dairy goats in the San Marino and Laguna Beach stables so that Billy could have fresh goat's milk. It didn't seem to her that there was much more to learn. When Emery Adair, a local dairy farmer, contracted rheumatic fever and had to sell out, Pancho agreed to buy his cows and equipment, floating another loan to do so. With her one hay barn, she wasn't set up to operate a dairy on her spread, so the Adair Dairy stayed where it was, seven miles away across the desert, and Pancho's young hired hand, Tony King, rode a horse out there every morning and every evening to hand-milk the cows.

Tony had started working at Rancho Oro Verde when Pancho first moved out to the desert. They met, appropriately enough, on horseback, when they were both riding in the Alfalfa Days parade down the main street of Lancaster, the nearest town of any consequence to Pancho's place. Tony was not much older than her own son, but he was already a seasoned ranch hand who earned his room and board breaking horses for a local rancher. His mother had died when he was very young. His father had been killed in a rodeo accident when Tony was still in grammar school. Ever since then, he'd been on his own. Pancho realized immediately how good he was with horses, seeing how he sat in the saddle, how he held the reins, how he calmed the horse when the parade got noisy. She told him there was work for him out at her place. The next morning, the fourteen-year-old boy saddled up his horse and rode the twenty-five miles to Pancho's, where he was immediately installed as head horse wrangler. Pancho had the two shires plus four saddle horses, one of which wasn't yet broken. Tony quickly accomplished the job, then took responsibility for all feeding, shoeing, and doctoring of the animals. His job expanded when Pancho bought the dairy, and it turned out, luckily, that he knew something of cows, as well.

The cows at the old Adair Dairy were played out, Tony told Pancho. They were incapable of producing enough milk to make the business worthwhile. Pancho listened to the boy's advice and traveled north to Washington again, money in her pocket from mortgaging alfalfa futures, to buy out a dairy up there. She had sixty Holsteins shipped down to the ranch, huge animals, twelve hundred pounds apiece, that gave ten to twelve gallons of milk a day. Pancho, Tony, Granny, and some hired help built a dairy barn and a wood-and-stucco building to house the milking equipment they brought over from the Adairs'. Pancho raised the money for construction by mortgaging the herd she had just bought. Now they had a complete operation at the ranch. But although they had cows that produced the quantity of milk they needed, Tony was concerned about the quality. He persuaded Pancho to buy ten Guernseys, cows known for giving particularly creamy milk. All these big, heavily producing cows were great for starting a dairy business, but they quickly presented another problem. They went through Pancho's hay faster than she could grow it.

She started buying hay from a ranch on the other side of Rosamond Dry Lake. The rancher there would get his young cousin to load up a truck with three or four tons of hay and haul it across the lake, delivering the load to Pancho and collecting a check. Al Houser, the cousin, didn't mind the job. He got a kick out of Pancho. He thought she was something else. They had met under unusual circumstances a few months before. Al and three friends were sitting around the living room of a rancher's house late one night when they heard noises outside. Al flicked on the porch light and went out to investigate, but peering into the black desert night, he could see nothing. He stepped to the edge of the porch to look around, and down beside the house, he saw what he thought was a man, squatting. Then he heard a rough voice.

"Turn out that sonuvabitchin' light. Can't you see what I'm doing?" the voice yelled.

Al hurried back inside. A minute later, there was a knock on the front door and in walked someone wearing an old cowboy hat, a torn jacket, and dirty Levi's.

"That's Pancho Barnes," one of his friends whispered. Al had never heard the name before.

Pancho turned to the group in the living room. "Now, which one of you bastards turned the light on?" she asked. She was pretending to be mad, but there was a big grin on her face. Al didn't really know what to make of her, but he admitted that he was the culprit. She walked over to him, trying to keep a straight face. "Why'd you have to stare?" she said. "Haven't you ever seen a woman take a piss before?" In fact, Al had not, and he figured he wasn't alone in that. He just stood there wondering how to react until this odd woman in old, dirty clothes started to laugh. Then they all laughed.

Al was happy to run the hay over for his cousin because it was an excuse to see Pancho again. She always had a story to tell, or a dirty joke. The only problem was, the checks Pancho gave him invariably bounced at the local bank. He would have to come back a few days later and tell her, and then she would write him a new check. That one would bounce, too. Al's cousin, the rancher, wasn't upset—this was the Depression, and farmers were broke and living on goodwill and credit—but he needed his money. He would send Al back a third time. "Pancho," Al would tell her, "we've got to have cash." She would dig through her pockets, an old purse, and her dresser drawers and come up with the money in change and crumpled bills. A few weeks later, she would need more hay and start writing more bad checks. They kept selling it to her because that was the way you did business during the Depression. She always paid, but never the first or second time.

It wasn't because she was broke. It was, rather, because she didn't know how to handle money or how to keep a checking account. In fact, in the mid- and late 1930s, Rancho Oro Verde wasn't doing too badly. Pancho had contracts to sell her milk to the Muroc Elementary School, to the Army Air Corps encampment on the other side of the lake, to a Navy base up north at China Lake, and to Pacific Borax, which operated a huge mine just outside the town of Boron. She charged forty cents a gallon for cow's milk and forty cents a quart for goat's milk, although she bartered and traded a lot, especially with the military men.

But the dairy was only one part of the operation out at the ranch. Pancho also started a hog business when she saw that the men at the isolated encampments at Muroc and China Lake needed meat. They were good, steady—and grateful—customers. Moreover, the government, unlike much of the local citizenry, actually had funds to pay for goods and services. She started with a dozen registered Hampshire pigs, the finest stock, and went on from there. The pigs were for breeding and butchering, but Pancho loved all animals, including hogs. She quickly found two favorites, whom she named Brandy and Benedictine, saving them from the harsh future of their pen mates. When Benedictine had trouble delivering a litter, Tony stayed up all night with the sow, comforting and stroking her. He put each piglet she delivered in a gunnysack and rubbed it to keep it warm while Benedictine struggled on. The next morning, the sow and her piglets were doing fine, and Pancho was so impressed with Tony's care and compassion that she promoted him on the spot, at age fifteen, to ranch foreman.

Pancho's hog operation grew quickly, and soon there were more than three hundred animals. When the hogs grew fat, she had some of them butchered and sold the meat to the men at the Army and Navy bases, combining her milk deliveries with ham and pork shipments. Some of the hogs she sold to the Los Angeles stockyards. When her breeding sows were played out, she got money for them at a local slaughterhouse that made bologna.

For a woman so bad with money, Pancho was turning out to be a promising entrepreneur. She had the requisite quick mind and restless spirit. She was full of ideas and excitement, willing to try anything, seeing opportunities and connections where others were blind. Some homesteaders ignored the military encampments. They were distant and invisible, way off on the desert hardpan, easy to ignore. Some saw them as nuisances and intrusions. Not Pancho. She liked the military. She had flown into Army Air Corps bases in and around Los Angeles for years. Her Women's Air Reserve had operated out of one in Long Beach. In the 1920s, she had met and made friends with young pilots like Jimmy Doolittle who were now military brass. She had what she considered a distinguished military pedigree courtesy of her Civil War hero grandfather. He hadn't actually been in the military, but that was a minor detail. He was, she told the guys as she delivered milk and ham and pork, the most-shot-at man in the war, the man who invented aerial reconnaissance. She thought of the military men as her buddies. But she also thought of them as potential customers.

Her next business move was as inspired as something could be that had to do with garbage: She contracted to pick up the kitchen waste at Muroc and China Lake. Back at the ranch, Tony and the hired men cooked the garbage in huge vats four feet off the ground, then poured it into immense cement troughs to feed the hungry hogs. These were some of the same hogs she butchered and sold back to the military for food, thus completing a brilliant entrepreneurial circle. She was doing very well for herself, bringing in as much as $1,200 a month from her dairy, hog, and garbage operations with expenses of only $500 a month. And she was doing it mostly by herself—not the physical labor so much anymore, but oversight of the entire operation. She had Tony, of course, but he was just a kid. She had depended on Granny Nourse, but in 1936 he had gone back to Missouri to visit family and ended up working in Kansas City for a year, where he met a woman he wanted to marry. When he came back to the ranch and told Pancho, their relationship ended. She hadn't wanted to marry Granny, but he had been her lover, and she couldn't help feeling betrayed. He stayed on to help for a few months and then left to start his new life. Pancho was alone, taking care of business. She was making as much as $700 profit a month, "with nowhere to spend it," she told a friend.

— ⋅⊨◈⊨⋅ —

But Pancho would always find a way to spend money. It seemed that every month she had a new scheme, another business idea she pursued impulsively and wholeheartedly until a new idea came along the next month and she lost interest. She was long on beginnings but short on follow-through. Her schemes kept her and everyone around her hopping as they soaked up any capital the more established businesses were able to generate. She decided to use some of her irrigated acreage to grow corn rather than alfalfa, thinking that would be more profitable. A local man was hired to do the job, but by the time the corn was up, Pancho had moved on to another idea. One day she came home with some new hogs for the ranch and neglected to pen them. They went out into the cornfield, ate everything, and trampled the ground. The hired man quit in disgust, and that was the end of that venture. Another time, she thought to add chickens to the ranch so she could sell eggs along with meat and milk to her military customers. But after the chickens were installed in their laying house, she put in a new diesel pump for a nearby well that made such a loud noise and set up such strong ground vibrations that the chickens wouldn't lay. At least, that was what Tony thought. No one else could explain why all those prime layers just sat and squawked all day. Pancho abandoned the egg venture as quickly as she had started it, letting the chickens wander around the barn eating the grain the horses spilled. Then, one by one, the chickens showed up at the dinner table. In a moment of weakness for a magnificent animal—such moments were common for Pancho—she bought, at considerable expense, a registered Hereford bull from a famous breeding ranch in Long Beach. But once she got the bull back to

Oro Verde, she took no interest in him. Instead of putting him out to stud, which would have been a lucrative business, she allowed it to free-range, impregnating all the cattle in the valley, Pancho's and everyone else's. Meanwhile, she spent $500 to lease a stallion to improve her small string of horses. Pancho also loved dogs and indulged herself by buying top-quality springer spaniels and Dalmatians, which she bred, presumably to sell. But when the time came, she always gave away the puppies to friends and visitors. It was another business venture that ended up costing money rather than making it.

Pancho was also busy buying land. She loved the idea of ownership, the notion of herself as overseer of a great estate. With more land, there would be more possibilities, more plans, more ventures. In 1937, she bought 120 acres to the west of her original eighty-acre spread, signing a trust deed for $6,500. The land had belonged to George Hannam, Ben's brother. In 1940, she bought sixty acres to the west and north that belonged to Ben and his sister. The next year, she added another eighty-acre parcel. Within six years, Rancho Oro Verde grew from eighty to 360 acres. What funds Pancho wasn't spending on animals and land, she spent on improvements. She expanded the original four-room farmhouse, knocking out the walls herself with a sledge-hammer and adding a large dining room to accommodate the hired help. She hired local men to build stables and new outbuildings for the livestock. She hitched up the two shires and dug a hole for a swimming pool—an amenity for her Hollywood visitors, an extravagance unheard of, unimagined, by her neighbors. Her energy was limitless. She was a dynamo, as much a force of nature as the desert windstorms. Pancho Barnes was fast becoming a local legend.

11

Something Out of Nothing

The people of Muroc were accustomed to a degree of eccentricity—the desert attracted characters—but they had never seen anyone like Pancho Barnes. She came into Charlie Anderson's store in Muroc smoking a cigar, and people talked about it for years. She ambled down the main street of Lancaster in patched blue overalls, her bare feet thrust into Mexican sandals, and the local newspaper found it noteworthy. She gassed up her Cadillac at Carl Bergman's Union Oil station, a big, luxurious car among the ranchers' battered pickup trucks. But when he looked in the back, Carl saw that the plushly upholstered seat had been yanked to make room for half a dozen dogs. That kept conversation going around the pump for weeks. When she was stopped by a highway patrol officer on the main road because her headlights were so far out of alignment that she was blinding oncoming traffic, she didn't just take the five-dollar ticket and go on her way. She cursed out the cop and went to court to fight the violation.

Pancho did her best to promote her image as someone rough-and-tumble in both word and deed. When she was invited to tea by the Muroc ladies, she knew well how she was *supposed* to act. She was, after all, a former Pasadena debutante. But she chose instead to regale the neighbor ladies with heavily embroidered tales of her Mexican adventures, telling them that she'd served in the Mexican navy, spicing the stories with words the women had heard only when their men accidentally hit their thumbs with hammers.

When the locals found out that she was the wealthy scion of an important family, they were even more baffled. Some whispered that she must be illegitimate. Others believed, instead, that her parents were paying her to stay away from home. A story circulated in the valley that Pancho's family owned all the movie theaters in New York City. That was the Loews, not the Lowes, but the rumor persisted for years. Despite all the talk, and despite Pancho's strikingly unfeminine behavior, she was generally well liked by her neighbors. She was a character in a land that appreciated characters. And, if she liked you, she was very generous. Pancho had been overgenerous with her friends in Los Angeles, feeding and housing them, lending them money, doing them favors. She hadn't done this to ingratiate herself but rather because she loved to be at the center of things, enjoyed being the person others could come to. She was generous in the nonchalant way that the very rich can sometimes be generous, because money doesn't matter. Now she was no longer wealthy, but she did have things her neighbors didn't have, and her willingness to share made her popular. In the early years, she had the only telephone in the area, and neighbors were free to use it when they needed to. She always had a well-stocked larder and a cook to make meals for the hired hands. There was always food for whoever dropped by. Then there was that Hereford bull, which improved everyone's stock. Pancho was community-minded as well, which also won her favor. When locals were discussing how to promote the first-ever Antelope Valley Fair, Pancho took the lead, literally. She put herself at the head of a long conga line that snaked in and out of the stores in downtown Lancaster, beating drums and chanting to announce the opening of the fair.

But not everyone loved Pancho. In fact, she made lifelong enemies of her immediate neighbors, the Grahams. Some of the squabbling was the result of typical farmer-rancher problems. When Pancho's

dogs strayed onto the Grahams' property and did some damage, Mr.
Graham did what farmers often do: He picked up a shotgun and ran
them off. When a few of the Grahams' cattle wandered over to Pancho's, she retaliated by filling them with buckshot. The feud escalated
when Pancho trucked three of Graham's trespassing calves ten miles
out into the desert. By the time he rounded them up, they were near
starvation.

But these spats were the symptoms of their poor relationship, not
the cause. Graham had not welcomed Pancho to the valley. She was an
interloper, as far as he could see, a woman who clearly came from a different world and didn't know the rules of this new one. She didn't act
like any of the other women on the Muroc homesteads. He was personally offended by her foul mouth and told his children many times to
stay away from her place.

When she first moved to the ranch, she had wanted to hire Graham
to do some electrical work. She saw that his own operation was in trouble, that he was struggling to make ends meet, and she thought the
extra money would help. It wasn't a matter of charity—she did need
the work done—but, she thought, of friendly, neighborly concern. It
was Pancho being generous, as she always had been. Graham agreed to
do the work but refused the pay, telling her, with pride, that he "didn't
hire out to anyone." He had his own place, he reminded her. He was not
going to work as her hired hand. Both of them managed to be offended
by this initial contact, and the stage was set for their rocky relationship.
Pancho made things far worse a few years later. In a financial pinch, she
had borrowed money from Erich von Stroheim when he came out to
the desert for a visit, pointing over to the Grahams' ranch and telling
him she would use it as collateral for the loan. When she didn't repay
on time, Von Stroheim, out once again for a visit, marched over to the
Grahams' farmhouse to tell the man he believed to be a hired hand to
get off the property because he, Von Stroheim, was going to foreclose.
Graham was so furious he could hardly breathe.

When Pancho bought George Hannam's property, Graham told his
children that she had purposely deprived the Hannams of water in

order to run them off and get their land cheaply. George Hannam didn't have a well on his property and had always depended on the well belonging to his brother, Ben. When Pancho bought Ben's property, that responsibility fell to her, but she was less careful with her water than Ben Hannam had been. Her workers sometimes absentmindedly ran the pump all day, flooding the back field out of carelessness. That meant less water to share with Mr. Hannam, especially during the long, dry summer months. Graham was right—Pancho had made water a problem—but it wasn't a calculated or purposeful move. It was an old story: She just had too many things going to pay attention to details.

<hr/>

From her arrival in the desert in the mid-1930s to the beginning of World War II, Pancho immersed herself in dirty, sweaty, smelly money-making schemes, operations far removed from her upper-class background. It was true that her father had raised animals, but he had been a gentleman farmer, a dilettante of agriculture and animal husbandry who dabbled and experimented and then returned home to his San Marino mansion. He had never slopped pigs and cooked vats of garbage. Pancho did these things because she needed money, more money than most, to support the free-spending lifestyle she refused to give up even in the worst of times. She did these things because that's how people supported themselves out in the desert, because that's where the opportunities were. But she also did them to prove she could, to show she was as tough and resourceful as any man, maybe tougher, to create something out of nothing, the way her grandfather had. On the one hand, she threw herself into these ventures joyfully, wholeheartedly, and thoughtlessly, like a child. On the other, she chose to act in certain ways, to talk rough, to roll her own smokes, to bale her own hay, as part of a willful act of self-re-creation. She was building her own new public identity as much as she was building any business.

Many of her schemes made money, and she would have done fine through the last years of the Depression had she known how to hold on to it. But for Pancho, money was for spending. This had gotten her into trouble in San Marino and Laguna Beach, and it would get her into trouble out in the Mojave. Her neighbors saw her building and expanding, and they whispered to one another about her great wealth, her deep pockets. But in fact, she had not been at the ranch more than a month or two before she started living beyond her means, borrowing money against her land to buy farm equipment, mortgaging her cattle for quick cash. She used her eighty acres as collateral to buy $2,000 worth of lumber. The next year, after she failed to make payments on the loan, the lumber company threatened to foreclose. She scraped through that mess only to remortgage the same land to the same lumber company two years later, always managing to keep herself in debt, regardless of her income.

The land she bought she could ill afford. When she failed to make payments on one trust deed for eighteen months, she almost lost the 120 acres she had bought from George Hannam's widow. To help her over that hump, she mortgaged eighty-six head of cattle and two hundred tons of alfalfa for $4,000. She also, reluctantly, sold her house in San Marino. She had managed to rent it out for two summers, but the rest of the time it remained vacant, and it had been badly vandalized. She got $5,500 for the thirty-five-room mansion, and promptly spent it all on more land and improvements to her water system.

A few months later, she faced another financial crisis. Back before she moved out to the desert, she had taken out a loan for $5,000, using her Travel Air Mystery Ship as security. At first she had resolved to sell the plane. Then she changed her mind and tried to trade it for one of Howard Hughes's aircraft. When that didn't work out, she put the Mystery Ship on the market again. But in the depths of the Depression, no one could afford the price tag, so she ended up using the plane as collateral. Now the loan was due, and she didn't have the money to pay it. She signed the plane over to Paul Mantz, the man she had helped become a member of the stunt pilots' union in the early 1930s. Now Mantz was the most successful stunt pilot in Hollywood. He took the plane and paid off her debt. If only she could have stalled her creditors a little longer, she might have been able to keep her Mystery Ship.

If only she could have held on until the inheritance she knew was coming finally materialized.

* — ⚊◆⚊ —•

Caroline Dobbins, Pancho's maternal grandmother, had died in 1935 at age ninety-four, leaving a substantial fortune and a will that enraged all her grandchildren. The will set up a trust with her son Horace in charge. He would receive all income from the trust, with the principal, more than $500,000, going to the California Institute of Technology after he died. Each grandchild, Pancho included, would receive a pittance of $2,000. Caroline's will was three pages long. The four years of legal maneuvering that followed produced more than 750 pages of documents. In August 1935, Pancho and her first cousins, Carolyn Banks and Dean Banks, filed suit, contesting the will on the grounds that their grandmother had been "extremely weak in body and mind"—incompetent and unduly influenced by their uncle. Horace, through his lawyer, countered that Caroline had been mentally alert until the end, overseeing her considerable estate by herself until three months before her death. That the will provided little for Pancho and her cousins was understandable, Horace contended, because Caroline had openly disapproved of "the manner in which her grandchildren had dissipated monies received by them." She was, Horace claimed, especially critical of Pancho.

Some or all of Horace's claims may have been true, but his lawyers knew he was fighting an uphill battle. The case against the will was textbook perfect: a wealthy, aged woman; a single relative with disproportionate access who benefited disproportionately. Juries didn't like relatives who were sole beneficiaries. Juries had great sympathy for those left out of the will or shortchanged by it. The case never went to court.

In the agreement hammered out by the lawyers, Cal Tech received $75,000 outright, Horace received $30,000 outright plus a share of Caroline's real estate holdings, and two of the grandchildren were granted title to other valuable property. The remaining six grandchildren, Pancho, Carolyn, and Dean included, shared equally in the rest of the estate. For Pancho, that meant about $10,000 in cash and $35,000 in stocks, bonds, certificates, and real property. It took a little more than a year to reach the basic agreement, but no one saw any money until 1939. The estate was large and diverse, the property difficult to appraise and divide. The family was contentious, even after the agreement. Horace's ex-wife surfaced and complicated matters by making claims. Pancho waited impatiently. She was in debt. More than that, she had big plans. She needed her $45,000 share, which was a considerable sum in those days.

<hr/>

The dairy operation, the hog farm, the garbage hauling—all these businesses brought in money and exercised Pancho's entrepreneurial spirit, but they were not the reason she had moved to the desert. The reason she had moved to the desert was the flying. She had her little airstrip, and she had her private plane. She flew for pleasure, and her Los Angeles friends flew in on weekend jaunts. But late in 1939 the opportunity came for her to do something important in aviation again, and she grabbed it.

Germany had been building superior airpower through the 1930s, creating the best-trained, best-equipped force in the world. None other than Charles Lindbergh, personally inspecting the Luftwaffe, had declared it that. In the summer of 1939, in response to Hitler's military buildup and German aggression in Europe, President Franklin Roosevelt asked Congress to allot $500 million to bolster national defense, most of it earmarked for increasing U.S. airpower. Out of this came a full-scale, federally funded aviation project, a huge, nationwide vocational program designed to train pilots. Civilian pilots, little operators like Pancho, were being hired, on contract, to do the work, from providing airplanes to teaching ground school to instructing in the air.

The Civilian Pilot Training Program (CPTP) officially began in the fall of 1939, and Pancho got in on the ground floor, securing a government contract to supply planes and instructors for the area's first class, beginning that winter. Pancho traveled to Wichita to buy planes and hired first an ex–Army Air Corps lieutenant and later a former RAF pilot to handle the flight instruction. Pancho herself wasn't a certified flight instructor. Her job was to oversee the operation, which meant that sometimes she was personally attentive, knowing all the would-be pilots by name, involved every day in what they learned on the ground and in the air, and other times they wouldn't see her for weeks. That was how Pancho approached all her enterprises, with intermittent enthusiasm.

At first, because she didn't have the necessary facilities at the ranch, Pancho's flight school was housed at Palmdale Airport, more than twenty miles away. But during the second class, in early spring 1940, she used some of her inheritance to build a forty-foot-by-sixty-foot steel-arched hangar and make improvements to the airstrip. Then she was able to move the flight instruction out to the ranch. That second class of students included two women, there because Pancho very much wanted them to be. Women were not barred from participating in the pilot training program, but neither were they encouraged. Some instructors still thought women incapable of learning how to fly, and government overseers were eager to fill the program with men who could enlist in the military after their civilian training. Women in the CPTP were a rarity. Pancho registered her two women students by their last names and first initials only, masking their gender from the government inspector until it was too late for him to object. One of the women, Irma "Babe" Story, went on to serve as a WASP (Women's Airforce Service Pilot) during the war, one of two thousand specially trained female pilots to fly everything from colossal B-29 Superfortresses to lightning-fast P-51 Mustang fighters, ferrying planes for the military and flying noncombat missions. Had Pancho been younger, she would have been up there with the WASPs. This was just the kind of opportunity for women pilots she had hoped for when she founded the WAR.

After two classes, Pancho's flight school had taught everyone in the sparsely populated Antelope Valley who wanted to learn. There just weren't that many. To keep the operation going and hold on to her government contract, she started to advertise for students in the Los Angeles newspapers, offering room and board at the ranch in exchange for light chores. One young man who took her up on the offer was a poor Armenian kid from Fresno named Kirk Kerkorian. He couldn't officially enroll in the flight school because he hadn't finished high school, but Pancho took an instant liking to him and agreed to give him flying lessons in exchange for his help around the ranch. She was like that. Men would show up at her door, strangers, transients, passersby, and if she liked them, how they carried themselves, how they talked, how they looked, she would find work for them. It drove her foreman Tony King crazy, although, of course, he had been the recipient of just such impulsive generosity.

Kerkorian was as eager as he was penniless. Pancho saw ambition in him, and she was right. The man who went on to become a commercial airline pilot, the owner of Western Airlines, the CEO of M-G-M, and one of the most fiercely independent billionaires in the world started his career shoveling manure in Pancho's stables.

Fifteen young men, mostly in their early twenties, enrolled in that third class, which began in June 1941. They slept in a bunkhouse Pancho had built—one long room with cots, attached to the main house—and they ate together in the big dining room she had built for the hired help. They'd get up before dawn to milk the cows and slop the hogs, then eat breakfast with the ranch hands before being driven into town, where they attended ground school at Antelope Valley Junior College. In the afternoon, they were back at the ranch for flight instruction. They stuck close to Pancho's all evening, eating dinner with the hands, hanging around the dining room for hours afterward to talk and smoke, drawn to the place not just out of necessity, not just because they had no money and no transportation, but because of Pancho. They were fascinated by her. She sat there, night after night, telling them stories, some true, some embroidered, about the old days of flying, about the air derbies and barnstorming and stunting for Howard Hughes. She was living history. The men would sit, transfixed, speaking only to ask the right questions, the questions that would fuel wild stories about Mexico and blind flying, about Prohibition and Hollywood parties. Pancho told them she'd been in the merchant marine, and they believed her. They believed everything she said.

Two members of that third CPTP class got special treatment. The other men noticed it immediately. Pancho, who was not a certified instructor, nonetheless gave the Nichols brothers private flying lessons. They were with her, not the regular flight instructors, every afternoon. But there was more. The men noticed that Pancho behaved differently around the Nichols brothers. She was friendlier, warmer, more intimate, especially around Robert Hudson Nichols, Jr., the guy everyone called Nicky. Nicky was a short, average-looking man in his mid-twenties, a quiet fellow with a Southern drawl and a talent for taking machines apart and putting them together. He tore apart a Model A Ford out at the ranch and got it running again on diesel fuel. He tinkered with the airplanes, too, but he wasn't much of a pilot. One morning that summer, the men woke up in their bunkhouse and noticed that Nicky's bed had not been slept in. They exchanged looks, but they didn't talk about it among themselves. They knew where Nicky was sleeping, and they figured they knew why he was there.

Nicky was not handsome, and he was not particularly bright. But he did have one thing going for him that made him irresistibly attractive to Pancho. The men couldn't help but notice this about Nicky. Tony King actually did a double-take, as in the movies, when he first saw Nicky standing naked in the shower. Tony had been around long enough to know that Pancho was a woman with a healthy sexual appetite and that she didn't like to go hungry for very long. In Nicky, at least fifteen years her junior, she found a willing, energetic, and particularly well-endowed partner. And that's what he would have stayed, a casual liaison, like Granny Nourse or Bob Short or Ira Reed before him, if Rankin Barnes had not filed for divorce.

The filing took Pancho by surprise. She hadn't seen Rankin in years. They hadn't lived together since 1928. But the marriage was the one constant in her otherwise changing life. Men came and went; businesses came and went; money came and went, but she remained Pancho *Barnes*. The divorce complaint, written by Rankin's brother, Stanley, a San Diego lawyer, listed "extreme cruelty" as the grounds. The "plaintiff alleges," it read, "that upon more than one occasion during the marriage of said parties, defendant has committed an act of adultery . . . that upon occasions too many to enumerate the defendant has associated with men other than the plaintiff and has occupied the same bedroom and bed with such various men." Rankin, the complaint alleged, had suffered "great and grievous mental and physical anguish and suffering."

But mental cruelty wasn't the reason behind the divorce. Pancho and Rankin had enjoyed an amiable long-distance relationship for years. Rankin wanted a divorce because he was in love, and he had decided, at age fifty, to choose personal happiness over career aspirations. He had met a good-looking New York City society woman and had chosen divorce and remarriage over the rank of bishop. Instead, he would return to California and assume the rectorship of his father's old church in San Diego.

It didn't make sense for Pancho to be hurt by the divorce, but she was. She was tough, but she pretended she was tougher. Bravado had taken her a long way. She didn't want anyone feeling sorry for her, the homely woman finally divorced by the husband who marries an elegant, red-haired beauty and lives happily ever after. She didn't want to feel vulnerable that way, exposed. So she made a story out of the divorce. She left out the beautiful society woman. She left out the complaint of extreme cruelty. Instead, she told people that *she* had initiated the divorce, that she had gotten Rankin to let her out of the marriage by parading through a deacons' meeting in the nude. They believed her. They thought she was just crazy enough to do something like that.

In December 1941, three months after the divorce became final, Pancho married Robert Hudson Nichols, Jr., in a civil ceremony in

Yuma, Arizona. Pancho's bookkeeper figured she married Nicky because he was good in bed. Her foreman thought the same thing. But Pancho didn't need to marry Nicky to keep him as a bed partner, and given her station in life and his, it would have been to her disadvantage to do so. She married him to prove to herself that she could secure the affections of a man, to prove to Rankin that he had not hurt her, that she could go on just as he had. The marriage, it is said, lasted two weeks. One day, Nicky was there; the next he was gone.

That winter was also the end of Pancho's flight school. After Pearl Harbor that December, the government closed down all private airports within 150 miles of the Pacific coast. Pancho's operation was out of business for the duration.

12

The War

On December 7, 1941, Pancho was outside in the chilly desert morning watching radio-controlled aircraft from Muroc zoom across the hard blue sky. The men at the small facility were always testing something, and Pancho always seemed to know what, when, and where. She had developed close ties with the "Foreign Legion" at the bombing and gunnery range, not just because she sold them milk and meat and collected their garbage but because she knew and cared about airplanes and was invariably curious and interested when she visited. There weren't many women who could talk airplanes the way Pancho could. So she knew about the test that morning. It was not until later that she found out what had happened at Pearl Harbor, in Hawaii. Just about the time she was staring up at the Mojave sky, the Japanese had attacked the U.S. Pacific Fleet 2,200 miles and half an ocean away. Across the country, people sat by their radios, stunned, listening to the latest details of the surprise attack, learning over the course of the next few weeks that the bombs had sunk or damaged seventeen ships and killed 2,400 people. They feared a second attack, this time on the U.S. mainland, and nowhere did tensions run higher than in the Pacific coast states, where people imagined themselves the next victims of Japanese bombers. The greatest anxieties were felt on and near military bases, the obvious targets for such second strikes.

In the days after Pearl Harbor, everyone near Muroc was on edge. Military guards were posted, and they were nervous and trigger-happy. When they saw a car or truck nearing the facility, they would yell, "Halt!," and reach for their guns. But it was December, cold as hell in the desert, and everyone's windows were rolled up, the heater blasting. Guards shot at seven vehicles that month. Billy Barnes came back to the ranch from a milk run one afternoon with a bullet hole in the delivery truck. He hadn't heard the command. From then on, he and Pancho drove with the windows down, regardless of the weather.

Everything moved faster now. The day after Pearl Harbor, the United States declared war on Japan. Three days later, the country was officially at war with Germany and Italy. Within a few weeks, the small, obscure Army Air Corps detachment at Muroc was transformed into a hub of activity, a center for combat training for hundreds of fighter and bomber crews. In December alone, more than ten thousand men arrived at Muroc, including two dozen bombardment, reconnaissance, and antisubmarine squadrons accompanied by several hundred B-24 bombers. In the following months, twenty more fighter squadrons with their aircrews, maintenance staff, and command personnel and P-38s arrived in the desert. As the war escalated, fifty aircrews a month completed their combat training at Muroc, many of them practicing their attack skills on a 650-foot all-wood replica of a Japanese heavy cruiser, christened the *Muroc Maru*, that "floated" on the dry lake. All this was happening three miles down the road from Pancho's ranch, where she was trying to make ends meet with her dairy and hog businesses.

While combat crews trained at the southern edge of the lake, the Army installed a top-secret airplane-testing program on the north end. Army flight testing had been centered at Wright Air Field in Ohio, but increasingly congested air traffic there and nearby housing developments made it a poor choice for hazardous test missions. The experimental planes needed enormously long runways, and the desert floor and dry lake were perfect. In mid-September 1942, crated pieces of a top-secret airplane were removed from railroad cars along a siding adjacent to Muroc Dry Lake and transported to a single, unmarked hangar. Engineers and technicians from Bell, General Electric, Lockheed, and Northrop set up shop. They would be working on a new kind of airplane, a turbo-powered jet. Across the lake bed, at the Army base, no one knew of the project. The secrecy of the jet tests rivaled that surrounding the Manhattan Project's development of the atomic bomb.

Meanwhile, the Muroc Army Air Base, as the main facility on the south end of the lake was now officially called, was growing so fast the Army could not keep up with it. There were no hangars for the hundreds of planes that kept arriving. Maintenance was done at night, outside, when the sunbaked aircraft had cooled sufficiently to keep crews from being burned on contact. The men lived in hastily constructed forty-man tar paper barracks haphazardly heated by kerosene stoves. The bachelor officers' quarters were little better: small, stark rooms furnished with only a bed, a chair, and a chest of drawers. The men ate in mess halls built almost literally overnight. Every meal was one part food to two parts sand. They categorized the notorious desert windstorms according to the size of what the wind whipped up: dust, pebble, stone, rock. Whatever it was, it hammered against the tar paper and seeped in through the cracks. When they wrote home to their parents and sweethearts, the men described their temporary quarters in a single word: grim.

When they weren't training or testing new aircraft, the men at Muroc were looking for R & R. Movies were shown on base, which might take up part of an occasional evening, and there was a designated place to drink, euphemistically called a club, but there was little else the unmarried men could do to escape isolation and tedium. Muroc, the men joked, was centrally located: It was in the middle of nowhere. The nearest town was Rosamond, a grubby little desert burg with one main street and a few windswept shacks. Twenty miles away was Lancaster, a small, sleepy community of barely a thousand spread out wide across the desert. Los Angeles was a hundred tortuous miles of single-lane asphalt away. Gas was rationed, and there were few cars on base anyway. The men were not allowed to hitchhike.

If pilots or navigators or engineers or, for that matter, commanding officers wanted a decent meal or just a few hours away from the base to forget about the training and the testing and the war and their buddies who had already died, they could go to Ma Greene's, a combination gas station and counter-service café in Muroc, just down the road from the base. Ma Greene wore huge hats and size 44 dresses and yelled at everyone who came in the door. "Sit down," she would order, pointing to a stool. When locals came in wanting coffee, she told them she could spare only a single cup: "I'm saving it for the soldier boys," she told them. But she wasn't all that much more generous with her military customers. She would stand behind the counter, looming over coffee drinkers, doling out the sugar and cream herself to make sure nobody used too much. She was a gruff, unsociable woman, prone to screaming at kids and scolding grown men. But, the men reminded one another, she made a good hamburger, and her place was nearby. Then there was Pancho's.

Pancho's place was already set up for visitors. Her Los Angeles and Hollywood friends had been coming out for years to ride her horses, swim in her pool, and eat big Western meals in the cookhouse. She loved to entertain. She loved company. She loved men, and she especially loved fliers. With Muroc Air Base bustling just down the road, it was inevitable that Pancho's life would connect with the military's in new and deeper ways. Men on the base knew Pancho, or at least knew of her, in part because she was there delivering milk and meat. But she was also somebody everyone talked about: the heiress who dressed like a ranch hand and cursed like a sailor, the woman who had flown open-cockpit airplanes in the old days when guts, not instruments, kept you in the air. Her ranch, with its Thoroughbred horses and its luxurious swimming pool, was a desert landmark.

It didn't happen all at once, or even by design, but Pancho's place became a popular off-duty spot. Men would catch a ride over from the base and come knocking on her door, asking if they could take one of her horses out into the desert for a ride. Riding was one of the few available sources of recreation, that and hunting jackrabbits. Pancho didn't know the men by name, but she knew they flew and worked on airplanes, and that was good enough. She always said yes. On hot days, they came by asking if they could go for a swim. She let them cool off in the pool, then handed them a scotch and sat and talked aircraft all afternoon. She served them thick steaks from her own butchered cattle, steaks they dreamed about at night, steaks they talked about for years afterward, and they went back to the base and spread the word. We're in the middle of a war, Pancho told her friends, and these boys are getting killed. I want to make a place for them to have some fun.

She did, with that same combination of off-color conversation and offhand generosity that had made her the center of attention in San Marino and Laguna Beach. She doted on the pilots, listened to the engineers and mechanics, quizzed the aircraft-company contractors, swapped flying yarns with the seasoned officers, and deferred to no one. At first, they couldn't figure her out. She was as plain as homemade soap, one guy said. She was as ugly as a mud fence, said another. Some of them thought she was a man, even after seeing her several times. But she had an energy and a vitality that charmed them, a deep-throated laugh, a sense of fun and adventure and abandon that they saw in themselves and admired in her. It wasn't just that she could put them at ease. They were used to women going out of their way to do that. Pancho was different. They could tell her a dirty joke, and she would answer with an even filthier one. They could talk shop, and she would understand. They could drink and smoke and carouse, and she was right there with them. And they could do it all for free.

The men spread the word, but what really put Pancho's on the map in the war years was its popularity with one particular man, a dashing, good-looking pilot who had flown in the old days as a crew member for Howard Hughes. A charming, outgoing man who loved to have a good time as much as he loved to fly, Colonel Clarence Shoop was the commanding officer of Muroc's Flight Test Center. Shoop elevated Pancho's from mere hangout to important establishment by frequenting the place himself and especially by using her facilities to host dinners and parties for visiting dignitaries and awards banquets for his own men. He even told one of his flight engineers, who was having trouble finding a temporary place to stay, to go out to Pancho's and see if she would put him up. But Pancho was less than enthusiastic. The man had his wife and kids with him. "It would spoil the atmosphere," Pancho told him. "People come out here to raise hell."

In the early war years, Pancho didn't run her place as a business. It was her private home, with men from the base dropping by to partake of her generosity. They ate their steak not in a restaurant or a café but in the ranch-style kitchen Pancho had built years before to feed the hired hands and her constant stream of guests. But as the base grew and the number of visitors—and mouths to feed—increased, Pancho saw opportunity. In 1942, she renovated the old cook's shack, creating a clubhouse with dancing and dining areas. The large room featured a piano, a jukebox, and a double-sided fireplace. She even installed a slot machine in the corner. A small counter separated the dining area from the kitchen, so that guests could watch their steak sizzle on the big gas grill.

In front of the grill was the best cook in the valley, a six-foot-tall, 250-pound black woman named Minnie, who lived in a little cabin by the side of the clubhouse. Late Saturday nights, when the men would get particularly rowdy, she would stomp out of her cabin, stand with hands on her ample hips, and dress them down for relieving themselves against the wall. Early Sunday mornings, she hitchhiked into Rosamond to go to church.

Minnie was a fixture at Pancho's. Her meals were better than any home cooking the men had left behind. While they ate, someone played the piano: "Smoke Gets in Your Eyes," "Lili Marlene," "On a Wing and a Prayer." Sometimes girls from the base would be there, clerks and secretaries and teletype operators on the arms of pilots who had just returned from tours of duty in the South Pacific or were just about to go. They danced. Sometimes they brought their own beer; sometimes they drank Pancho's whisky. At the end of the evening, the closing tune on the piano was always the same: "We live in fame or go down in flame / Nothing can stop the Army Air Corps."

Horseback riding was popular with the men from the base, so Pancho added Arabian and Irish Thoroughbred stallions to her stables, hired a pretty young wrangler named Dorothy to take the men out on guided trail rides, and started charging hourly and daily riding fees. She built a little arena next to the stables and held small rodeos on the weekends, nothing fancy, just another reason to go out to Pancho's for a good time. To accommodate overnight guests, military or otherwise, she bought two surplus buildings from the Army, moved them onto her property, and, after minor renovations, used them as motel rooms.

As her guest ranch flourished, her farming operations were all but forgotten. She wasn't growing nearly enough hay for her horses and livestock, and she didn't seem to notice. How she could love her horses so much and not care about feeding them was a mystery to her young wrangler. But in between entertaining at home and traveling regularly to see friends in Los Angeles, Pancho lost interest in the daily routine of operating Rancho Oro Verde. It seemed that every time she left the ranch, there was another alfalfa crisis, hungry animals, no cash left behind to buy hay. At one point during the war, Pancho traveled east on family business and came home with two men in tow, Doc and Reggie, who claimed to be successful New Jersey farmers who were going to use their expertise to fix up the place and increase hay production. Instead, unsupervised, they sat on their haunches in the shade all day. Tony King, Pancho's foreman since the mid-1930s, would have taken control of the situation, but he had enlisted in the Navy in 1942. It would have been difficult for anyone to oversee Pancho's diverse and ever-expanding operations, but now the job fell to the person least likely to succeed at it: Pancho herself. Her enthusiasms often overtook her business sense. Her generosity consistently outstripped her resources. She was spontaneous and impulsive, disorganized and undisciplined. It was all part of her charm. But it made her a terrible manager and an even worse boss.

Even as she upgraded the place, spending money she didn't have to transform her private spread into a public watering hole, she couldn't help giving away what she should have charged for. Although she wasn't much interested in renting cabins to families, she opened her place during the day to the wives and children of aircraft company employees. The men of General Electric, Republic, Bell, North American, and Douglas now found themselves out in the Mojave working on the jet planes that were being tested on the north edge of the dry lake. Their families lived in pressboard houses, miles from any amenity, baking in the desert sun. Pancho invited them to swim in her pool, ride her horses, and eat her food. She entertained a number of other nonpaying guests as well, old friends from Hollywood whom she wouldn't have dreamed of charging—Duncan Renaldo, Ramon Novarro, Bill Boyd, and Erich von Stroheim, who would arrive with an entourage of young, pretty girls. She had new friends, too, who also took her generosity for granted, like Roy Rogers, Buck Jones, and Ronald Reagan.

To those who ate Minnie's grilled steaks and rode Pancho's Thoroughbreds and sunbathed around her sparkling rectangular pool, the operation looked as prosperous as the finest country club. But Pancho, as usual, was in deep financial trouble. Her government contracts for milk, which had brought her a good income for years, had now become unprofitable. A wartime ceiling on milk prices meant she was selling at a loss while paying top dollar for hay to keep the animals fed. The ranching operation was rudderless without Tony King. She was expanding and renovating, building a business without running it like one, and her profligacy caught up with her. In 1942, she was sued for defaulting on a mortgage payment and ordered to adhere to a strict schedule. A few months later, she was sued for failing to pay a $3,500 bill for lumber and other supplies. The court put a lien on her property. The next year, she lost another judgment for an unpaid supplies bill. Then she was sued for $1,400 and had another lien slapped on her land. A few months later, the Bank of America took her to court when she defaulted on a $2,000 promissory note. She was ordered to pay or lose a piece of her property. At the ranch, she bounced checks to her employees.

But Pancho didn't care. She was soon going to be rich. She was literally banking on yet another inheritance, the last she would get from her mother's family. She had rapidly spent all of the money from her grandmother on land, improvements, and horses. But there was more to come, and Pancho knew it. Besides holding a personal fortune, Caroline, along with her son Horace, was trustee of the estate of Richard J. Dobbins, Caroline's long-dead husband. Richard's will called for the trust to be divided equally among his children when Caroline died. Pancho's mother, had she lived, would have received a quarter of the estate. As her only living heir, Pancho was set to inherit that share.

While she didn't know how much her grandfather's estate was worth—both Caroline and Horace were close-mouthed about it to the end—she knew it was substantial. Richard J. Dobbins had invested his money wisely. The estate included considerable property, including one of the top hotels in downtown Philadelphia, the Broadwood, an impressive twelve-story stone-fronted structure with a grand ballroom and the city's most exclusive health club. The estate should have been settled soon after Caroline died in 1935, but her own will took precedence, and the nasty fight over it had lasted more than four years. After Caroline's money was disbursed, it took another three years for Richard's estate to be put in order. Horace, the lone living benefactor of the trust, was receiving annual income from it and was in no great hurry to see it dissolved. As the legal proceedings inched forward, Pancho became more and more eager to see her inheritance and more willing to spend as if she already had it.

Finally, in June 1942, the courts completed the considerable paperwork. The Richard J. Dobbins estate, Pancho learned, was valued at more than $1.3 million. Her share would be about $340,000, a fortune at the time, enough for a moderately wise person to live on, in style, for the rest of her life. That was the good news. The bad news was that the bulk of the inheritance was stock in the company that ran the Broadwood Hotel. The only liquid assets, the only actual cash she would receive, totaled less than $15,000, hardly enough to pay her debts, splurge on a few horses, and throw a lavish party. It had been frustrating to wait this long for the settlement, and the wait had strained the already poor relationship between Pancho and her uncle Horace. Worse yet, instead of freeing her from responsibilities by delivering a huge sum of cash, the settlement gave her new responsibilities in a business three thousand miles away. Now, on top of entertaining military flight crews and test pilots and engineers and her Hollywood pals, in addition to expanding the ranch and overseeing, however maladroitly, its operation, Pancho found herself traveling to Philadelphia for business meetings several times a year.

━ ⊨◆⊨ ━

There, in the late summer of 1944, she met a strikingly handsome man named Don Shalita. Six years younger than Pancho, he looked like a cross between Clark Gable and Robert Taylor with an overlay of Ramon Novarro: a head of thick, wavy black hair, intense, wide-set eyes, and a pencil-thin mustache above lips almost too sensual to be a man's. Shalita had those dark, exotic looks that defy categorization. He might have been South American, Greek, Italian. In fact, he was Persian. He and his family had escaped the Turks in 1916, fled on foot across the Elburz Mountains, and made their way to America circuitously, by way of Bombay. He was twelve when they finally landed at Ellis Island, seventeen when he married for the first time, and in his early twenties when his career as a dancer took off.

Shalita moved with sinuous grace. Appearing as either Don Shalita or Jose Shalita throughout the 1930s, he danced what was billed as a "Symphony of Movement" with a female partner at the best hotels and clubs in Los Angeles, Chicago, Philadelphia, and New York, and on cruise ships to Cuba. He was a star attraction with Ted Lewis and His Melody Masters, a headliner at the Palmer House. He auditioned with Rita Hayworth and dated Ida Lupino. Now in his late thirties, with the best of his performing career behind him, he had opened a dance studio off the main ballroom in the Broadwood Hotel. That was where he and Pancho met.

She was immediately smitten, strongly attracted not only to his matinee-idol looks but equally to his charm and ebullience. Shalita could not have found Pancho beautiful, but he did find in her what he hadn't found in all the glamorous women who had surrounded him for most of his adult life: a kindred spirit. They were outgoing, fun-loving, social animals, both of them. They loved to go places, do things, see people, drink, stay out until dawn. They spent two glorious, fast-paced weeks together in Philadelphia, hardly out of each other's sight, after which Pancho invited him to accompany her back to California. Shalita hardly hesitated. His dance studio was languishing. There was nothing to keep him in town. Pancho was one of the most interesting women he had ever met, so gregarious, so indefatigably social, so spontaneous. He never knew what she was going to do or say next. He was a man who loved adventure, and California, the desert, the ranch, the wild times Pancho described to him, sounded like more fun than he'd had in a while. It certainly occurred to him, although it did not matter as much as he thought it would and as much as others suspected, that she was a rich woman.

Back at the ranch, Dorothy, the young horse wrangler, couldn't take her eyes off him. He was the best-looking man she had ever seen. Lounging around the pool, smiling with impossibly white teeth, joking, always with a drink in his hand, he was the talk of the place. Shalita was equally enamored, at least at first, with his new life. A showman at heart and by profession, he embraced the role of desert rancher, buying a cowboy hat and Western shirts, learning to ride, learning to shoot a .22. He loved the constant stream of people who came to Pancho's—the Hollywood folks, the parties, the dancing to the jukebox and piano tunes. He loved to cook, to circulate among guests, to be the always charming host. He and Pancho clearly enjoyed each other's company. They would drink and laugh and tease each other, then literally ride off into the sunset on two gentle saddle horses. Shalita took an interest in the running of the place, too. He helped plan events, helped Pancho develop the rodeo and horseback-riding operations.

They could have just enjoyed themselves, let a good thing alone. Instead, on July 29, 1945, they got married in Reno. No one, least of all the two of them, could figure out why. Those who thought Pancho needed a marriage license to hold on to Shalita didn't understand her particular brand of uninhibited charm. Those who thought Shalita was marrying for money found out they were wrong. The marriage was a mystery, but it was a short-lived one. Four months after the civil ceremony at the district courthouse, it was all over. Shalita packed his bags and moved to Los Angeles. He missed the city. He missed the civilized, posh-hotel-lobby life he was used to, the life of tuxedos, not Levi's, the smell of perfume, not horse manure. He was tired of playing the rancher part. Pancho was rough and dirty and coarse, and it wore on him. Still, they parted good friends and remained so for many years. He didn't ask for a penny in the divorce. After the split-up, he often visited. When Pancho was in Los Angeles, they had dinner together.

Pancho missed Shalita, but it was not in her character to have regrets or to look backward. There had always been men in her life, and there always would be. The relationship with Shalita, like that with her second husband, Nicky, was momentarily exciting, momentarily mutually beneficial, but then it was over, a brief interlude rather than a life-changing event. Toward the end of the war, with Shalita gone, Pancho devoted her prodigious energies to the expansion of her new guest business. She could now well afford the project, for in 1945, despite her distrust of and animosity toward her uncle Horace, Pancho sold him her one-quarter interest in the Broadwood Hotel. Some of the money went where most of her money usually went—to entertainment and trips to Mexico and free food and drink for her many friends. But she also used her new wealth to make major improvements. The first involved her true love, aviation.

13

Pancho's Fly-Inn

When the war ended and the U.S. government lifted the ban on civilian flying, Pancho quickly moved to reopen her field. But to her astonishment, her application was rejected when a Muroc pilot training commander intervened, insisting that there was not enough room in the area for civilian hobbyists in addition to the military and test pilots. Enraged, Pancho immediately went over his head, working her connections in the upper echelons of the military. After a few well-placed phone calls, her permit was issued. She had won easily, but that initial brush with Muroc was an inkling of what was to come, the beginning of what would be a monumental turf battle over who belonged in the desert and who owned the sky.

With permit in hand, Pancho added two more runways to her little airfield to make landing in desert crosswinds safer and easier. They were lit by kerosene lamps that Billy or one of the workers would set out at dusk every night and collect again at dawn. With the hangar she had built for the Civilian Pilot Training Program before the war and the new runway improvements, Pancho had a sizable private airfield adjacent to her expanding guest facilities. She renamed the entire operation "Pancho's Fly-Inn" and established an open-door policy at the airfield. Anyone could tie down his plane for free, providing he agreed to buy gas and oil from Pancho. Her Los Angeles and Hollywood flying friends jumped in their cockpits, zipped over the San Gabriel Mountains, and came out for fun. Military pilots, now discharged from the service, hangared their little recreational planes at Pancho's. They had railed against the desolation of the Mojave when they trained here, but the desert pulled them back. As fliers, they could not resist the clear weather and the vast sky and the growing community of like-minded aviation hobbyists.

Pancho was soon hosting so many guests that she had to make additional improvements, spending considerable money renovating and re-modeling the two Army surplus buildings she had placed on the property to serve as motel rooms. Always delighted with any excuse to buy horses, she added even more to her stables, which now featured a dude string of twenty Thoroughbreds she rented out to guests. She expanded the small rodeo arena and made grand plans to build an even bigger facility that would host nationally sanctioned competitions. As the fighter pilots and their crews left Muroc, the test pilots, engineers, and aircraft company men came in even greater numbers. The base quickly, almost effortlessly, changed from a wartime training center to a big, literally booming, jet-testing facility. The attendant social whirl at Pancho's correspondingly intensified.

She closed down the dairy business for good—it had been costing her money for years—and concentrated on providing the men of Muroc with a place to have an unfettered good time. But word of mouth was spreading even faster than Pancho wanted it to. Serving her Hollywood friends and the new Muroc arrivals, the dashing young test pilots she had a permanent weakness for, was one thing. But now the Fly-Inn was being visited by people Pancho didn't know, friends of friends of friends, sometimes "city people" whom Pancho deemed un-desirable because, as she later told a friend, "they shoot guns . . . they take pictures . . . they drive in and walk all over you." Pancho loved people, but the crowds at her place were getting out of hand. Even as she proclaimed an open-door policy at the airstrip and expanded the guest ranch operations to accommodate more visitors, she decided to limit access. It wasn't really that she wanted fewer people. She just wanted to make sure she attracted only her *kind* of people. Pancho's Fly-Inn would from now on be a private club, admission by membership only. Pancho herself would issue and sign every member's card after reviewing written applications.

The first membership was honorary. It was issued, without application, to her old friend and flying buddy Jimmy Doolittle. Pancho had known Jimmy since the early thirties, when they were both speed racers and cross-country daredevils. Now he was the nation's biggest flying hero, the man who, at age forty-five, had led a daring mission to attack Tokyo, the man who had bailed out over China and come home to a Medal of Honor, the man who, as Lieutenant General James Doolittle, had commanded the 8th Army Air Force in Europe and the Pacific during the last year and a half of the war. Jimmy Doolittle's membership set the tone for Pancho's place. It was the unofficial but unmistakable seal of approval from the highest, most credible source possible, and it invested the place with both status and allure.

⊷ ✦ ⊶

From the air, Pancho's 360-acre spread was a single green square sewn into a brown-gray desert quilt that blanketed hundreds of miles. From the ground, set off the dusty two-lane road that ran ruler straight between the two dry lakes, it was an extraordinary sight, a lush, sprawling oasis shaded by cottonwoods, Chinese elms, poplars, and bamboo. Like her grandfather, old Professor Lowe, who had spent several fortunes bringing his personal vision to life in the canyons and crags of the San Gabriels, Pancho was both imaginative and excessive, spending whatever it took to leave her mark on the desert. A three-story Spanish mission–style tower, cement roughened to look like authentic stucco, set the tone for the place. A curved archway led to a courtyard planted with yucca, dwarf palm, and Virginia creeper, the centerpiece a four-tiered rock fountain whose waters cascaded into a fifty-foot fishpond in the shape of the Army Air Corps emblem. The courtyard was flanked by the best-appointed motel rooms in the Antelope Valley. Pancho had remodeled them in redwood paneling with rustic beams, equipping each with the unheard-of luxuries of air-conditioning and private, attached baths.

Outside the courtyard was the large swimming pool, surrounded by an ample patio. Nearby buildings housed the dining room, with its huge stone fireplace, the dance hall, and the bar with its custom-upholstered cowhide stools and a wall of framed and autographed photos featuring Pancho's most illustrious friends. Off to one side of the property, the stables and corrals housed her ever-growing string of horses, from poky saddle horses she rented by the hour, to the fine quarter horses she had just started breeding, to Trigger Boy, her champion bloodline stud stallion. Now she added two racetracks, a circular one for rodeo events and a straightaway for quarter horse racing.

Four hundred yards from the main buildings was the airport, which had come a long way from the little dirt strip she had scraped out of the hardpan fifteen years before. The runway was more than half a mile long now, with three hangars that housed offices, a repair shop, and a lounge. Crop dusters wintered their planes here, and two little local airlines and a private flying school had set up shop in one of the hangars. But the main users of the airport were the friends and customers who flew in for the day, the weekend, or the week, transported from their private planes to their quarters at the guest ranch in conspicuous Western style by antique stagecoach, buckboard, or hay wagon.

Pancho said she was concerned about too many guests and visitors overrunning the place. But even while she was devising a plan to make the bar and grill a private club, she was aggressively advertising her guest ranch in Los Angeles newspapers. One ad gave the air miles and directional readings from five L.A.-area airports, showing which passes would safely take pilots over the San Gabriel Mountains. Another touted her "modern flying dude ranch" with its "pure city comfort in a high desert plateau." A third, which captured both the ambiance of the place and the personality of its owner, was styled as a conversation between a "tired city dweller" and a knowing "Grandma" who, not surprisingly, speaks a lot like Pancho.

"What I need is a vacation!" says the tired city dweller, beginning a page of dialogue. "I want to find a place where I feel I'm a million miles from nowhere." Grandma, of course, knows just the spot. In fact, she tells the tired city dweller, she flew her plane out there just a while ago. It's a place, she says, "where you can do whatever you damn well please." She mentions everything from quail hunting in the desert to wiener roasts around the campfire to musical chairs played on horseback, but the flavor of the place comes through best when Grandma, late in the long conversation, admits to tossing back a few and "shooting a hot game of craps under the stagecoach with the handsome cowboys." It all sounds wonderful to the tired city dweller, but he fears it will be too expensive. Grandma tells him that a week's stay, including a room with twin beds, three meals a day, and horseback riding, costs only $49 per person.

In addition to placing newspaper ads, Pancho sent flyers advertising the guest ranch to all the top hotels in and around Los Angeles and as far north as San Francisco. Business, particularly during the summer months, when the desert promised cool evenings, was brisk. It was not unusual, in those immediate post–World War II years, to see a hundred planes tied down at Pancho's airfield.

It was a big, bustling operation, and Pancho ran it in her characteristic style—with complete abandon and almost joyful disdain for orderly commerce. She kept haphazard records, taking cash from customers and writing few receipts, paying for supplies with crumpled bills scrounged from her purse and her dresser drawers. She was running a complex series of businesses—private club, guest ranch, airport, horse and dog breeding, hog farming—but she didn't know whether she was making money, didn't pay attention to filing income tax returns, and didn't remember where her bank accounts were, let alone how much money was in them. And she spent extravagantly. If she liked the look of a horse, it didn't matter what the price was or whether she had the money or whether she needed the horse, she bought it. If she had fifty dollars in her pocket, one of her ranch hands used to say, she'd spend sixty. But much of her spending was not self-indulgent. She threw an enormous catered party for a local boy she'd taken a liking to. She gave a loyal friend the down payment for his house. She bought a car for another. She gave handouts to a variety of deserving and not-so-deserving souls who showed up at the ranch. One day, an old, crippled man, badly burned and broke, presented himself at her doorstep. He turned out to be Blackie Rowan, a mechanic who had worked on her Travel Air Mystery Ship years before. She took him in and gave him room and board and cigarette money for the rest of his life.

Personal generosity was one thing. But Pancho had to have been one of the few business owners actually to advertise her largesse. In a flyer promoting summer activities at the ranch, she added this, after listing the cost of accommodations: "If you happen to feel a little broke—don't stay away—we want you anyway." Money was always secondary to having fun. If it took an open hand and loose purse strings to keep things moving at the ranch, to keep the level of excitement high and the dance hall packed, then so be it. Money, whether she was making it or spending it, had never meant much to Pancho beyond the thrill of the moment. No matter how many times in her life she overspent, overextended, was hauled into court for nonpayment of bills, transferred property to stay one step ahead of the tax man, sold something expensive—a horse, a car—at a terrible loss because she needed, she *wanted* cash that moment, she never learned the obvious lessons about handling money. She was long accustomed to the indulgence of spontaneity, in finance as much as in life. She simply enjoyed spending. She enjoyed being Lady Bountiful among the desert rats. It was too late to learn otherwise. The imprint of her wealthy childhood and her wildly extravagant grandfather was deep. Even though she was now in her forties, with three marriages behind her and multifarious businesses to oversee, her attitude had not changed. "Come on out," she wrote to an old friend, inviting him to stay at the ranch. "We will ride a pony, fly a kite and light cigarettes on hundred dollar bills."

For all the effort Pancho put into the guest ranch, fixing up and adding on to the facilities, hiring wranglers and ranch hands, dreaming up activities and promotions, creating flyers and writing advertising copy, her true love was not the guest ranch with its city slickers and weekend pilots but her bar and grill with its Muroc clientele. During the war, that clientele had been Army Air Corps pilots and their crews training for battle in the Pacific theater. Now, her visitors were young test pilots and their crews, as Muroc transformed itself into the premier test flight center in the nation.

They flew everything out over the Mojave, these seemingly fearless young men: jet-powered planes and bombers, one-of-a-kind designs from snub-nosed bullets to graceful flying wings, gliders, Thunderjets, rocket wings, ships with names like Tornado and Skystreak, Black Bullet and Shooting Star, Mixmaster and Chain Lightning. Muroc was known as the Indianapolis of the Air, where every day, as a matter of course, pilots were doing something that had never been attempted—or even thought of—before. They were ex–war pilots, intense, driven, hardworking men, mostly in their mid- and late twenties, but they were also hotshots with attitude, with "the Right Stuff," as that potent mixture of bravado and casual sangfroid would later come to be called.

There was the legendary Bell test pilot Tex Johnson, one of the few old enough to know better, who would get roaring drunk the night before a flight—usually at Pancho's—show up dazed and bleary-eyed at the hangar the next morning, slip into the cockpit of his plane, and breathe pure oxygen through his mask for half an hour until he was alert enough to take on the challenges of the day.

There was Chuck Yeager, a young, good-looking fighter ace just home from the war, who amazed even his fellow pilots. One morning, Bill Bridgeman, an ex–Navy pilot, was test-flying the Skyrocket with Yeager in the chase plane. The desert sun, blasting through the cockpit, blinded Bridgeman so that he couldn't see his own instrument panel. Then, all of a sudden, a shadow fell across his face, and he looked up to see Yeager's plane slightly ahead and above him, dipping its wing in front of the sun to shade Bridgeman's eyes. It was an astonishing feat of precision flying as the untested planes hurtled through the sky at unheard-of speeds. Bridgeman was speechless. Yeager's voice came over the headset, a lazy drawl, as if he were talking over the back fence to a neighbor on a summer day: "Is that better, son?" That's the way they all were, more or less, full of themselves so they couldn't be full of fear.

They were in the air every day, every day a new plane, a new test not just of these extraordinary machines but of the pilots' control over them and over their own fear. A pilot would take his plane up tens of thousands of feet above the desert floor and then point the nose downward, diving at a thousand feet per second, hoping a plane he'd never before flown would pull out of the dive and bring him home. The pilots' daily lives were full of harrowing tales of superheated cockpits, flaps that wouldn't go down, out-of-control rolls and shakes, emergency landings, and fellow pilots who didn't make it, who "augered in," nose first into the desert hardpan. They never said "crashed"— that word was too explicit, too real. When they came home to their families after a day's flying, back to the ugly little houses their wives tried to make livable, they would be asked, "What happened today?" And, whether they had almost suffocated in a 150-degree cockpit or barely kept the plane together in the sky, they would say, "Nothing. Nothing happened, honey." The wives found out about the close calls later, on their own.

When the pilots weren't flying, they were hanging out with the engineers talking airplanes. When they weren't on base talking shop, they were at Pancho's talking shop, just as the pilots before them, the World War II trainees, had done. Her bar—informal, convenient, well-stocked—became their unofficial debriefing room. Over beer or scotch or whatever was being poured that night, the pilots traded flight test data. They talked about thermal thickets and weightlessness and control reversal while the engineers drew wing designs on cocktail napkins. Pancho's was a comfortable place. The food was good. The door was always open. But the main attraction was Pancho herself. She was not a barkeep, not a hostess, but one of them: a flier. She would work the room, circulate, slap a few backs, make sure they all had what they needed, and then she would sit at one table or another and listen. The men would be talking about a test they'd done that day or a new plane they might get to fly, and she'd listen intently and ask the kind of questions only a fellow pilot would know to ask. She was smart about planes, and she was funny, a great storyteller who knew a past they'd never experienced. But she also knew their present almost as well as they did. Although the experimental test flights at Muroc were top secret, and great pains were taken to keep them that way, Pancho seemed to know everything that went on at the base.

When Bill Bridgeman showed up at Pancho's the night before an important test flight, he did so gingerly, not knowing what sort of reception he might get. He was an ex–Navy commander flying a Navy project in direct competition with the Air Corps program that everyone knew was close to Pancho's heart. He figured Pancho would probably kick him out. When he walked in the door, he spotted her standing by the piano listening as a young lieutenant played a Cole Porter tune. She had one arm draped around a portly major.

Pancho watched Bridgeman come in and let him settle himself before she sauntered over. "I hear you're going to fly the Skyrocket tomorrow," she said matter-of-factly. Bridgeman didn't know how to respond. How did *she* know about the secret test flight? Before he could figure out what to say, she surprised him again. "You checked out on the F-80, didn't you?" she asked, referring to an earlier test flight, also secret. She took down a picture of the airplane that she had hanging above the bar and had Bridgeman autograph it. Navy or not, Bridgeman was a pilot.

It seemed to the elite group of test pilots that Pancho's was their private den, their personal playroom, their own fraternity house. She knew what they needed: not just time by themselves to debrief, but time to blow off steam; drunken, rowdy evenings playing liar's poker, eating steaks, and ogling the pretty girls who served the drinks. The celebrations were many and memorable. After every milestone flight—and, with new aircraft constantly being designed and redesigned, there were milestone flights practically every day—the pilots would gather at Pancho's to celebrate. At one such gathering, a barmaid whom the pilots had voted "The Girl We'd Most Like to Land On" hit an airman with a heavy stool, hospitalizing him with a broken nose. It was just another night at Pancho's, a few hours of escape from the danger and dread and death that surrounded them.

There were so many crashes in those days, so many deaths. The technology, as advanced as it was becoming, was several paces behind the daring of the test pilots. During the day, they'd look out from the flight line and see a plume of smoke in the distance, and they'd know that yet another plane had augered in. The dirt roads that ran through the base were named for the dead pilots until there were no more roads to name. Muroc itself was rechristened Edwards Air Force Base after one of the dozens of test pilots killed during the late forties, a thirty-year-old World War II hero named Glen W. Edwards.

—•—⊨♦⊨—•—

Of all the test pilots who frequented Pancho's in those days, there was one with whom she formed a special attachment, and who became the yardstick by which she measured all others. Chuck Yeager first met Pancho when he flew into Muroc from Wright Air Field in Dayton, Ohio, in the summer of 1945, on temporary assignment to test a new aircraft called the Shooting Star. One afternoon, he and three other pilots went rabbit hunting out in the desert, accompanied by two girls who worked on the base. When they got hot and thirsty, one of the girls suggested they go over to Pancho's. She'd been there before, during the war years.

Like most men, Chuck didn't know what to make of Pancho at first. He thought she was the ugliest woman he had ever seen, but he was almost immediately taken by her stories. She had the foulest mouth he'd ever heard, but she was also a charming and engaging hostess. He had never met anyone like her. As for Pancho, she took an instant liking to

Chuck. He was her kind of guy: casual, cocky, a good-looking young war hero whose most exciting times were yet to come. If Pancho was his link to the past, then Chuck was her link to the future. They sized each other up and liked what they saw.

Their backgrounds couldn't have been more different. Chuck, who was twenty-two at the time, was a Depression-era kid from one of the poorest counties in West Virginia. He spent his early childhood in a three-room house, sleeping in the living room on a fold-out couch with an older brother. His father made home brew; his mother cooked squirrel stew for dinner on a good night, if Chuck brought home the squirrel. But their personalities, forged a generation and a class apart, couldn't have been more similar. Chuck was, by his own admission, stubborn, strong-willed, and "opinionated as hell." Like Pancho, he had a take-no-prisoners, full-tilt approach to life, courting danger and calling it fun, playing hard, barely tolerating those who lived tame lives. He could have been her son. She wished he was. The bond was immediate, but it wasn't until two years later, in July 1947, that their friendship had time to mature. That was when Chuck came back to Muroc for what turned out to be a seven-year tour of duty during which he averaged more than three flights a day and a hundred flying hours a month. For all the time he spent in the air, he maintained with some degree of pride that he spent more time at Pancho's.

Chuck, his very pretty wife, Glennis, and their two young sons at first lived in a one-bedroom adobe house at a ranch thirty miles from the base. Pancho, who didn't normally get involved in the domestic lives of the men who frequented her place, went out of her way to be generous to them. She put the whole family up in her motel several times, for a week or more, refusing payment. She invited Glennis and the children over during the day to cool off in the pool. The boys learned to ride horses at Pancho's. The Yeager family pet was a Dalmatian pup, a gift from Pancho. To Chuck himself, she was even more generous, never letting him pay for food or drink, presenting him with an old Triumph motorcycle he used to tool around the desert, and regularly taking him on hunting and fishing expeditions. On one such trip,

Pancho flew him down to Hermosillo, Mexico, in her plane, where the mayor greeted her warmly and set out numerous bottles of tequila, which the three managed to empty that night. The next morning they set off on horses for a remote Indian village where Pancho was once again welcomed like visiting royalty. Then she flew him to Guaymas, where they went marlin fishing with an old friend. It was Pancho's idea of a grand time, and, as it turned out, it was Chuck's too. She was enjoying herself, but she was also trying to impress him. She succeeded.

Glennis wasn't jealous, and unlike some of the other wives of the pilots who spent so much of their free time at Pancho's, she didn't complain. Pancho was good to her and her family, and she was confident that—regardless of her reputation and her affinity for younger men—the Fly-Inn's proprietor was no threat to the Yeagers' marriage. Glennis was right, but for the wrong reasons. She found it impossible to be threatened by so homely a woman, but Pancho had other charms. She had no designs on Chuck other than friendship, but if she had, she just might have succeeded.

Glennis also had to contend with Chuck's friendship with the charming, attractive, and wealthy Jacqueline Cochran, a longtime rival of Pancho's. Cochran, a few years younger than Pancho, was a fiery, competitive pilot who had won numerous cross-country races and national awards in the late thirties and had, like Pancho, moved to the desert to create her own personal oasis. Cochran, by dint of marrying well, had a thousand-acre spread near Palm Springs, a self-contained paradise thick with groves of tangerine and grapefruit trees and sporting a skeet range, tennis courts, an Olympic-sized pool, a private nine-hole golf course, and six guest cottages, one of which housed the Yeagers on many occasions. Jackie lived the way Pancho could have lived had she not blown her fortune.

Back in 1933, Jackie had attended one of Pancho's San Marino parties, and the two had taken an instant dislike to each other. Years later, when they were both Chuck's confidantes, they would delight in insulting each other through him. "How can you stand that old bitch?" Pancho would ask Chuck about Jackie. A week or a month later, when

Chuck was spending time with Jackie, she would say of Pancho: "That disgusting bitch, how can you stand her?" Chuck met Jackie Cochran at about the same time he met Pancho, and she admired him with the same intensity and opened her home to him and his family with the same inordinate generosity. For years, the two women vied for Chuck's attention.

14

Blow and Go

When Chuck came out to Muroc in 1947, scores of new planes were being tested every month, but the big deal was supersonic flight and the big question was whether man could fly faster than the speed of sound. Some thought the sound barrier was an actual barrier, an impenetrable wall that, when encountered, would destroy both pilot and plane. Others thought supersonic flight was possible but didn't know if a machine could be constructed to withstand the stresses of such speed. The hotshot pilots, Chuck being one of them, just wanted to go up there and try. A civilian pilot named Chalmers "Slick" Goodlin had been testing the Bell X-1, a small, needle-nosed, torpedo-shaped experimental rocket plane that he'd managed to get close to supersonic speeds. Unlike the military pilots, he was being paid good money for his efforts. Now, it was rumored that he was demanding a $150,000 bonus to try to take the X-1 to Mach 1, the speed of sound. Pancho, who knew everything, knew about the secret test flights and about Goodlin's paycheck. Slick put in his time at Pancho's along with the military fliers. One night, after she learned that Chuck would also be testing the X-1, she lit into Goodlin in front of a packed house.

"Do you know what Yeager makes?" she roared at him. "Two-fifty a month. Do you know what he's getting to fly the goddamn X-1? Two bucks an hour." Still, she fed Goodlin steak and scotch and set it up so that he talked with Chuck and his chase pilot, Bob Hoover.

She was no less vocal with anyone who doubted Chuck was equal to the challenge. When he first arrived at Muroc, in the summer of 1947, the rumor was that he had been chosen for the supersonic tests because he was the most junior man in the flight test section at Wright Air Base and therefore the most expendable. That was either professional jealousy or sour grapes on the part of the other pilots. In fact, General Al Boyd, chief of flight testing at Wright and one of the most well-respected pilots in the military, had hand-picked him for the job. Chuck and Bob Hoover were two of the hottest fighter jocks in the Air Corps. Pancho obviously thought so, too. One night, just before their first flights in the X-1, a civilian test pilot came over to Chuck and Bob, who were, as usual, sitting at Pancho's bar.

"What makes you think you young fellas can fly faster than sound?" he asked. Pancho overheard the query and leaped to their defense.

"These two can fly right up your ass and tickle your right eyeball, and you would never know why you were farting shock waves," she said, without taking a breath. That ended the conversation.

By mid-October of 1947, with a number of preliminary flights under his belt, Chuck Yeager was ready to try to break the sound barrier. The night before the attempt, he and Glennis went over to Pancho's for dinner. In the early evening, as the sun set and the heat dissipated, they went out to her corral, had two horses saddled up, and rode out in the desert for an hour. By the time they decided to race each other back, the moonless sky was ink black. That was why Chuck, who was out in front, didn't see that the corral gate was closed until he was almost on top of it. He pulled hard on the reins, jerking the horse aside, but it was too late. The horse's flank hit the gate, and Chuck was airborne, knocked unconscious. The next thing he remembered was Glennis leaning over him, that and the intense pain in his side.

He knew something was wrong, and he knew if he went to the base doctor to find out what, he'd be grounded the next day. So he drove the dusty back road to the little town of Rosamond to find a local doctor, who told him he had broken two ribs. The doctor taped him up, cautioning him to keep his arm and shoulder motionless for the next few days.

The next morning, in severe pain, Chuck realized that, once seated in the cockpit of the X-1, he wouldn't be able to lean over to lock his own cabin door. But he wanted to go anyway. He knew he could do it. He knew if he didn't do it, someone else would. Telling no one about his injury, he had the flight engineer saw off a length of broomstick and took it with him into the tiny cockpit. He held his body rigid and used the stick to reach over and lock the door. The little rocket, sitting in the belly of a B-29 bomber, ascended to twenty thousand feet. Then the bomb bay doors opened, and the X-1, painted a bright orange, became a flaming torch against the deep blue desert sky. For the next fourteen minutes, Chuck Yeager was alone with his $6 million toy. He fired all four rockets, climbed to 42,000 feet, and, bracing himself against heavy buffeting, watched the Mach meter climb—0.83, 0.88, 0.92, 0.98— until, with no jolt, no impact, nothing special to signal the moment, the needle passed off the scale, and man, one man, was, for twenty seconds, flying faster than the speed of sound. Down on the ground, Pancho heard the sonic boom, the first ever. She knew what it was, and she knew Chuck had made it.

That night, October 14, 1947, Chuck, Bob Hoover, engineer extraordinaire Jackie Ridley, B-29 pilot Bob Cardenas, and the rest of the X-1 team congregated at Pancho's to celebrate their triumph. It was the first of many such parties for pilots who, over the next few years, would equal Chuck Yeager's feat. They called themselves the Blow and Go Club, these supersonic jockeys, and they always came to Pancho's to claim their bragging rights, a free steak dinner and as much liquor as any of them could hold. That night, Chuck stood up on the bar, steadying himself by leaning against the back wall, as the group toasted him again and again. The celebration stayed private. The historic flight was considered top secret, and the Air Corps, which was just in the process of officially becoming the United States Air Force, kept a lid on publicity for more than two months. When Pancho learned that there would be no official announcement, no immediate public glory for Chuck and "her boys," she railed against "those assholes in Washington" and got on the phone to her good friend General Jimmy Doolittle, informing him that "by the time the Air Force gets off its ass, the Navy will probably have flown Mach 2."

After the supersonic flight, Pancho and Chuck became even closer. Any test pilot who dared to criticize Chuck in her presence was thrown out of the bar. She persuaded the Motion Picture Pilots Association, her old group of movie stunt fliers, to award Chuck an honorary membership, and she hosted a huge party at the Roosevelt Hotel in Hollywood to celebrate the occasion. When the public finally heard about Chuck Yeager's achievement, his picture made it to the cover of *Time* magazine. Pancho framed it and hung it over the bar.

Chuck and his flying buddies were the fuel that powered Pancho's in the late forties and early fifties, but her place wouldn't have attracted the brass and the visiting dignitaries and the president of Bell Aircraft, among many others, had it not been for General Al Boyd. Boyd, who had learned to fly at March Field in the late twenties, was, like so many of the higher-ups in the Air Force, an old friend of Pancho's. "The test pilot's test pilot," Boyd had flown more hours in more different planes than any other military pilot in the world. He was a tall, lanky man with a hard, weathered face made almost handsome by a boyish grin his men rarely saw. The chief of the Flight Test Division at Wright Field before he took command at Muroc/Edwards in the late forties, Boyd commanded, and demanded, enormous respect on base. He was a stern, disciplined man—Yeager considered him the toughest person he'd ever known—but he also liked his fun. Pancho's was where he had it.

One Saturday morning just before dawn, Chuck Yeager and fellow pilot Pete Everest took off in a pair of F-86 jets to do an air show for the Navy at a nearby base. As the pilots often did on takeoff, the two buzzed Pancho's motel, literally shaking the shingles off the roof. When Chuck landed back at base that afternoon, there were two messages waiting for him, one from Pancho, the other from General Boyd. Pancho had called, mad as hell, to tell him that General Boyd was still at her place when they buzzed it. When Chuck personally reported to Boyd, the general frowned at him over his desk. "I thought I issued strict orders not to buzz Pancho's," he said. Yeager was probably the only man under Boyd's command who would have dared reply as he did. "General," he said, "how did *you* know that I disobeyed orders? I buzzed that motel at five this morning." Boyd let a grin out, then quickly squelched it, cursing Yeager and ordering him out of his sight.

Just as Clarence Shoop had legitimized Pancho's during the war, elevating the place from a rowdy hangout to sanctioned meeting and banquet hall, so did Al Boyd in the postwar years. His personal use of Pancho's facilities gave the place more than class and distinction; it secured it a niche in the history being created at Edwards by the Blow and Go Club. His friendship with Pancho gave her unusual access to the base and to its centers of power, confirming for all her position as friend, confidante, even "mother" of the Air Force, a title she later claimed.

Between Chuck Yeager's close friendship, General Boyd's unofficial stamp of approval, and the intensity of activity at Edwards, Pancho's was so popular that she felt she was losing control over the clientele. The place was a business now, but it had just recently been her private domain, her big ranch kitchen where she invited friends in for a hearty meal and a couple of laughs. She loved the crowds that came now; she loved the attention. But she also wanted to preserve something of the old days, at least in spirit. That was why she decided to make her bar and grill a private club. Private-club status also conveniently circumvented paying for a liquor license, and if Pancho delighted in one thing above all else, it was circumventing authority. Of course, she also loved being the boss. Approving each written application for membership and personally signing each card proclaimed and reaffirmed that position. Ironically, what making the club private didn't do was limit the crowds. Pancho knew and liked too many people. At its peak, her club had nine thousand card-carrying members.

The club to which these thousands of men belonged wasn't called Rancho Oro Verde or Pancho's Fly-Inn. Those names remained to describe her ranch and her flying resort. The bar and grill was called the Happy Bottom Riding Club. Given the presence of the pretty barmaids and the uninhibited late-night partying, the name seemed more salacious than equestrian, but Pancho, often with a wink, insisted it wasn't. She said it had to do, literally, with horses. In one version she told about the derivation of the name, she credited Dr. Fred Reynolds, an eye surgeon at the base who was a regular customer. Reynolds was said to have made the remark that old-timers at Pancho's had "happy bottoms" because they had ridden her horses so frequently that they'd toughened up their own hides. In the other version, Pancho said that Jimmy Doolittle named the place after a long ride on a spirited horse. When she asked him how he liked the ride, he replied, "It gave me a happy bottom." In fact, relatively few of the nine thousand members ever rode a horse at Pancho's. Pancho understood and enjoyed the double entendre. The club's logo was a rear view of a buxom cowgirl astride a horse, casting a come-hither look over her shoulder. It was racy. It was good advertising. And it may have had more to do with Pancho's operation than she willingly admitted.

⊷—⊷ ⊨◊⊨ ⊶—⊶

Amid all the wild success of the Happy Bottom Riding Club, Pancho met her next husband. She first saw him when he came to the ranch in the spring of 1946 with a group of fliers just back from overseas. Eugene McKendry, or Mac as everyone called him, was tall, handsome, and strong-jawed, with auburn hair, hazel eyes, and the casual Western good looks of a singing cowboy, the kind who appeared in Saturday morning serials. Born in Canada and raised in rural Washington State, he came to his love of aviation early, sweeping floors and washing airplanes at a local airport to pay for flying lessons. In the early war years, he worked as a flight instructor for military pilots in Florida. Then, for almost two years, from early 1944 to late 1945, he served as a flight officer with the U.S. Army Air Corps, assigned as a personal pilot to a

commanding general. He arrived home, honorably discharged just before Christmas, to discover that his wife was about to serve him with divorce papers and leave him with sole custody of their four-year-old
son.

Bob Dennis, Mac's navigator during the war and his closest friend,
saw that he was in bad shape. Mac needed a new start, a new life, Dennis thought. Mac needed, most immediately, a place to live, a place to
raise his son, and a job. Dennis also knew, through the grapevine, that
Pancho could use help. She hadn't had a steady foreman for the ranch
since Tony King left to enlist in the Navy. Dennis introduced Pancho
and Mac that spring, hoping they could do each other good.

Pancho was immediately attracted to Mac and used her influence in
the entertainment business to get him a part-time job flying a DC-3
called the *Mystic Lady* around the country for a magician named John
Calvert. Then she offered him a job at the ranch, a home, and her bed.
It had been several years since her divorce from Shalita, and although
Pancho never went without male company of some sort, she was ready
for a more permanent arrangement. Mac was twenty-six, about the age
of Pancho's son. Pancho was forty-five.

She was, as she had been with Don Shalita and Nicky Nichols,
proud of the age difference. Far from being a desperate older woman
clinging to a young lover, Pancho enjoyed the relationship with gusto
and did not curtail her other regular dalliances for the sake of her new
man. She regularly rode off into the desert with one or another Hollywood visitor. She had a serious crush on cinematographer Leon Sham-
roy and pursued him vigorously. But she also, simultaneously, threw
herself into a relationship with Mac that included caring for his young
son. Richard McKendry called her Mom, and she tried, in her way, to
live up to what that implied. She taught him to ride a horse, took him
to dozens of area horse shows to compete, just as she had done as a
child, and even ran a summer riding school for six-year-olds to provide
him with companionship. He took to ranch life with the enthusiasm
one would expect from a little boy. When he was old enough to start
school, he wore cowboy boots every day, and he smelled of horses so

often and so strongly that his teachers suspected he slept in the stables. Pancho may not have been concerned with Richard's hygiene—she was not much concerned with her own—but she did take an interest in his education, teaching him the multiplication tables and more than once bailing him out of trouble by marching into the principal's office and intimidating school officials. She bought him a telescope, and for years, every night, he would scan the desert skies looking for UFOs. Richard was her second chance at motherhood, and this time she did better.

Meanwhile, her relationship with her own son, Billy, became increasingly strained. Then in his mid-twenties, Billy lived and worked at the ranch, spending most of his time overseeing the airport operation. In 1945, he had married a pretty, vivacious young woman named Betty Swan Campbell, a horse enthusiast whom he had met at a party in North Hollywood the year before. Billy was taken in by her good humor, her energy, and her thick, curly black hair. But Betty was also a young woman with a past. She had already been married and had a young daughter. And, at the time she met Billy, she was deeply in love with a man who had left to fight overseas, the man for whom she would leave Billy three years later.

From the beginning, Betty was unhappy at the ranch. She felt that she and Billy were living on Pancho's handouts, and increasingly, it seemed that way to Billy, too. He had his own ideas for the ranch, his own plans for the airport, which Pancho did not allow him to pursue. He had not, as an adult, ascended to the role of second in command, as he might have expected or hoped. He got along with all his mother's boyfriends, including Mac, and he liked and was good to Richard, teaching him how to shoot and taking him rabbit hunting in the desert. But it could not have been easy for him to see his mother pay more attention to someone else's son than she had to her own. It could not have been easy to see Mac ascend to second in command.

Thaddeus Sobieski Constantine Lowe—Civil War hero, pioneering balloonist, renowned inventor, and self-made millionaire—was Pancho's maternal grandfather. In 1910, when she was eight, he took her to the first aviation exhibition in America. "Everyone will be flying when you grow up," he told her. "You'll be a flier too."

Florence Mae Dobbins, Pancho's mother, was the daughter of a Philadelphia architect who came west by private railway car, servants in tow. The
old-money Dobbinses considered the Lowes slightly gauche but did not
stand in the way of the marriage between Thaddeus's favorite son, Thad, Jr.,
and Florence Mae.

Pancho, a headstrong, rebellious girl, was sent to a series of increasingly strict private academies, boarding schools, and convents. When that didn't work, the Lowes promoted her marriage, at nineteen, to a straitlaced Episcopalian minister, the Reverend C. Rankin Barnes.

UNIVERSITY OF SOUTHERN CALIFORNIA HEARST NEWSPAPER COLLECTION

Pancho never settled into life as a minister's wife. Leaving her husband and five-year-old son behind, she cropped her hair, donned men's clothing, and signed on to crew a banana boat bound for Mexico. She and a fellow adventurer jumped ship and tramped cross-country on foot and astride burro, returning home almost seven months later on the *Rajah*, a New Orleans freighter.

When Pancho learned to fly in the spring of 1928, aviation was high adventure: Lindbergh had crossed the Atlantic only the year before. Pancho flew a single-engine, open-cockpit plane, stick and rudder, with few instruments.

AIR FORCE FLIGHT TEST CENTER
HISTORY OFFICE, EDWARDS AFB COLLECTION

Pancho (third from the left) was a regular at the dozens of small airfields that sprung up in the twenties in and around Los Angeles. Female pilots were a rare breed, but with her fearless flying and salty conversation, Pancho won the respect of her fellow aviators.

Of the more than 4,500 licensed pilots in the United States in the summer of 1929, only 31 were women. On August 18, they had a chance to race one another in the first women's cross-country flying derby. Pancho (extreme left), Amelia Earhart (third from the left), and Gladys O'Donnell (in helmet) were among the contestants in the eight-day, 2,800-mile event.

Pancho was the envy of every pilot when she purchased the fastest sport plane of the day, the Travel Air Model R, known as the "Mystery Ship" because of the secrecy that surrounded its development. With a top speed of more than 200 miles per hour, the low-wing, snub-nosed monoplane, painted a flashy scarlet, was, one observer quipped, "so fast that it takes three men to see it."

The Betsy Ross Corps, founded in the early thirties, was a national organization of female pilots intended to function as an auxiliary to the Army Air Corps. Pancho (kneeling, second from left) joined immediately but was disappointed by the lack of activities. She took the initiative and, with a fellow pilot, founded the Women's Air Reserve to give female pilots an opportunity to train and serve, as male reservists did.

Pancho was not an attractive woman, but the photographer George Hurrell performed magic in this dramatic image. Hurrell, who was barely making a living photographing artists and their work when Pancho met him, was a regular at her Laguna Beach parties. She was so pleased with his portraits of her that she introduced him to her Hollywood friends. Through these connections, Hurrell began a sixty-year career as M-G-M's chief still photographer.

Ramon Novarro, a leading star at M-G-M in the twenties, became one of Pancho's closest friends. Novarro was warm and attentive, but Pancho soon discovered that his romantic intentions were reserved for men.

When Pancho first moved to the Mojave Desert in the mid-thirties, the facility that would later become one of the most important air bases in the country was an isolated tent encampment known locally as "the foreign legion of the Army Air Corps." Pancho made friends with the men who had the misfortune to be stationed there.

When Pancho moved to Rancho Oro Verde in the Mojave, she took her son, Billy (left), with her. He had been in his father's charge for years, but Pancho and Rankin agreed that ranch life would be good for the boy. She also took along her current lover, Logan "Granny" Nourse (center), a pilot and airplane mechanic.

Pancho loved outdoor work and prided herself on her physical strength. At one time, she simultaneously managed a dairy farm, extensive hog and cattle operations, a horse-breeding business, a garbage-hauling business, and an alfalfa ranch. She dressed rough and talked dirty but kept her hands perfectly manicured.

Pancho became the Mojave's premier entrepreneur. What started as an eighty-acre alfalfa ranch became, with enormous effort and extravagant spending, a Western-style resort with a guest ranch, bar and grill, dance hall, weekend rodeos, and private airstrip.

Pancho's bar and grill became the unofficial headquarters for the first generation of supersonic test pilots, the daring and arrogant young men who were to define "the right stuff." They treated Pancho's as their private fraternity house, spending long hours drinking, debriefing, and blowing off steam. Pictured around the piano with Pancho are (from left) Jack Ridley, Ike Northrup, Pete Everest, and Chuck Yeager. Gus Askounis is at the keyboard.

Pancho's bar might have been just another desert watering hole had it not been for the force of her personality. She was the consummate hostess, bear-hugging old friends, playing jokes on newcomers, entertaining all with tales of her early flying days.

PANCHO'S RODEO

3 NIGHTS

FRIDAY, SATURDAY SUNDAY - 8:00 P.M.
July 28-29-30

5 BIG RODEO EVENTS - Cutting Horse Contest
Every Night   -   Stock Furnished by Cline

HOLLYWOOD STARS - Special Events Galore

Friday, Children Free   Saturday, Big Surprise Night
Sunday, FREE BARBECUE, 6:00 p. m. until Show Time

Free Camp Space. Bring the Whole Tribe and Spend the Weekend! Swimming Too

Highway 6 to Rosamond, Then East 12 Miles
Barnes Airport on CAA Chart - 24 Hour Service

Kitchen And Cocktail Bar Open 6 a. m. To 2 a. m.

LANCASTER   CALIFORNIA

Pancho's locally famous rodeo was one of the many ventures that, under her management, lost rather than made money. Thousands attended the three-day extravaganzas, which featured fireworks, barbecues, burlesque shows, and, one year, a naked "Lady Godiva."

Pancho often entertained Hollywood celebrities at the ranch, but sometimes the movie community came not to play but to work. The crew or cast of a number of productions stayed at Pancho's in the early fifties, which gave the Edwards pilots yet another reason to hang around. Left to right: Jack Ridley, Jimmy Doolittle, Jr., Chuck Yeager, Shelley Winters, Russ Schleeh, and Pete Everest.

The Los Angeles *Herald Examiner* called Pancho and Mac's wedding "one of the most flamboyant . . . in the state's history." They were married in two ceremonies, the second presided over by Chief Lucky and Little Snow White, members of the Blackfoot tribe. Guests then made their way down a thirty-foot banquet table, complete with massive ice sculptures, and were later entertained by a Hollywood character actor, a waddling duck, and Lassie.

When the Air Force tried to buy Pancho's property to make room for the further expansion of Edwards, she fought long and hard, mounting three successive lawsuits against the U.S. government. Acting as her own attorney, she waged what was dubbed "the War of the Mojave" not just for her land but for her way of life.

On November 14, 1953, in the midst of her litigation, Pancho's house and dance hall mysteriously caught fire. She lost everything in the house—furniture, artwork, clothes, jewelry, and a gun collection— and much that was in the barn. Several prized stallions died, trapped in their stalls.

After the fire and her move to an isolated ranch north of Edwards, Pancho lived in virtual obscurity—and increasing poverty—for almost fifteen years. Then, in the late 1960s, she was "rediscovered" and became a frequent and honored guest at functions on the air base, including a special Pancho Barnes Recognition Day.

To Walt
a Real Joy
to know
Pancho Barnes

Back in the limelight, accompanied by her new friends and "co-discoverers" Ted Tate and Walt Geisen, Pancho became a popular banquet speaker, spinning yarns about the old days and telling off-color jokes to appreciative audiences. She spoke at banquets for the Experimental Aircraft Association (where this photo was taken), the Society of Flight Test Engineers, and the Silver Wings Club, as well as at the fiftieth-anniversary celebration of the McDonnell-Douglas Aircraft Company.

Pancho's life was all about contrasts: the socialite upbringing that clashed with her rough-and-tumble ways, the vigorous life that belied her ill health, the lack of beauty that could never overshadow her great charm. Perhaps nowhere was the contrast more visible than in the homes in which she began and ended her life. As a child, she spent a great deal of time with her grandfather Lowe at his 24,000-square-foot mansion on South Orange Grove Avenue (known as Millionaires' Row) in Pasadena. In her later years, she lived in a small stone shack in the desert.

15

Did She or Didn't She?

Pancho lived a vigorous outdoor life, riding and training horses, pitching hay and hunting jackrabbits, overseeing the ranch, the stables, and the guest accommodations. Her social life was equally strenuous, with a barrage of visitors, all-night parties at the ranch, and weekends alternately spent entertaining at the Happy Bottom Riding Club, hotel-bar hopping in Los Angeles, and flying to her favorite Mexican haunts. She seemed inexhaustible, unstoppable, invulnerable. But she wasn't.

Her mother had died of a stroke brought on by high blood pressure before she was fifty, and Pancho had inherited the condition. Symptoms had laid her low once, many years ago just after her mother died, but Pancho had been misdiagnosed as having a "nervous condition" and sent to bed. Now nearing the age at which her mother had succumbed, Pancho didn't know she suffered from extreme hypertension. It is, in fact, a mostly symptomless condition until something serious happens.

For Pancho, that something happened one sunny afternoon in the fall of 1946 when she was at Compton Airport. She had driven into Los Angeles to hang around the local airports, checking out the new planes, snooping around the hangars, and trading stories with the pilots. At Compton that afternoon, she was staring at a big metal airplane gleaming in the California sun when she suddenly felt a blast of light explode behind her eyes. The pain was considerable, but she didn't take it seriously at first. She thought she'd just gotten a bad headache from the sun reflecting off the silver body of the plane. At Glendale Airport, her next stop, her eyes bothered her so much that she bought a pair of aviator's sunglasses to cut the glare. As she tried them on, closing first one eye, then the other, she discovered that she couldn't see out of her right eye. She didn't know it at the time, but a blood vessel had burst behind the eye, the result of blood pressure later tested at an astronomical 265/135. While staring at the plane on the Compton runway, she had suffered a retinal hemorrhage. This is what doctors call a hypertensive emergency, a life-threatening situation. But Pancho had no love of doctors and didn't go to see one. She went home, where she would have ignored the incident entirely had she not collapsed a few days later. Her ranch hands put her to bed and called a doctor.

In those days, there were no drugs to control hypertension. The preferred treatment for dire conditions like Pancho's was to remove pints of blood and thus lessen the pressure on the whole system. This dangerous and drastic measure provided only temporary relief, of course, because the body shifted into high gear to quickly replace the missing fluid. There was one other, even more extreme treatment for cases like Pancho's. Lying in her bed at the ranch, she remembered reading about it in the *Reader's Digest*. It was a grueling operation called a sympathectomy, in which the nerves that sent blood-pressure-raising flight-or-fight signals to the brain were cut. The Mayo Clinic in Rochester, Minnesota, was one of the few places that performed this difficult procedure. Mac McKendry flew her as far as Des Moines in the big plane he used to shuttle Calvert the magician to his shows. From there, Pancho went on alone to the clinic.

The operation involved making an eighteen-inch incision on one side of the spinal column, from under the shoulder blades to the tailbone. Ribs were removed or pulled back so the surgeon could locate the nerves. First one side of the body was operated on. Then, after a lengthy and painful recuperation, the procedure was repeated on the other side. Pancho was alone and miserable in the hospital after the first operation. The nerve cutting scrambled signals to her circulatory system. She was cold on one side of her body and warm on the other. She contracted pneumonia. Confined to her bed in the small hospital room for weeks, she suffered from claustrophobia.

She had never really *needed* any of the many men in her life before. They had been nice to have around for companionship, for laughs, for sex, but Pancho was seemingly self-contained, a fiercely independent woman who relied emotionally on no one other than herself. But in the hospital in Minnesota, weak, sick, and alone, she hit bottom. Only Mac was there to cushion her. He flew in from Detroit, where Calvert was putting on a show, and accompanied her into the operating room for the second procedure. He kept her company on and off during her recuperation. Then, the day after her stitches were removed and doctors measured her blood pressure at 125/80, Mac took her home on a commercial flight. Billy was waiting at the Lockheed air terminal in Burbank. He had blanketed the backseat of the car with pillows to make his mother more comfortable for the 120-mile drive back to the desert.

Back at the ranch, Pancho proceeded to put herself on display, lying facedown in bed while some of the most famous pilots in the United States Air Force filed by to have a look. She didn't want anyone pitying her, and this public showing, with Mac narrating the details of the operation while she cracked jokes for anyone who had the stomach to listen, was her way of proving her toughness. She wanted them to shake their heads and talk about what a character she was. She wanted them to laugh with her. She wanted anything other than for them to feel sorry for her.

Pancho did not stay in bed long. Although her circulation and sense of balance were still impaired, two weeks after flying home she pushed herself to get on a horse and take a desert ride. She gathered her strength to make an appearance at the ranch bar, carrying on as usual until someone forced her back to bed. On Labor Day, about six weeks after her second operation, she flew to Cleveland to attend the first National Air Races held since the beginning of the war. She spent several days enjoying the festivities and seeing old friends, who slapped her on the back and yelled, "Good ole Pancho!" while she alternately laughed and winced. With four ribs partially removed, she was still in considerable pain. She figured her recovery would be complete only if she had an adventure. It had worked before, when she set out cross-country as a young woman, getting up from a sickbed the doctors said she would never leave. It would work this time.

The adventure was, as Pancho later called it, "the cruise to end all cruises," a two-month, four-thousand-mile voyage in a forty-six-foot fishing boat from San Pedro, California, down the coast of Mexico to Cabo San Lucas. Roger Chute, the man who had named her Pancho twenty years before, came along for the ride. Billy and his wife, Betty, were on board, as was Mac. It was a wild trip. The waves were gigantic, almost tossing them from their bunks. During one particularly heavy storm, the propeller shaft broke, and Billy and Roger had to dive into the fiercely choppy waters to fix it. Billy's mechanical abilities, which were considerable, were taxed to their limits as he worked to keep the engine running through all kinds of difficulties. The boat rolled and pitched, and Pancho was convinced that the constant exercise she got keeping herself from going overboard helped complete her recovery. Whether for that reason, or thanks to the sea air or just the passage of time, when the boat docked in San Pedro again, she was her old self: healthy, invigorated, and ready for action.

<hr />

In the late 1940s, the Happy Bottom Riding Club was all action. Pancho bragged that she had a "three-ring circus going on," a "real jumping joint," with big meals and lots of liquor and live dance bands three times a week. On Wednesday nights, the Kings Four—a trumpet, sax, clarinet, and piano quartet from the base that later became a popular Los Angeles dance band—played in the lounge. All the pilots and their wives came, the engineers, the designers, the crew—anyone who had a membership card or was friends with someone who did. The crowd grew to as many as four hundred on these nights. But the real action was on weekends, when guests would fly in or drive in from Los Angeles, and the guys at the base would make the short hop from their quarters to Pancho's front door.

She thrived on the spontaneous, out-of-control atmosphere and fed it, throwing impromptu barbecues, loading up the hay wagon for surprise rides into the desert, celebrating any occasion she or anyone else could think of—first flights, milestone flights, promotions, retirements, departures and arrivals, anything that could be toasted. Pancho stayed up most of the night, every night, then took a long siesta with her dogs during the day.

The parties quickly became legendary. At one New Year's Eve celebration, Pancho rode her horse into the lounge at midnight and shot off a gun. For another party, she imported three exotic dancers from Hollywood who performed, as Pancho said, "a total strip tease right down to their lovely naked bodies . . . and not a goddamn thing wrong with it, either." During the long, hot Saturday afternoons, it was common to see girls diving into the pool naked, and men, overcome with lust, alcohol, and high spirits, splashing in after them, sometimes stripped to their underwear, other times fully clothed in suits and ties.

Most of Pancho's booze was flown in illegally from Mexico, so she paid no taxes on it. Just as one of these clandestine shipments was being delivered, she was tipped that some "civilian federal boys" might be making a surprise visit to the ranch. She and one of the hands took the crates of liquor out into the desert, used a tractor to dig a hole, and buried them all. That night, a gullywasher wiped out their landmarks, and the next day, despite hours of searching, they could not find the stash. They never did find it. But there was more where it had come from. Alcohol scarcity was never an issue at Pancho's. She dispensed the inexpensive stuff to the nightly revelers, saving a bottle of premium whisky for herself and special friends like Al Boyd and Chuck Yeager. She kept the bottle behind a removable stone on the side of the fireplace. One night, when she reached in for it, she was bitten by a spider.

She pulled her hand back, cursing loud enough to be heard above the din. "That goddamn thing will die for biting me," she said, and no one in the bar doubted it.

The bar at Pancho's was well stocked, within its limits. If you wanted a drink, you got scotch, a highball, or a beer. If anyone asked for something else, a cocktail or something fancy, the bartender looked at him as if he'd gotten too much desert sun. There was no formality, no etiquette, no pretense. The bar, like Pancho, like the desert, was rough, coarse, and unceremonious. One night, a customer made the mistake of complaining when he saw the bartender stir his highball with an index finger. "Hey, buddy," the bartender replied brusquely, "the alcohol will kill the germs. What are you worried about?" The customer accepted the drink.

Pancho had a special bath mat she kept rolled up under the bar, a prop she brought out when she thought the evening needed a spark or when she figured she could embarrass the hell out of a young officer or a new waitress. The mat was a sheet of sponge rubber made of falsies, row after row of pink rubber breasts glued together. Sometimes Pancho would unroll it on the bar, laughing raucously and waiting to see who blushed. Other times, she would blindfold one or another of the men, preferably a youngster who was new to the Happy Bottom Riding Club, and have the embarrassed kid take off his shoes and socks and walk up and down on the mat.

One amateur pilot who flew in for the weekend was so completely inebriated by Sunday afternoon that Pancho ordered him put to bed and locked in his room so he wouldn't attempt to fly home that night. Undeterred, the man crawled out the window of his motel room, staggered over to the airstrip, got in his plane, and took off. He crashed a mile from the hangar, but with the odd luck that occasionally accompanies those too drunk to take care of themselves, he walked away from the wreck with nothing but a bloody nose. Another evening, two pilots who were getting noisily drunk at the bar and boasting of their aerial skills made a bet about which of them could shear off Pancho's weather vane with a wingtip. The weather vane stuck up about six feet from the peak of the barn roof. They got in their planes, took off and buzzed the ranch repeatedly, swooping low over the barn. The weather vane survived the evening; so, miraculously, did the two pilots.

Alcohol also fueled more than a few fights, old-fashioned, chair-smashing, nose-flattening brawls, the likes of which most of the men had previously seen only at the movies. Some of the almost monthly altercations were small enough for Pancho to handle. "Get your ass out of here," she would order some disorderly customer who looked ready to take a swing at someone. She might punish a troublemaker by taking away his membership card or have friends physically toss him out of the place. But some fights required outside intervention, the most noteworthy of which was a classic collision between Army and Air Force men who found themselves at the same place at the same time roaring drunk. It was a tear-'em-up brawl that no one could contain. Pancho watched them destroy her bar, breaking bottles and windows and one another's jaws, and then she did something characteristically Pancho: She went right to the top. She didn't bother with the marshal on base, or with the commander. She called one of her bigwig friends in Washington, D.C., an Air Force buddy from the old days with whom she was on a first-name basis. The next day, the Air Force sent an investigating crew out from Washington, which did nothing to endear Pancho to the base commander. Pancho's was put off-limits to all base personnel, which was something she hadn't planned on. But she weathered the setback, filling the place with civilians and her usual complement of Los Angeles visitors. Soon enough, she was open for military business again.

Pancho constantly invented entertainments and novel events to draw new customers and keep regulars interested and coming back, fun, not commerce, being the real motivator. She expanded the lounge by opening an outdoor bar on the patio. She ran an illegal casino in one of the outbuildings, bringing in a couple of dealers from Las Vegas to operate the blackjack table and the roulette wheel and installing one of her prettiest barmaids at the poker table. It was all hush-hush, one of those secrets that everyone seemed to know but that somehow never got as far as the authorities. She instituted Sunday afternoon deep-pit beef barbecues. She organized and advertised a foxhunt across the open desert, with riders jumping obstacles as they pursued a pack of hounds pursuing the prey. The night before, they had all partied in the lounge at a gala hunt ball.

One summer she dreamed up an airborne treasure hunt, with pilots taking off from her airstrip to land at four different fields looking for clues to the location of a treasure chest filled with one hundred silver dollars, a gold belt buckle, and a silver brooch. Billed as the "Big Air-Real Treasure Hunt," the event began the night before with a "Pirates Dance" and ended late in the afternoon with a beef barbecue. "Be sure to wear your buccaneer clothes," instructed the flyer Pancho created for the weekend extravaganza. "Fly in, tie down for free, camp for free or see if we can sardine you into a bunk," the invitation read. Each treasure hunter had to sign an entry form, which deftly combined Pancho's disdain for authority with her acknowledgment of same. "I will observe all CAA [Civilian Aeronautics Association] regulations and do my best not to make a damn fool of myself," read the form. "I will wait until the hunt is over and my plane is safely tied down before I so much as sniff a small smell of alcohol." Later that same summer, she organized her own air races with cross-country flying, spot landing and bombing contests, parachute jumpers and stunt fliers. The event was a huge success, but it was merely a warm-up. That fall, in 1949, the national Bendix Air Races started at Rosamond Dry Lake, just a few miles west of Pancho's, and the racing greats, past and present, came out to the desert. Pancho, of course, threw a huge party.

In the late 1940s, Pancho's big horse barn caught fire. A fire truck from the base responded quickly, but there was a railroad train blocking the tracks that crossed the road to the ranch. The truck set off across the desert, got stuck in the sand, and never made it to Pancho's. Meanwhile, the barn blazed, and ranch hands were unable to save two big stallions caught in their stalls. Thousands of dollars of tack and saddlery burned, too. Pancho mourned the loss of her five-gaited stallion and her gray, but she remained undeterred from her grand plan to make horses even more of a focal point at the ranch.

For several years she had hosted a little rodeo almost every weekend, a few events held in the corral, with onlookers perched on the fence. Now, in 1949, she built a real rodeo facility with chutes, an arena, and grandstands, and she gained the endorsement of the Rodeo Cowboys of America Association. To advertise the three-day event, she hitched her matched pinto ponies, Tip and Top, to the ranch stagecoach and drove up and down the main street of every small town in the area. She mailed out a flyer that promised, in addition to the rodeo events, a stage show with "our Hollywood celebrities, gorgeous girls (legs 'n all) and burlesque." As another enticement, Pancho purchased a new Chevrolet to be raffled off during the event. A few days before the rodeo, she rented huge searchlights and set them out around the arena. The beams could be seen for thirty miles. Then, on Friday, Saturday, and Sunday, August 5–7, 1949, almost five thousand people came to the ranch to watch professional rodeo cowboys ride Brahma bulls and bucking broncos, rope calves, and bulldog steers. Pancho expected to make a lot of money and have a lot of fun. She had a lot of fun. Although the stands were packed every day, the event lost $13,000. In her desire to create an extravaganza, Pancho had overspent on everything.

Undaunted, she launched plans for another rodeo the next year, which she envisioned as even grander. She had a great time producing a raunchy, twelve-page mock newspaper for the event, the *Happy Bottom Blister,* which featured on its front page the familiar club logo of a buxom cowgirl astride a horse. Inside, there were jokes and anecdotes set in typed columns with headlines, like news stories. In one story, titled "Young Lady on Way to Lover Suffers Brutal Attack," the victim, "Ruth Rodent," is caught up in a combine while crossing the field to visit her boyfriend. When he sees her, shaken, torn, and disheveled, and asks what has happened, she replies: "I've been reaped!" In another story, a sex-starved G.I. hides along a jungle path and grabs what he thinks is a native girl. When he discovers he has instead grabbed an old man, he exclaims: "I've half a notion to let you go!" These and the other stories were quintessential Pancho, the kind of off-color, mildly offensive stories she loved to tell in the bar not just to get a laugh but to show that she was a different kind of woman than anyone within earshot had ever met. But Pancho also covered her bases. In a boxed story on the same page, she proclaimed, "We just aren't responsible. Among other things, we're not responsible for the interpretation you care to place on the stories in the BLISTER."

One story in particular caught everyone's attention: "Godiva Rides Again for Same Damned Reason." The story described Lady Godiva as a "blonde babe" who once rode through the streets of Coventry naked to protest high taxes. She would ride again, promised the story, and "while it's not expected that she'll get your taxes lowered, she'll make you forget them." Rodeo-goers read this item as a joke, like all the others, but it was, in fact, an announcement of one of Pancho's wilder schemes. During intermission on the final day of the rodeo, a pretty young woman with long blond hair came out of one of the chutes, riding bareback on a horse. She circled the arena at a gallop, and people in the grandstands couldn't believe what they were seeing. The young woman was completely naked. The Godiva spectacle was the talk of the rodeo, which lost only $9,000 that year.

Morals at the Happy Bottom Riding Club were always a matter of debate. After the war, when Pancho expanded her business and began catering to larger and larger primarily male crowds, she started hiring pretty young hostesses to tend bar and wait tables, with the understanding that they would also converse and dance with the men. "My girls are the sugar to catch the boys," she used to say. Pancho would advertise for hostesses in the Los Angeles papers—"Girls, vacation with pay on Dude Ranch"—looking to attract personable, good-looking young women in their twenties. She was partial to girls who could sing or play the piano, who were outgoing, intelligent, and unabashedly flirtatious. Many of those who answered her ads were out-of-work Hollywood showgirls, would-be actresses, and unemployed models, some still wide-eyed and naive, others quite hard-boiled. Just before the busy summer season, for which she needed to hire a gaggle of hostesses, Pancho would drive down to Los Angeles, stay at the Beverly Hills Hotel, and conduct interviews. Each girl brought with her an eight-by-ten glossy, which Pancho took back to the ranch to lay out before her informal panel of experts—her hotshot pilot friends—who would go through the photos one by one, discussing the physical attributes of one girl after another before choosing the ones they thought Pancho should hire. A few of the hostesses stayed for a year or more or returned to work every summer, but most lasted only a single season. The desert was too hot and too desolate. Their accommodations at the ranch, a long, narrow dormitory building lined with double bunk beds, were less luxurious than they might have hoped. The job was not, in fact, a "vacation with pay," but a hectic, sometimes nonstop, whirl of social activity that could be exhausting.

All the hostesses worked at night, which was defined as late afternoon, when the serious drinking began in the lounge, to whenever the ongoing party broke up, often in the predawn hours. Their days started deceptively slowly as they meandered into the ranch kitchen to drink coffee, eat steak and eggs, and gossip about the ever-changing Who's Who of guests. Some girls were off-duty during the day—Pancho allowed them four days off a month—and they swam or rode horses or caught up on their sleep. Most had no transportation and were stuck at the ranch unless Pancho organized a shopping trip into town for them. Those who were on duty might provide companionship to male guests poolside, on horseback, or in the restaurant and lounge. On weekends, some men would fly in not to stay at the ranch but just to refuel and pick up a hostess or two to accompany them to Las Vegas. The girls could make their own decisions about who wanted to be with whom. The men paid for the weekend's activities, giving the girls extra money to gamble. Pancho had to approve all comings and goings, but she was a lenient boss who was as caught up in the spontaneity and social swirl of the place as any of her guests. All she wanted was for the men to have a good time, a *very* good time.

That often meant going out of her way to devise as outrageous and memorable an experience as she could. People came to Pancho's expecting wild times, and they rarely left disappointed. On one occasion a couple of two-star generals called Pancho from their base in Ohio, telling her that they'd be flying out and were interested in "the finest steak, some good scotch that wasn't one of her Mexican refills, and a couple of willing girls who were first-class 'eating stuff.' " Pancho met the challenge. She had two big aluminum serving trays made and commissioned a baker in town to create two giant loaves of bread. When the brass arrived, she served them big steak dinners and the best liquor, and told them the girls would join them directly. Back in the kitchen, the cook was busy making sandwiches from the loaves of bread, using two nude girls as the filling. A few ranch hands were called in to hoist the serving trays on their shoulders and present them to the astonished, delighted, and undoubtedly embarrassed generals, who had gotten more than they bargained for. Pancho loved shocking the people to whom others would have deferred: generals, Hollywood personalities, millionaires. She loved actively, purposefully creating what would become the legends of the Happy Bottom Riding Club, stories she and others would tell later, many times, embellishing even the seemingly unembellishable.

But wild events like these, while they kept Pancho's guests coming back, also fueled the suspicion that something more than drinking, dancing, and clowning around was going on at the Happy Bottom. Locals were convinced, in fact, that the club was a house of ill repute, where Pancho's bevy of Hollywood hostesses regularly traded intimacies for cash. Everyone in the neighboring towns of Rosamond, Lancaster, and Palmdale knew, or thought they knew, the truth about Pancho's. Didn't all the girls go by fake names? Hadn't Pancho surnamed them all "Smith," assigning days of the week or months of the year as their first names? The locals whispered about the prices each girl charged and made up stories about hand-painted signs nailed over the front doors of the cabins to advertise the favors that could be procured within. They whispered about a local lady who stormed out to Pancho's to bring her daughter home. They whispered about how the principal of the on-base grade school walked toward Pancho's on Monday mornings carrying a stick with a nail at the end of it so she could pick up all the discarded condoms on the road before the kids saw them.

Everyone had a story: the pretty wrangler who was hired to work with the horses but supposedly asked to put in time at night in the cabins; the new hostess who, it turned out, had just been released from the Tehachapi prison after serving time for prostitution. Some said that when you rented a hotel room, a girl came with it. Others said you negotiated at the bar. Some said the services were open to all comers; others said you had to be a friend of Pancho's. Local opinion was divided not on whether prostitution existed at the Happy Bottom but only on whether Pancho encouraged it or merely tolerated its existence, whether she took a cut of the girls' earnings or was content that these extracurricular activities brought in more bar-and-grill customers. In private, Pancho, they said, made no bones about what was really going on out there.

But to a man, the military pilots, most of whom had wives and children at the base, maintained the purity of the Happy Bottom. Sure, it was raunchy at times. Sure there might be naked women in the swimming pool. But there was no sex for hire, they insisted. The pilots' wives knew better. Glennis Yeager called Pancho's "little more than a desert whorehouse. She knew it and so did I." Another pilot's wife burst into Pancho's one night, spotted her husband at a table, dumped a salad bowl over his head, and marched out the door. Most of the wives were unhappy, to varying degrees, when their husbands spent their off hours at the club.

Did she or didn't she run a brothel? She seemed to want it both ways. On the one hand, she encouraged gossip with her nude water ballets and Lady Godiva stunts. She even drove a pickup truck with a new crop of girls in the back down the main street of Lancaster, showing them off in their shorts and halter tops. But, on the other hand, she seemed offended when accusations were made about the behind-doors goings-on at the club. On various occasions, she defended the innocence of the girls—"I kept them like virgins in a harem," she told a newspaper reporter—but she was particularly distressed when her son, Billy, married one of them.

After Billy's first marriage had ended when his wife's old flame returned from the war, he met a woman named Gladys at the ranch. She had been working at a nightclub in Alaska and quickly became one of Pancho's top hostesses. Regardless of Gladys's skills as a barmaid, or perhaps because of her skills elsewhere at the Happy Bottom, Pancho vehemently disapproved of the marriage. "I don't like his wife," she wrote to her old friend and traveling companion Roger Chute. "She worked for me and I know her better than Bill does." Pancho called her new daughter-in-law an "old bitch" and kicked her—and her son—off the property.

Pancho made much of the "house rules" she set for the hostesses: "We permit you to accept tips and gifts while performing your regular duties. But NEVER are you to accept money in remuneration for the more intimate aspects of romance." She posted regulations for the girls that prohibited sitting on guests' laps, necking in public, or permitting a man to come to their rooms "at any hour for any reason." But over the bar she posted a "Notice of Nonresponsibility," which clearly acknowledged that she knew something was happening at the ranch beyond drinking and dancing. "We're not responsible for the bustling and hustling that may go on here," read the notice. "Lots of people bustle, and some hustle. But that's their business, and a very old one." When Pancho was asked if there was sex for sale at her place, she hotly denied it. But then she would wink and add, "But what those girls do on their own time is their own business." Of course, everyone who knew Pancho knew that she *always* knew what went on at the ranch, both in public and in private.

For years, she delighted in both fending off and encouraging the salacious gossip. It was good for business, and it fit her persona: the freewheeling, libidinous thrice-married woman who could drink any man under the table while simultaneously keeping him amused with a steady stream of dirty jokes. She figured she knew firsthand what many of the men wanted who came to the Happy Bottom Riding Club, and she intended to give it to them, from the big, thick steaks to the highballs to the girls. She chose the hostesses personally, selecting those with the prettiest faces and deepest cleavages. Some of them were serving more than drinks, and she knew it. It was all part of the Happy Bottom experience, just like the hayrides and the barbecues. But Pancho didn't solicit, and she didn't take a cut. She rarely did things for the money. She was a good-time gal, not a madam.

16

Just Do It

I t didn't seem to make any difference how many hundreds of customers she had, how many were attracted by her ads in the Los Angeles newspapers, how many came to the Wednesday night dances or the endless stream of special events. Pancho always managed to spend more than she made—not that she knew how much either sum amounted to. One day she would be broke, scrounging through her purse to find money to pay the man who delivered cases of soft drinks to the ranch. The next day, she'd sell a horse or make a deal, and she'd have several hundred dollars in her pocket. "That's enough to buy gas," she'd tell Mac or Chuck Yeager or her friend and employee Cliff Morris or her fellow adventurer Roger Chute. "Let's go to Mexico."

That afternoon, they'd be airborne. If there were only two or three of them going, she'd take her little Stinson plane. When she wanted a bigger party, she'd load up the twin-engine, the Bamboo Bomber, as it was nicknamed. Regardless of who accompanied her on these trips or what airplane they took, the first one on board was always Barney, her Dalmatian. From the early days, when she used to strap a miniature parachute onto her favorite Chihuahua and take him on cross-country air races, Pancho was rarely in the air—or in a car or in her house—

without one of her dogs. She loved the uncomplicated companionship they provided. Most of all, she loved their loyalty. People might come and go. Husbands *did* come and go. But her dogs were a constant.

With Barney in the back, they'd fly down to San Felipe, on the Gulf side of the Baja Peninsula, or continue farther south, to La Paz. Sometimes she'd fly over the Gulf and stop at Guaymas, where she knew one of the wealthiest men in town, who would unfailingly entertain her and her guests in grand style. She never tired of the warm reception and the cold beer, and her companions, no matter who they were, were always impressed.

Often, the assembled group would go down with nothing more in mind than fishing and cantina-hopping. But sometimes Pancho created a more adventurous agenda. Early in 1950, she flew with Roger Chute to Acapulco to view the jungle country through which they had hiked and horsebacked on their grand adventure almost a quarter of a century before. Roger was one of Pancho's strongest ties to her predescrt past. They had kept in touch over the years through letters and visits. Pancho had tried hard to persuade him to move to the ranch and take a job managing the lounge, touting the opportunity, telling him he was the only one she could trust, pleading with him to help her out. Roger, as much as he liked and enjoyed Pancho, thought she was crazy when it came to money. The last thing he wanted to do was become one of her employees. Still, he got a kick out of going on south-of-the-border exploits with her.

In February 1951, Roger, Pancho, and Mac set off in the Stinson for San Felipe and then on to the San Pedro Martyr Mountains to circle Mount Calamahue, at over ten thousand feet the tallest peak in Baja. They did it because they weren't sure anyone had ever done it before. Then they flew to Mazatlán and on to a tiny island Pancho had located on a map. She wanted to see if she could land on a small sandbar nearby. Roger joked that she would probably crash the plane, but he consented to her plan anyway. "If she wants to chance it," he wrote to his mother, "I'm willing." It was Pancho's show, as usual, which meant that no one but she knew what would happen next. They had made plans, of course, but Roger understood Pancho well enough to realize that spontaneity always ruled. "Any part or all of this may change any moment," he wrote to his mother, sketching the itinerary a week before their departure. "That's Pancho." As it happened, they landed safely on the sandbar and, after exploring the island, moved on to wild times in Puerto Vallarta, Acapulco, Mexico City, and Matamoros.

Pancho usually insisted on doing all the piloting herself, regardless of the fact that by then she no longer held a valid pilot's license. It had come up for renewal years before, but she had not gone in for the necessary medical exam or taken the flight test. For a woman to whom flying was the ultimate joy and the ultimate freedom, this was odd behavior, but it was also characteristic. Partly it was the result of her fecklessness. Partly, it was because she was afraid she couldn't pass the physical exam. At least, that was her excuse before the operation that cured her high blood pressure. But mostly she didn't renew her license out of a combination of defiance and annoyance. The rules and regulations for flying and licensing had become increasingly complex during her decades as a pilot, and she hated the forms and the bureaucrats and the way flying seemed to have been taken over by desk jockeys who had never seen the inside of a cockpit. Back in the days before the federal government had become involved in controlling the skies, Pancho had known and flown with everyone. It was a small world, a free-for-all world that celebrated risks and courted dangers, winked at idiosyncrasies and venerated individualism. That world, her world, was disappearing, and Pancho did not want to admit it. She did not want to become part of the new order. Flying without a pilot's license was her brand of protest. She held only a student's certificate, essentially a license to keep on taking instruction, which presented few bureaucratic hoops through which to jump. And she flew the way she had always flown, at two speeds: fast and stop. On the jaunts to Mexico, she would fly as fast as whatever airplane she was piloting would go, open throttle all the way. She did not gently taxi, but came to an abrupt, we're-down-let's-get-the-hell-out-of-the-airplane stop. It was hard on her passengers. They thought she took too many risks, flew a little too fast and loose. On a trip to La Paz with Cliff Morris and Mac, Pancho was fly-ing too low over a particularly tricky oceanfront airstrip when she swiped the plane's undercarriage on a palm tree. She thought it was funny. Cliff and Mac didn't.

⊹⊱•≒◈≒•⊰⊹

When she wasn't flying off to Mexico, Pancho was entertaining a grow-ing number of Hollywood celebrities at the ranch. The list of regulars included Errol Flynn, Tyrone Power, Dick Powell, Veronica Lake, Nicky Hilton and Elizabeth Taylor, Danny Kaye, Shelley Winters— even Lassie. Bob Cummings would pilot his own plane, flying in often and taking part in Pancho's airborne treasure hunts. Others would be ferried out by private plane or come by chauffeur-driven limousine, their shiny black cars making a stir as they zipped through the sleepy desert outposts of Palmdale, Lancaster, and Rosamond.

Edgar Bergen came out to the club to entertain, taking the train from Hollywood to Lancaster and waiting at the station for Pancho to pick him up. When she showed up one too many times in a ranch truck or a ramshackle car, he complained, half seriously, that it "just wasn't fitting." The next time Pancho was in town, she went to the car dealer-ship and bought a luxurious new Cadillac Fleetwood. On the way back to the ranch, she remembered she needed some hay. She stopped at the feed store, took out the car's backseat, and loaded up. She never both-ered to put the seat back in. When she went to pick up Bergen a few weeks later, she ushered him into the back of the impressive new car, where he sat on what remained of a bale of hay.

Others came out from the movie community not to play but to work: the directors, actors, and crews of a number of movies that called for desert locations. The ranch and surrounding terrain were particularly inviting for production companies making Westerns. Cost-conscious producers appreciated that Antelope Valley was only a two-hour drive from the studio. Directors loved the vast, flat dry lakes where a camera mounted on a truck could take long, uninterrupted footage of gallop-ing cowboys and Indians or runaway stagecoaches without worrying about running out of road or bouncing on uneven ground. The dry lakes were smooth and endless. And of course, everyone had heard of Pancho's.

When William Wellman filmed *Westward the Women* in 1950 at Rosamond Dry Lake, the cast—including Robert Taylor and Denise Darcel—stayed at Pancho's. That same year, *Passage West*, a wagon-train adventure, was filmed in the area, with the entire company living at the ranch for three months. *Son of Paleface*, a notable Bob Hope–Jane Russell comedy, was filmed in and around the Happy Bottom Riding Club, and part of the crew was housed at the ranch. Two Roy Rogers movies were also based in the area and made use of Pancho's lodgings as well as her horses and equipment. Howard Duff and Dan Duryea starred in the movie *Johnny Stool Pigeon*, which was filmed, in part, at Pancho's airport. Through the late forties and early fifties, had Pancho been paying attention to such things, she would have realized that the movie business was bringing in quite a bit of money. To Pancho that simply meant more horses, more airplanes, and more trips.

⊷ ⊨✦⊨ ⊶

It's hard to know how she found the time, but Pancho began a new—if abbreviated—career in the early 1950s: songwriting. She did not have an overwhelming talent. Her lyrics tended toward the banal; her tunes were unsophisticated. But she showed her usual fearlessness in trying something new, the character trait that separated her from most others. She loved music, which she viewed more as a social activity than an art, and she loved the piano. Why not just sit down and compose? Others might stop themselves, or hesitate long enough to let the moment of inspiration pass. They might doubt their abilities, question their talent, shy away from taking the risk. Pancho suffered no such trepidation. She just did it.

At least nine of her songs were recorded, many by Stan Worth and His Orchestra or by the Kings Four, both successful and well-known bands on the Los Angeles scene. "Moon Crazy," one of her favorites, a song regularly sung around the piano at the bar, was recorded several times and sung on national television. Songs like "Hello Heaven," "Yippee It's Rodeo Day," "You Can't Get Me Down, Down, Down," and "Turn That Page," a New Year's ditty, words and music by Pancho Barnes, were full of spirit and optimism.

The song she was most attached to, "Song of the Air Force," she wrote in 1950 with the hope that it would become the Air Force anthem. Although it included a standard jingoistic verse about fighting for liberty, most of the lyrics celebrated the accomplishments of the high-flying, faster-than-sound, circling-the-earth pilots whom Pancho knew and loved. It was a rousing, singable military march, simple and catchy, with a nod to Stephen Foster. The pilots sang it loudly and happily at the club. She was disappointed that the Air Force didn't adopt it but tremendously pleased that her songwriting credits were being recognized elsewhere. She was elected to the American Society of Composers, Authors and Publishers (ASCAP) as well as the American Guild of Authors and Composers, both elite groups.

But although Pancho was good at everything she tried, she rarely stayed with any activity—competitive flying or horseback riding, political campaigning or songwriting—long enough to perfect it. She was a starter, not a finisher. Within a year or two, despite the success of seeing a number of her songs recorded, she tired of composing and moved on.

Among her many and varied activities in the early 1950s was the planning of an enormous wedding, her own, her fourth. It would be the biggest, grandest party she ever hosted, with 650 guests, Hollywood celebrities flown in to entertain, whole roasted pigs, and dancing until, literally, dawn. She was marrying her ranch foreman, Mac McKendry, a man she had lived with for close to six years—and, as with all her marriages, no one could figure out why. The impending union was much discussed around the corral and at the base and in town at the grocery store and beauty shop. Those who didn't know Pancho, but just knew the "facts"—she was homely and wealthy and fifty-one; he was handsome and poor and thirty-two—assumed she was being taken for a ride. But no one took advantage of Pancho, except perhaps a man with a beautiful horse to sell. Those who knew Pancho well also knew this. Still, it was such an odd match, the pilots said to one another, shaking their heads as they drank Pancho's scotch.

But their relationship was far less of a mystery than their friends and acquaintances made it. Pancho was, as her ex-foreman and loyal friend Tony King used to say, "man-crazy—and proud of it." All her life, she had enjoyed having men around, both as friends and as lovers, especially the latter. All of her husbands had been handsome men, the last two younger than she was, although the age difference was less pronounced than it was between her and Mac. Others might whisper nastily about that. But to Pancho, it was a source of pride. The old gal could still rope 'em in and keep 'em interested—that was how she thought of it. Mac's attraction to Pancho was also easy to understand, if one looked beyond the purely physical. At Pancho's, he had found a comfortable home for both himself and his young son. But Pancho offered far more than that. She was, quite simply, the most exciting thing that had ever happened to him. The ranch, the club, the airport, the people he got to meet, the trips he got to take . . . it was all so much more than a quiet, unassuming farm boy could ever have dreamed of.

But why marriage? Even those who understood what brought these two together didn't understand *that*. Pancho had three failed marriages behind her. Just a few years before, she had ruined what seemed to be a great relationship with Don Shalita by marrying him. Years later, Mac would say that they got married to end complaints from the brass at Edwards that there were morality problems at the ranch, not just with the "hostesses" but with the owner herself. That's what her buddy Roger Chute thought, too. She had to marry Mac for appearances' sake, he wrote to a friend a year after the deed was done. But no one on the ranch, no one who really knew Pancho, bought this explanation. Pancho didn't care what other people thought about her various liaisons. If anything, she relished being talked about as a woman living in sin with a man barely older than her own son. It showed just how much sexual power she had. It made all those guys who called her ugly rethink their criteria. It added to the Pancho legend.

But she got married anyway. She needed help at the ranch, and marrying her foreman would ensure some consistency. But there was more to it, and more than the regular sex, which she also wanted to ensure. Mac had stood by her after her stroke. Pancho had never been vulnerable as she had been when she was ill. She had never before needed anyone to take care of her, to take charge. Mac had been there, and he stuck. He flew her back to the Midwest. He stayed by her bedside. Pancho had a lot of good-time cronies, folks who came around when things were flush, who liked to laugh at her jokes and drink her liquor. But she didn't have a lot of stormy-weather friends. A wedding was also a wonderful excuse for the kind of enormous, excessive party Pancho had always wanted to give herself.

The festivities began early Saturday evening, June 28, 1952. Edwards Air Force Base came to a standstill. Pancho had invited all the brass and all the pilots, with Al Boyd, then the commanding officer, selected to give the bride away and Chuck Yeager serving as the best man. The bride, whom most had never seen in anything other than dirty jeans, wore a floor-length dress of white chantilly lace with full-length sleeves, a high-roll collar, and buttons to the waist. In her hair was a silver jeweled tiara. In her hands rested a spray of orchids. Judge J. G. Sherrill of Mojave officiated over the fifty-eight-second ceremony under the glare of movie lights and the popping of flashbulbs, courtesy of the Los Angeles media. After the bride and groom had exchanged rings, and the assembled crowd had broken into cheers, hand-clapping, and whistling, Pancho and Mac took their vows a second time in an Indian ceremony presided over by Chief Lucky and Little Snow White, members of the Blackfoot tribe dressed in full beaded and feathered regalia. That accomplished, Pancho excused herself, informing the crowd that her feet were killing her, and reappeared a few minutes later, looking relaxed and happy, in jodhpurs, a gray silk blouse, and cowboy boots.

As for the wedding feast, if Busby Berkeley had been a caterer, he could not have orchestrated a more flamboyant, excessive banquet. The thirty-foot table to which the hundreds of guests flocked sagged under the weight of four whole roasted pigs, four roasted turkeys stuffed with rice, four baked and stuffed salmon, bonito, yellowtail, and cod, eighty pounds of potato salad, eighty pounds of macaroni salad, sixty dozen hard-boiled eggs, sixteen gallons of fruit Jell-O, seventy dozen dinner rolls, and a three-tiered, fifty-pound wedding cake. In the middle of the table was an ice sculpture that, even in a wedding full of conversation pieces, not the least of which was the bride, still made an impression. The sculptor, who had been imported from Hollywood, spent the day carving human figures inside separate blocks of ice. When each block was filled with red wine, the figures came alive. The wine didn't last long enough for the ice to melt.

But even two wedding ceremonies and a banquet were not enough. For an hour or so, Pancho's guests were entertained by the movie character actor and early television personality Vince Burnett, a dancing duck that waddled in time to a piano number, and Lassie. When the show was over, the dancing began with music provided by the Kings Four, who featured Pancho's own "Moon Crazy." The celebration lasted longer than most of the guests were able to remain standing. Some of the locals, hired to keep the food and drink coming, called the party a "drunken, rowdy mess." The Los Angeles *Herald Examiner* called it "one of the most flamboyant weddings in the state's history."

Whatever it was, it was Pancho's swan song.

17

The War of the Mojave

Suddenly, it seemed to Pancho that everything around her was changing. For her generation of fliers, especially the handful of women, taking to the skies had both literally and symbolically marked their freedom. But by the 1950s, aviation was a complex, highly regulated industry, with just as many rules in the sky as there were on the ground. That was even more true out in the Mojave, where the tremendous postwar expansion of Edwards Air Force Base led to tighter controls and more and more airspace restricted by the military. Pancho's place, only three miles from the base, was increasingly hemmed in. It was no longer possible to take off from her airport, point the nose of the ship north, south, east, or west, and, without a thought, just fly. Now Pancho was being dogged by the Air Force for traffic violations over the restricted airspace. Her connections with the top brass didn't matter anymore. The rules did. Even her friend Al Boyd, the man who gave her away at her wedding, the commanding officer of the base, could not bend them for Pancho. "It would be very much appreciated if you will bring to the attention of your pilots and guests the fact that the air space over Edwards is restricted and that violations cannot be tolerated," Boyd wrote Pancho, threatening to report infractions to the federal authorities.

Edwards itself was unrecognizable. Pancho still cherished the memory of the old tent encampment by the dry lake with its dozen or so outriders who welcomed her as much for her company as for the milk she delivered. She had played cards with them, lent them money, kept track of their movements. They were her boys, and through the years and the changes at Edwards, she had never lost that proprietary feeling, that sense that the Air Force was somehow hers. But if it ever had been, it wasn't now. Edwards was no longer a lonely outpost. It was a vast, bustling facility covering hundreds of thousands of acres, including more than a dozen football-field-sized hangars, technical facilities worth $150 million, modern barracks, hundreds of family homes, two churches, several clubs, and more than 17,000 Air Force personnel.

By the early 1950s, the brash camaraderie of the war years was giving way to the spit and polish of the modern military. The cocky, risk-taking test pilots who flew with broken ribs and hangovers were mostly gone. In their place were managers of technology, controlled, buttoned-down, college-educated men who understood and played by the rules. No one symbolized the new Air Force better than Brigadier General J. Stanley Holtoner. He was a test pilot who had learned to fly in the early thirties and served during World War II, but unlike many of that ilk, he did nothing by the seat of his pants. He was an ordered, organized, formal man, a New York University graduate in aeronautical engineering, a man more comfortable with rules than with people. When he took over command of the Air Force Flight Test Center at Edwards early in 1952, he was forty years old, a careerist on the way up, a boss who never let anyone forget that he was one. "Strictly military" is the way the men thought of him.

He certainly had more on his plate than any previous commander, overseeing thousands of people and scores of test projects. But he also oversaw—and in many ways instigated—the change in social atmosphere at the base, from freewheeling informality to a straitlaced conformity that mirrored the zeitgeist of the new decade. At the suggestion of his wife, Mary Jane, Holtoner established a new dress code on base. Women could no longer dash over to the commissary in shorts with their hair in curlers. They had to be dressed, even in the middle of the Mojave, even at the height of summer, in skirts and stockings.

Not surprisingly, neither Mary Jane nor her husband was much pleased with the existence of Pancho's, a place renowned for just the kind of unorthodoxy they were trying to squelch at the base. Past commanders like Al Boyd and Clarence Shoop had not just tolerated Pancho's, they had personally enjoyed her hospitality. But General Holtoner considered the place unseemly, a vulgar nuisance, like its owner. It was an attitude the general expressed early on and with great clarity. When Holtoner first arrived, Pancho showed up at his new office to welcome him to the base and invite him out to the ranch to eat and ride. It was, as far as Pancho was concerned, a courtesy call from the unofficial Mother of the Air Force to a newcomer. She had enjoyed easy access to generals for such a long time and was so accustomed to the privilege that she no longer thought of it as one. Holtoner reminded her. He kept her waiting in the outer office. When she was finally ushered in by his secretary—a formality she had rarely had to go through before—and allowed to say her piece, he was silent for a long moment. Then he gave her a cold stare. "Oh yes," he said, referring to the contract she still held to collect kitchen scraps from the base to feed her hogs, "you are the garbage collector." The relationship went downhill from there.

Edwards and its leadership were changing, aviation was changing, and something even closer to home was changing: home itself, the little settlement of Muroc, the desert outpost Pancho and a handful of ranchers and farmers had made their own. The postal service changed the mailing address to "Edwards" and, literally overnight, Muroc officially ceased to exist. The action had a practical purpose but was also symbolic, a heavy-handed message issued special delivery to the old homesteaders: Move over, Muroc. Edwards was in charge now.

In fact, the Air Force had been working quietly and diligently for al-

most a decade to make the settlement disappear. The growing air base
wanted miles and miles of clear airspace and miles and miles of no
neighbors. Under the constitutional provision of eminent domain, the
government has the right to take private land for public purposes. And
this was just what was happening around Edwards, as the federal government began to condemn various properties, offering their longtime
owners modest compensation for the land. As far back as 1942, the government had condemned 160 acres owned by the Adairs, dairy farmers
who had sold cows to Pancho many years before, paying the unhappy
family $5,000 for the property. Pancho and her neighbors watched the
government closely, keeping track of what land was condemned,
grumbling among themselves, wondering just how much property the
Air Force needed.

When Pancho learned that the Army Corps of Engineers was out
surveying her neighbors' property, the first step toward establishing
the price the government would pay when it took over the land, she immediately called on her nearest neighbors, the Grahams. There had
been years of tension between them, fights over grazing land, altercations over wandering calves and dogs and horses. But Pancho didn't
care about that now. Saving the land was what mattered. Pancho proposed an alliance that day, but Graham had had enough of his voluble
neighbor over the years. Whatever Pancho suggested, he wanted no
part of. He didn't want to lose his property, but neither did he want to
join forces with Pancho to fight the government. As it turned out, the
government offered the Grahams $90,000 for their entire homestead,
including the house, the barns and outbuildings, 160 acres in alfalfa,
and more than a thousand acres of rangeland. Dickering by himself,
Graham got the offer increased to $103,000. Any sense of victory he
might have felt soon dissipated when the Air Force started charging
him $300 a month because he hadn't been able to move all his cattle off
the land as quickly as the government would have liked.

One of Pancho's friends, Al Houser, put up a fight when the Army
Corps of Engineers came out to appraise his place. He had eighty acres,
a wonderful well, three ponds that covered almost twenty acres, a big

tin barn, and a new three-bedroom home. He had just started a duck-hunting club on the property. The government's offer was $18,000, and it was unbudgeable. Houser tried everything he dared to keep the property. He ignored the government's letters. He railed at the appraiser. He wrote angry letters to everyone he could think of. Pancho egged him on, visiting him often to get an update on his battle. Houser held on for several months until a U.S. marshal knocked on his front door one morning and told him if he didn't vacate in thirty days, he'd find all his possessions out on the Sierra Highway. The next day, he conceded.

One by one, the homesteaders surrendered as the government stepped up its land acquisition in the early fifties. Most of the families had been working the land or running cattle on it before Edwards existed, before even the tent encampment at Muroc Dry Lake existed. Over the years they had watched the base grow, sometimes profiting from its expansion, sometimes bothered by it, but, especially during the war years, tremendously proud to have it as a neighbor. Now their neighbor was their enemy. Most homesteaders settled outright, taking what the government offered and keeping their anger to themselves. A few did a little negotiating. Four or five tried to put up a fight. But the old Muroc ranchers didn't feel they had much choice.

Pancho, of course, didn't see it that way.

Pancho did not want to sell what had taken her twenty years, tens of thousands of dollars, and three husbands to create. Unlike her neighbors, whose property might have a few outbuildings, Pancho had an enormous investment in the land. Her 360 acres was Rancho Oro Verde, the Happy Bottom Riding Club, and Pancho's Fly-Inn, a farm and a horse ranch, a resort and an airport, all in one. It was her desert oasis, her personal playground, her own backbreaking, bank-account-busting creation. But her emotional attachment to the land did not blind her to the reality she saw around her. She understood better than her neighbors the power of the Air Force, and she saw her future clearly. She knew she would eventually have to sell. She knew that even her well-connected Washington, D.C., friends couldn't help her. But she'd be damned if she'd let the Air Force buy her out for the pittance they were offering the others.

In the spring of 1952, the appraiser for the Corps of Engineers showed up on her property, as he had on the properties of so many of her neighbors, to survey, measure, and count trees. It seemed to Pancho that he came and went in an hour, giving the place a haphazard and cursory inspection. She waited impatiently for the results of the appraisal, for the dollar offer. Months went by. Pancho called General Holtoner's office but was handed off to a Colonel Shuler, who informed her that the appraisal process might take another few months. She wrote to him in July 1952 and then again in August, pressing for a decision. Her price, she told Shuler, was $3.5 million. She had turned down a $1.5 million offer several years ago, she told him. This may or may not have been true, but certainly Pancho believed that her property was far more valuable than her neighbors'. This was not just because Rancho Oro Verde had many and varied improvements and supported several businesses. It was because her property, sandwiched between the two dry lakes, one of which Edwards used as an airstrip, couldn't have been more strategically located. If Edwards was to continue expanding, it needed Pancho's land. "I want action," she wrote to Colonel Shuler, impatient to see what the government would offer, impatient to make plans that would most likely include moving and starting over again elsewhere. Then she added, in true Pancho style: "In case you do not fully comprehend what I am trying to say, I will now lapse into a fine old Anglo-Saxon phrase which everyone understands—'Either shit or get off the pot.' "

As she waited for the government's next move, watching the land-grab around her, she began to feel squeezed by the Air Force in other ways. It had started a few years back when then–base commander Colonel Signa Gilkey had placed her ranch off-limits to all military personnel for several days. Pancho always thought he'd done it out of spite because she went over his head to complain to her Washington, D.C., friends about some of his men. Whatever the cause, putting the place off-limits was tantamount to calling it a whorehouse. At least, that was what Pancho would later claim, insisting that "great hordes of disreputable characters descended upon the ranch" after the ban was lifted. Now the same thing was happening again under her nemesis, General Holtoner. Early in 1952 a young lieutenant named Ratcliffe wrote a letter to Holtoner telling him that he had paid a girl for sexual favors at the Happy Bottom Riding Club. The general, more than willing to believe the story, turned over the letter to the FBI, which mounted a three-month investigation including on-site interviews with all Pancho's hostesses. FBI operatives quizzed the girls, at one point presenting them with photos of Los Angeles and Hollywood call girls whom they were asked to identify. The investigation came up with nothing. Pancho was furious. "If I was really running a whorehouse," she told the FBI man in charge, "you could have found out about it in a couple of days instead of the fourteen weeks it took you to find out not a goddamn thing."

While the FBI was doing its work, Holtoner and his staff considered putting Pancho's off-limits again. They decided to await the outcome of the investigation, but for some reason, the Air Force base combo, Kings Four, didn't show up at Pancho's to play for several nights, and she suspected Holtoner was behind the absence. The relationship between the two, which had started out bad, became worse. Al Boyd, who was now at Wright-Patterson Air Force Base in Ohio, tried to persuade Pancho to make nice with Holtoner, but she would have none of it. "I personally requested several months ago that you bury the hatchet," Boyd wrote to Pancho, scolding her. "I was very disappointed to learn . . . that your relationship had again deteriorated to a very unsatisfactory level." Boyd and the rest of the Air Force would soon learn just how unsatisfactory that relationship was.

Pancho's anger ran deep. She felt slighted by Holtoner, mistreated by the Army Corps of Engineers, and picked on by the FBI. But most of all, most painfully, she felt betrayed by the institution she loved, the Air Force. Al Boyd had given her away at her wedding. Jimmy Doolittle had been her longtime buddy. The Air Force owed its life to her grandfather, and the test pilots at Edwards owed their sanity to her.

That was Pancho's line of thinking. Now she was being treated like a pest, some ordinary landowner whose property happened to stand in the way of expansion. Worse yet, the enterprise she had built from nothing, her desert monument to fun and freedom and good times, was under attack. She might wink and joke about the goings-on at the Happy Bottom Riding Club, but she would not tolerate an attack from anyone else, especially not from the Air Force, which for so long had taken full advantage of her hospitality. "They just picked the wrong girl to push around," she said in public. Privately, she was more direct: "I never ran away from a fight in my life, and I'm sure as shit not running from these peckerwoods."

<hr />

On March 10, 1952, while awaiting the buyout offer, Pancho filed a $1,483,000 lawsuit against the U.S. government, alleging that the Air Force had purposely harmed her business. Acting as her own attorney, Pancho submitted a rambling, seven-part, twelve-page complaint, an odd mixture of sophisticated legalese and personal pique, accusing the Air Force of various "negligent and willful acts," from illegally selling liquor on base to allowing civilian aircraft to land at Edwards. To each cause of action, she attached a dollar amount, an estimate of the business income she claimed to have lost—$50,000 in lost liquor sales, $10,000 in lost airport fees. Claiming to have lost $25,000 in business when her mailing address changed from Muroc to Edwards in 1951, she called the change of post office designation a "heinous act" and accused the Air Force of behaving in "an overbearing and illegal manner" with the goal of "crippl[ing] all private enterprise in the vicinity." Several emotional paragraphs later, she heatedly argued against the name change not of the post office but of the military base, *her* military base. "It may well be that more men burned in their planes at Muroc for their country than froze during the historic winter at Valley Forge," she wrote in the complaint, painstakingly typing each word on legal stationery. "Yet who would think of changing the name of Valley Forge."

Another cause of action accused the Air Force of willfully "throwing" shock waves in the direction of the ranch by repeatedly shooting off rockets, bombs, and other experimental explosives and buzzing her ranch with aircraft "capable of immense noise," all of which, she claimed, caused $205,000 worth of damage to her buildings and irrigation pipes. But the biggest cause of action was a $1 million complaint alleging that her business had been irreparably harmed by "inferences, implications and impressions" that she was selling more than liquor at the Happy Bottom Riding Club. Harking back to Colonel Gilkey's order putting her ranch off-limits for six days in 1947, she accused him of "caus[ing] or fail[ing] to correct the impression that the reason for the ranch being put out of bounds was that it was a whorehouse." She then proceeded to stake out the high moral ground in a way laughable to anyone who knew her. It must have greatly amused her even as she wrote it. She came from a "proud family" and was "carefully and gently reared and well educated," she wrote primly. She had been "greatly chagrined and humiliated" by Gilkey's action. Furthermore, the "impressions were so strongly put out at the time (and without one iota of cause) that . . . not a day elapsed that men have not come in their search to buy flesh."

In the pressroom of the federal court building in Fresno, Pat O'Hara, a veteran Los Angeles *Daily News* reporter, whistled when he read the complaint. "You don't actually expect to collect that much, do you, Pancho?" he asked her.

"Hell no," she said. "But I'm gonna worry them to death."

＊＋ ᙅ◊ᙁ ＋＊

But the Air Force didn't seem overly worried. Backed by a U.S. attorney and two assistant U.S. attorneys, the government presented a motion to dismiss the case, asserting that Pancho's claims for relief were invalid and that, in any case, the court lacked jurisdiction over the matter. Pancho countered by modifying and scaling down her demands, stripping the suit of its emotional content and most of its monetary claims. The amended complaint asked only $1,500 in damages for the post office name change and $8,500 for damage sustained by her irrigation pipes and swimming pool because of the Air Force's "negligent acts." Pancho's point was always more than money, anyway. It was to stand up to the Air Force, to fight what she thought was the good fight, meanwhile embarrassing them in the press and making them spend time and money to defend themselves. The point was to force them to pay attention to her, to respect her, not treat her as a local nuisance. As the case continued, Pancho was well pleased with herself, a private citizen on her own, keeping the federal government in court and off-kilter.

The government was not amused. The case dragged on, with the defense attorneys answering the latest complaint by denying that the Air Force had caused any structural damage to Pancho's property. The pool cracked not because of shock waves but because it was "built by amateurs" and exposed to weather, they said. And even if its activities did cause the damage, the Air Force was simply performing its mandated duties. Pancho would have to show "positive negligence," which she didn't, the lawyers argued.

Finally, just as the case was about to be heard in court, Pancho lashed out in an entirely new direction, filing an affidavit of bias and prejudice against the judge. In a three-page document that was later stricken from the record as scandalous, she called for Judge Leon Yankwich's disqualification from the case, claiming that he refused to see her in chambers, didn't allow her to finish her arguments, and had threatened her with contempt. Legal arguments aside, Pancho felt she had not been treated with proper respect in the courtroom. She was acting as her own lawyer—and damn proud of it—and wanted to be treated like one of the big boys. The judge didn't see it that way.

"I do not talk to litigants, and you are a litigant," he told Pancho sternly. She had just presented him with the document that accused him of "personal bias and prejudice," and he was not a happy man.

"I disagree with you, Your Honor," Pancho answered. "I certainly should receive the same consideration as a lawyer."

"We do not talk to litigants," Judge Yankwich repeated. "We talk to lawyers because lawyers know the ethics of the profession, and litigants do not."

The implication fueled Pancho's anger. She kept at it, pressing the judge to look at court opinions she had gathered to buttress her point, waving documents, playing the legal game in top form, she thought.

"All right," said the judge, "you may be seated." Pancho remained standing. "I am not going to engage in dialogue with you," Yankwich told her. "You will have to sit down."

The judge was in a huff, and Pancho was in her element—feisty, contentious, rule-busting, a lone woman against the odds. She was not winning the War of the Mojave. But she was not losing it, either.

18

Pushing the Envelope

Pancho had done almost everything in her life to excess. But nowhere was this tendency more pronounced than in her battles with the U.S. government in the early 1950s.

The $1,483,000 suit she filed in March 1952 was just the first skirmish in the War of the Mojave. Nine months later, while that case was wending its way through the courts, she filed another suit, this one for $1,253,000. In it, she accused the Air Force and the Army Corps of Engineers of, among other things, conspiracy, harassment, fraud, deceit, mismanagement, and stupidity. She also accused her once-beloved Air Force of what she considered the most heinous and personally painful crime: forgetting that it owed its success to private pilots, to people like Pancho Barnes.

Her new complaint, twenty-two pages of bombast, was, by turns, a finger-wagging lecture, a detailed engineering critique, a constitutional jeremiad, and a petulant harangue. She excoriated Edwards, calling the entire Flight Test Center "a waste and bad engineering" and "a disconcerted hodgepodge series of unrelated, expensive white elephants." But she reserved her sharpest criticism for the center's newest plan, a massive project that involved building a twenty-seven-mile-long airstrip from Rosamond Dry Lake to Muroc Dry Lake, cutting right through the middle of Pancho's land. In a thousand-word lecture that showed her extensive knowledge of aviation, from German rocket planes to Japanese Zeroes, from the supersonic Bell X-1 to British experiments in high-speed flight, she painstakingly explained why the proposed runway was a boondoggle.

She even argued against the continued existence of the entire base. For a woman who owed much of her business to her next-door military neighbors, a woman whose closest friends during the past ten years had been Air Force pilots and engineers, this was an almost unbelievable turnaround. As fiercely as she had loved the Air Force, she now disowned it, a scorned parent taking vengeance on an ungrateful child. She noted, pointedly, that a Navy test base, Inyokern, lay just forty miles north of Edwards, and that it was already four or five times larger than Edwards, with a great deal of undeveloped land.

Finally, twelve pages into the complaint, after lectures on aviation technology, the importance of civilian airports, the threat of nuclear attack, traffic patterns in the Los Angeles Basin, military security, and the future of aircraft manufacturing, she got to the point. The Corps of Engineers, she said, "falsely and fraudulently and with intent to deceive and defraud" made an unjust appraisal of her property. The appraisal was "slipshod," "inadequate," "haphazard," and "biased," and it in no way reflected the real market value of her much-improved land, she claimed. More than that, she objected to the length of time it had taken the Corps of Engineers to make an initial offer. She claimed that almost six months of uncertainty so affected the ranch that "most of the functional activity has come to a standstill." This, she claimed, was intentional. By purposely delaying, which hurt her business, the Corps was, in effect, reducing the value of her land so it could be bought at bargain prices. When an offer for $205,000 finally came in the late summer of 1952 and was rejected, the Corps, she said, had dared to suggest that she was being unpatriotic in refusing to sell. Sounding as if she were once again running for public office, she wrote: "The present setup is un-American and criminally unfair. The unfriendly great United

States government is using every force at its command to bewilder and mentally unhinge the small land owner without conscience." The oratory was inflated, but the sentiments were deeply and genuinely felt. Pancho was much aggrieved. She had been, she felt, ignored, abused, and humiliated. It was payback time.

But getting back at the Air Force was not going to be easy. Pancho could fight the government, but the "unfriendly great United States government" could marshal much greater forces to fight Pancho. Two months after she filed the second suit, the Los Angeles–based U.S. attorney whose office would be in charge of defending the Air Force wrote to his boss in Washington, D.C., with an idea. The FBI, he suggested, should be called in to conduct an independent investigation of Pancho's activities. That information could be funneled through channels to the lawyers preparing the defense.

FBI field agents from the Los Angeles office were on the job almost immediately, searching through crime records; credit reports; county, district, and Superior Court documents; state agency records; and newspaper and magazine clippings for anything they could find about Pancho. They interviewed a number of people, including her former secretary and her daughter-in-law, asking about possible illegal or immoral activities at the ranch. The investigation continued unabated, months stretching into years, with agents fanning out to Pasadena, Fresno, Bakersfield, and the Antelope Valley, compiling reports to send to the government lawyers. When it was over, Pancho's FBI file was almost two hundred pages long—but, to the lawyers' dismay, it contained very little that was incriminating. Pancho had bad credit, had been in and out of civil court, and was the subject of numerous salacious but unprovable rumors. That was it. Unproductive though it was, the investigation was intimidating. To Pancho, it was yet another instance of government authority used, with the heaviest of hands, against the little guy.

The U.S. attorneys on the case had criticized Pancho's original complaint because it was too long, too discursive, and more a narrative than a set of allegations. Now she filed a new document, scaled down to barely two pages and focused on a single allegation: The Air Force had, since the end of World War II, purposefully stunted the growth of her private, civilian airport, using "every means to hamper the plaintiff's business." This new complaint the government lawyers criticized for lacking detail. They were right both times. Pancho was smart. She knew aviation. She knew Edwards, and she understood more about the legal system than most nonlawyers. But she was outsmarting herself by acting as her own attorney. The trouble was not just that she lacked some of the specific lawyerly skills one needed to mount such a large case. It was that she didn't have the temperament. Fueled by anger and ego, she was deeply and emotionally involved, more interested in venting than winning.

Vent, she did. And lose, she did. When the case finally went to court, the judge did not take long to agree with the government that Pancho's claims were vague and unsubstantiated. Pancho, being Pancho, immediately appealed the decision.

In the middle of litigating the two cases, Pancho did the unthinkable: She filed a third major lawsuit, a $300,000 defamation claim against her nemesis, Air Force general and Flight Test Center commander J. Stanley Holtoner. Pancho had tried to get Holtoner replaced ever since their first unfortunate meeting in his office when he referred to her as a garbage collector. In March 1952, when the general had barely unpacked his bags, Pancho fired off a letter to a top Air Force administrator, calling Holtoner a "demoralizing influence" on the base. In characteristically forceful language, consequences be damned, she wrote: "To leave General Holtoner in his present position would be a heinous crime."

But nothing came of the letter except more ill will between her and the general. Now, in early 1953, she sued Holtoner and Lieutenant Colonel Marcus B. Sacks, filing another rambling complaint that was long on bile and short on facts. The essence of the suit was that Holtoner and Sacks had put the Happy Bottom Riding Club off-limits and "by innuendo indicated that the club was a place of prostitution," thus defaming Pancho personally and, she claimed, hurting her business. This was the same accusation she had made against a previous commander, Colonel Gilkey, in her first suit against the Air Force. This time, she claimed that the denigration of the club was part of a conspiracy cooked up by Holtoner, Sacks, and other military and civilian personnel after she refused to sell her land. They meant to "molest, obstruct, hinder and prevent" her from making a living. Further, she claimed that Holtoner had on several occasions publicly threatened to bomb the ranch with napalm.

As she had done in the other two suits, Pancho fired at will, accusing Holtoner of numerous other acts: preventing her from securing a renewal of her garbage-hauling contract; purposefully ruining a banquet held at the ranch for the Aviation Writers of America; and strong-arming the Automobile Association of America to exclude her place of business from its club maps. The top brass at Edwards wanted her off her land and out of their hair—and they were willing to do anything to make that happen. That's what Pancho believed.

Some of the accusations might have seemed far-fetched, but Pancho wasn't suffering from paranoid delusions. She was under siege. She was looking to connect all the little troubles and mishaps and slights that had come her way since the Air Force had begun going after her land. She was looking to hold someone accountable. She was looking for J. Stanley Holtoner to get his comeuppance. This was even more evident when she filed her amended claim, which reduced the damages to ten dollars *and a public apology.* She wanted respect, not money.

Once again acting as her own attorney, Pancho sought to subpoena General Holtoner so she could take his deposition. The idea of slapping the commanding general with a summons was irresistible. Actually doing so was, it turned out, quite difficult. First she sought the services of the constable in the little town of Mojave, adjacent to the base. But the man got only as far as the entrance gate to Edwards. There he was asked by the guards what his business was. There he stood fidgeting while they phoned the general's headquarters. And there he stayed, after being refused entry. "General Holtoner isn't here," he was told several times.

Pancho was temporarily outmaneuvered, until inspiration struck: She asked her loyal friend and occasional staffer Cliff Morris to serve the papers. Morris worked on base as a civilian employee and had a decal on his car that would get him through the gates without being questioned or stopped. The next morning, he took the subpoena, stuffed it in the pocket of his jacket, and drove from the ranch to Edwards where, instead of reporting for work, he asked his foreman for a few hours of leave. Then he drove to the main base and down to the flight line. Pancho had told him General Holtoner was flying himself to Washington, D.C., that morning. Morris knew Holtoner by sight. When the general came out to his airplane, Morris approached him.

"Are you General Holtoner?" he asked, because that's what summons servers are supposed to do.

"Yes," said the general.

"Well, I have a subpoena for you," Morris said. He handed over the document and then turned to walk back to his car.

Holtoner was carrying a parachute on his back. He let it fall to the ground, took one look at the summons, and threw it to the ground too. Then he followed Morris back to his car.

"Where do you work?" he asked, obviously enraged. His foot was planted on the car's front bumper. When Morris told him that he worked for the National Advisory Committee for Aeronautics (the predecessor of NASA), Holtoner immediately drove over to NACA headquarters, a few miles from the main base, where he had words with Morris's boss. Morris was sure that the general was trying to get him fired. But he had delivered the subpoena while on sanctioned leave from his job. He had done nothing illegal, had broken no rules. He could not be fired. The general could make his life less than pleasant, however. Holtoner took away his badge and had the base police scrape the decal off his car. For a month after he served the summons, Morris had to pick up his badge every morning at the entrance gate and return it every evening. He had to carpool to work.

At the preliminary hearing, federal judge James M. Carter listened as Pancho lit into Holtoner. She accused him of ruining her business and spreading lies about the club. She accused him of threatening to drop a bomb on the place. "I'd like Congress to answer for him," she told the judge. "They made him an officer but they didn't make him a gentleman."

Holtoner was clearly offended and very angry. "There is absolutely no foundation to her charges," he told Judge Carter. But the judge denied the government's motion for dismissal. Not only that, he publicly reprimanded Holtoner and his lawyers. He had listened carefully to Pancho's testimony about the general trying to evade being served with a subpoena, and he had read Cliff Morris's affidavit alleging that Holtoner had taken away his badge and decal. "Any legal papers issued by the court that are refused service I will consider an abuse of the processes of this court," the judge said, scolding Holtoner. "I expect to hear that all discrimination against Morris is ended." The government attorneys were quick to assure Judge Carter that his wishes would be heeded.

When the case finally came to trial, the newspapers were there in force. The Los Angeles *Herald Express* dubbed it "The Battle of the Mojave Desert." The *Los Angeles Times* focused on the alleged bomb threat. The Riverside *Daily Press* offered this sympathetic headline: WOMAN SEEKS MORAL VICTORY OVER OFFICERS. The trial itself was, if not exactly a circus, then certainly one of the livelier legal happenings of the year. Once again acting as her own attorney, Pancho came to court dressed in cowboy boots, riding britches, and colorful Western shirts purchased from Barry Goldwater's exclusive cattle-country dude store in Phoenix, a sartorial strategy meant to counter any impression that she might possibly be the operator of a bordello. Pancho took the trial seriously, in the sense that she had invested a great deal of time and money putting together her case, but she also didn't do anything that wasn't fun. This trial, however it turned out, would be fun.

Pancho paraded through twenty-three witnesses, from Don Dwiggins, a noted aviation writer who knew everything and everybody and testified to Pancho's righteousness, to Walt Williams, a NACA chief engineer and Happy Bottom Riding Club regular who testified that, while there might have been some "hanky-panky" going on at the club, it was just "normal boy-girl stuff that went on between any good-looking waitress and an admiring customer." Cliff Morris testified. Employees and customers, military and otherwise, testified, all vouching for the purity and sanctity of the club. But none had the impact of the witness identified only as "January Smith," one of Pancho's most beautiful and alluring hostesses. "Goddamn gorgeous" is how Pancho described her. She took the witness stand dressed like a cloistered Southern belle, albeit one with long, shapely legs that caught the attention of half the courtroom. She had been extensively briefed by Pancho and was dressed to play her part.

"Do you understand that we have been accused of operating a whorehouse?" Pancho asked her witness. January answered by uttering a little cry of dismay.

"Did guys make passes at you or pay you money to make love to them?" Pancho asked. January was shocked. Passes had been made, yes. But to make love for money? The thought alone made her ill. January was so sweet and pure up on the witness stand that everyone wanted to adopt her. At least, that's what Pancho told a friend.

January Smith was the hit of the proceedings, but Pancho also had other successes. When she cross-examined one of the government's witnesses, a warrant officer named Antone Padavich who was purported to have had his morals undermined at the club, he ended up recanting. Under Pancho's aggressive questioning, he denied that her hostesses were "street walker types." Other government witnesses, under cross-examination, could not offer concrete evidence as to the questionable morals of the club. Pancho was making some headway. She had, as she so indelicately put it, "nailed some of the lying assholes who claimed they bought sex at the ranch." Now she was going full throttle, sure she would win this battle, sure that at least *this* case would be decided in her favor.

But then the government introduced photographs of naked host-esses, presumably taken at the ranch—damaging evidence, particularly when coupled with the stories of nude swimming and the Lady Godiva stunt. Pancho was delighted, and surprised, when the judge ruled them inadmissible, saying that he couldn't tell whether the girls were actually naked or wearing flesh-colored tights and that, regardless of their at-tire, there was nothing to indicate that the pictures were taken at the ranch. Pancho figured she'd sewn up her case, or as she put it: "I knew I had them by the short hairs."

She was wrong. When Judge Carter handed down his decision, he ruled against every one of Pancho's allegations. There had been no conspiracy to injure her business. General Holtoner had not interfered with the renewal of her garbage-hauling contract. He had not put the club off-limits. He had not threatened or intimidated any military or civilian personnel who patronized Pancho's. He had not ruined her Aviation Writers of America banquet. And, although the judge ruled that Holtoner had, in fact, "made a statement to the effect that the plaintiff's ranch should be bombed," that statement was made "either in anger or in jest and without deliberation or intent to carry out the ac-tion implied therein." The judge also clearly took pity on the general. After sitting in a courtroom watching the Pancho Barnes Show for a few days, Judge Carter concluded, with polite understatement, that the general had "probably never encountered a public relations problem such as that of dealing with the plaintiff."

But Pancho did get something out of the judgment. The Happy Bottom Riding Club—deservedly or not—was officially cleared of all improprieties, and Pancho herself was extravagantly praised as a "courageous, forthright individual, a Native Daughter of California, a person with apparent great interest in the conduct and well being of the Air Force." Furthermore, and much to Pancho's delight, General Holtoner's hand was officially and judicially slapped for avoiding the subpoena servers. Pancho declared a moral victory. The fact was, she had lost the case. But she didn't think of it that way. The actual ruling mattered less than the fact that she had forced the government to take her seriously. It mattered less than the fact that she had embarrassed General J. Stanley Holtoner.

She took what comfort she could from this "victory." She needed comforting, for in the midst of all the litigation, the $1.2 million suit, the $1.4 million suit, and the Holtoner case, in the midst of running off to Bakersfield and Fresno and Los Angeles to make court appearances and file complaints and affidavits and depositions and briefs, in the midst of planning and strategizing and personally typing page after legal page, Pancho was, nonetheless, losing her land.

<hr />

Back in August 1952, when her first court case was pending and before she filed either of the other two suits, the government had offered Pancho $205,000 for her property. She turned it down immediately and vehemently, calling it an "inadequate and disgraceful sum." Two hundred thousand dollars was a lot of money, far more than the other Muroc homesteaders had gotten, but Pancho's property was undoubtedly worth more than theirs. Pancho called it "practically a small village," and she was right. With its motel, its seven bungalows and women's dormitory, its restaurant and two bars, its in-ground swimming pool, extensive rodeo grounds, and self-contained airport, the ranch was developed as no other Antelope Valley property was. Pancho took care to detail all its features in a six-page affidavit, calling special attention to its five wells and twenty-thousand-gallon water tank, its 366 planted shade trees and forty thousand square feet of buildings.

But even as she held out, staying on the land while her neighbors took the money and ran, filing suit after suit to keep the government busy on matters other than the appropriation of Rancho Pancho, she knew she would have to sell. She knew she would have to leave. She just didn't want to do it quietly. And she didn't want to do it on anyone's terms other than her own. But in February 1953, with all three cases pending, the government turned the tables and took the offensive. Pancho, who had been in control of the action, who had been the filer of suits, now became the defendant in a government-initiated suit ominously and impersonally entitled *The United States of America v. 360 Acres of Land.* Pancho's property, claimed the government, was "in the very center" of Edwards Air Force Base, where classified work was being carried out. This presented both security and safety problems, with a "grave danger of an accident, of a crash landing of planes" on Pancho's property. Then, of course, there was the proposed twenty-seven-mile, dry lake–to–dry lake runway slated to cut through the middle of the ranch.

Just three days after the suit was filed in Fresno, the U.S. District Court gave the government title to Pancho's land for the offered price of $205,000. Unintimidated and undeterred, Pancho immediately moved to stop the transaction, claiming, as she had in an earlier suit, that the expansion of the Edwards runway through her property was unnecessary and ill-planned. The government countered by filing for immediate possession. Early that fall, Judge Campbell E. Beaumont gave Pancho a reprieve, denying the government's application for immediate takeover and opening the door to protracted legal wrangling.

Elated, Pancho moved into action, notifying the court that she intended to subpoena General Holtoner and other top Air Force brass and demanding that they bring with them maps, documents, and the master plan for the air base. The government reacted swiftly, claiming that she was just trying to "embarrass, harass and annoy the commanding general . . . who has incurred her displeasure." While the judge was contemplating this, Pancho submitted another notice of intent to subpoena, this time targeting the Army Corps of Engineers appraisers. Again, the government countered, calling the new subpoenas "unreasonable" and "oppressive" and claiming that the appraisers' documents were confidential and privileged.

Thus began a paper battle so furious and so unrelenting that it consumed three U.S. attorneys, four judges, dozens of Air Force and civilian employees, and the indefatigable Pancho Barnes. An unbelievable amount of time and effort went into preparing the case on both sides. Pancho, occasionally soliciting the help of a Los Angeles law firm but mostly working alone, filed motions and countermotions, designations and counterdesignations, amendments, declarations, and subpoenas, statements, briefs, and appeals, working the system as hard as she knew how. By the fall of 1953, business at the ranch was at a standstill. Between the government's case against her and her three suits against the government, Pancho now had a new, full-time occupation: litigant.

19

Goodbye to All That

People later said they could see the plume of smoke twenty miles away. Pancho and Mac saw it on their way home from a quick shopping trip to Rosamond and figured another Edwards pilot had augered in. But it wasn't a downed aircraft burning in the desert that November afternoon in 1953. It was Pancho's house.

There were only a handful of employees working at the ranch that day, and they were scattered across the property, away from the main buildings. But they all heard the explosion. A few saw it raise the roof of the wood-frame dance hall two feet in the air. Some said the fire started there, in the rear of the dance hall. Others believed it started in the barn or in the summer kitchen attached to the ranch house. Later, the county fire marshal, sifting through the rubble and charred buildings, would say that the fire seemed to have been even throughout, "as though it was probably set."

By the time firefighters from the base and the neighboring towns of Mojave, Tehachapi, and Rosamond arrived, the dance hall was engulfed in flames, the roof of the house and summer kitchen were burning, and the barn was choked with smoke. They quickly exhausted their own water supplies and would have started pumping water from Pancho's pool to help fight the blaze, but the pool had been drained a few days before in preparation for a pre–holiday season cleaning. They might also have used some of the twenty thousand gallons of water in the cistern behind the clubhouse, but no one from the fire crews knew it was there. While the water from their trucks held out, they fought hard to keep the blaze under control, but it spread throughout Pancho's ten-room house and jumped to several of the nearby buildings. By the time Pancho arrived, it was almost over, the dance hall in ruins, the barn smoldering, her house gutted. She had lost everything in the house: furniture, artwork, clothes, jewelry, furs, and a gun collection. The firefighters had managed to save her more than two dozen Dalmatians, hurrying them out of their kennel before the smoke asphyxiated them. But the firemen and ranch hands hadn't been able to save the horses that were in the barn. All of the prize stallions in the box stalls died in the fire. Pancho also lost all the tack, including ornate saddles and trunks full of show harnesses. She estimated the loss at $300,000, $100,000 more than the government was set to pay her for the entire property. But a loss like this could not be measured in dollars. She thought of it in terms of years, as in the almost twenty it had taken her to build up the place. She thought of it in terms of people: the men who had lived there with her, the famous pilots who had bellied up to the bar, the Hollywood stars who had lounged by the pool, the hundreds and hundreds of guests who had kept the place hopping and kept Pancho at the center of things. In the end, she measured the disaster not in grief but in anger.

No one knew how the fire started, but everyone had a theory. One of her former employees, a young horse wrangler, was convinced a drifter was responsible. Pancho had recently hired the man, who showed up one day at the ranch drunk and out of work and proclaiming his expertise with horses. When she needed someone, Pancho wasn't picky. This drifter got cold that morning, so the theory went, and started a fire in the woodstove in the tack room. Then, as he started drinking and nodding off, the fire burned out of control. The fire marshal, on the other hand, was convinced the blaze had been set, probably in more than one place, and had been helped along by an accelerant. Pancho listened, and thought, and reached a conclusion of her own.

In years past, there had been a number of suspicious fires on or near Edwards. A sergeant at the base had been questioned by the police in connection with three fires in Lancaster in the late 1940s. Pancho was worried enough about the possible presence of an arsonist so near her place that, back then, she had asked for protection from both the local sheriff's department and the Air Force. When she got help from neither, she hired two off-duty sheriffs from Lancaster to guard her airplane hangars. Late one night not long after, the guards observed someone walking around one of the buildings. They stopped him, patted him down, found a concealed weapon, and hauled him off to the sheriff in Lancaster. He spent six months in county jail in Bakersfield. The man skulking around Pancho's airfield with a gun in his pocket was the sergeant who had earlier been questioned for the Lancaster fires. After his release, he had every reason to make trouble at the ranch. At least, that was what Pancho thought. She also thought that the brass at Edwards was well aware of this firebug and ignored the threat he posed. She went further, suspecting that the arson was part of an Air Force conspiracy to get her off her land.

The rumor mill went even further than that: The Air Force had napalmed Pancho's. After all, that was what Pancho had accused General Holtoner of threatening to do. Maybe, whispered the locals, he had followed through. But they also whispered something else: Maybe Pancho *herself* had set the fire. She had the $205,000 offer from the government. Now she'd collect on insurance, too. Maybe the fire was part of a scheme to make more money from the property. Or maybe Pancho, in her anger, was carrying out a scorched-earth policy. If she could not have the ranch, then no one could. She would burn it to the ground before she handed it over to the government. Whatever actually started the fire, the timing, everyone thought, was just too coincidental. It *had* to be arson. The evidence at the scene bore this out. But who did it, or why, was never discovered, even after a full investigation.

With the property severely damaged and the ranch house unlivable, Pancho temporarily moved into Lancaster. She was deeply disheartened and deeply angered by the fire and by what it clearly and irrevocably meant: the end of the Happy Bottom Riding Club, of Rancho Pancho, of the Fly-Inn, of everything she had built during the past two decades. Of course, she had known that she would eventually lose the place, but before the fire, she had figured that she could keep the government in court and her whole operation going for several years. Living on the land, riding horses out into the desert, continuing to entertain, she could pretend things were still all right. She could, while knowing the end was near, live as if it weren't. The fire destroyed that illusion.

But if the Air Force or the government lawyers thought she'd give up, they couldn't have been more wrong. All the energy that would have gone into operating the ranch was now redirected into her legal maneuverings.

━•━━━━◆━━━━•━

A few months before the fire, the government had filed a "declaration of taking," which Pancho had unsuccessfully tried to stymie. This gave the government legal title to her land, for which was deposited, in the spring of 1953, $185,000 of the $205,000 offering price. The deposit was, the court ruled, "without prejudice to the rights of any party to such additional compensation as may be found to be due." In other words, Pancho could continue her suit for more money. She did so, with alacrity. Just a few weeks before the fire, in preparation for the condemnation suit the government had filed against her, *United States of America v. 360 Acres of Land*, Pancho subpoenaed twenty witnesses, from the constable of Mojave to an executive at Lockheed, from a local real estate agent to the director of the Long Beach Airport. Don Shalita, who could testify to the postwar successes of Rancho Pancho, was also on the list.

But even as she prepared for this final fight, Pancho could not let go of her place. Less than two months after the fire, she was back on the

land again, overseeing the rebuilding of the dance hall and reconstruc-
tion of the massive outdoor fireplace. In early February 1954, the government got a restraining order to prevent Pancho from making any
improvements on the land. She not only ignored it, she mounted a
countersuit, again claiming that the condemnation of her land was un-
necessary. The complaint was a laundry list of allegations, written out
of anger and frustration and perhaps devilment. The court quickly decided it was not an actionable case and dismissed it. Pancho, persistent
as ever, took it to the Ninth Circuit Court of Appeals, where she lost
again.

Meanwhile, the government's case against her was heating up. Pancho, either not understanding or choosing not to understand that
United States v. 360 Acres of Land was solely about compensation for
the land and not about the legality of the condemnation, kept pushing
the latter point. In March 1954, the court short-circuited her, ruling
that by taking the government's money, Pancho "waived her objection" to the taking of her land. She appealed the ruling and lost. At
the same time, the court ordered Pancho to give up possession of her
property no later than May 22, 1954. She deluged the court with
statements and affidavits, and the possession date was moved back to
July. When July neared, another flurry of legal activity successfully
extended the possession date to August 7. But that was it. The court
would not listen to any further arguments. She had to be off the property by then.

Being ordered to leave was a legal defeat, a psychological blow, and a
logistical nightmare. Pancho had bought a new piece of property thirty
miles north of the old ranch and now had to figure out how to move six
hundred hogs, a hundred head of cattle, forty horses, thirty dogs, several airplanes, and all the supplies and equipment that went along with
her various operations. Before she could move the hogs, she had to get
all the sows vaccinated and build Health Department–approved feeding platforms at the new place. Before she could move the horses, she
had to construct corrals for the stallions and separate pens for the
mares. When she moved the dogs, her pedigreed Dalmatians, over to

the new property without first constructing a kennel, a number of them dug under the fence and trekked cross-country back to the old ranch, arriving three weeks later, emaciated and torn up. Ranch hands were needed at the new place, but there was no housing for them. There was also no electricity and no running water. Had Pancho admitted defeat earlier and planned for the move, it would not have been so hellish for her that spring and summer. But she hadn't, and it was.

Life was further complicated by the fact that she was also still working on whichever suits had not yet been dismissed—she could hardly keep them straight at this point—with particularly close attention to the federal suit against her. Now that she had finally lost the land, she focused entirely on the money issue. In new court documents, she argued that the $205,000 applied only to her land and not to her various enterprises. Fair compensation, she said, would include funds sufficient to duplicate forty thousand square feet of buildings as well as the rodeo grounds, the airstrip, and other improvements.

<hr />

After almost three and a half years of legal wrangling, the jury trial began in Pancho's fourth and final case on June 5, 1956. Although she had hired a Los Angeles firm for assistance, once again she represented herself and was involved in all aspects of the case. She was getting smarter now, understanding that who she was and how she presented herself in court could influence the outcome of the trial. She had dressed a part for the Holtoner trial, making sure that she looked nothing like anyone's image of a whorehouse madam—and it had worked. She had been able to claim a "moral victory" in that case. Now, once again dressed for court in britches, boots, and a Western shirt, she wanted to make sure the jurors were not put off. Women simply did not dress like this in public in the mid-1950s. The twelfth of her twenty-two questions to prospective jurors read: "If it develops in the course of this trial that said Pancho Barnes customarily wears frontier type trousers or flying pants . . . would that circumstance in any way prejudice you?"

When the trial began, Pancho knew its purpose was to determine fair compensation. The judge had made that clear in his rulings and his court statements. She was off the land. She had lost it. But time and again during the trial, she strayed from the money issue to attack the government for taking the land and attack the Air Force for what she saw as its betrayal of its most loyal supporter, her. "I flew over this territory before the Air Force was there," she told the judge. "It was I that opened up that territory and suggested it to the Air Force. . . . I went in and showed it to them."

The core of the trial was two full days of testimony by Pancho during which she was questioned in minute detail about the development and use of her land. Her own lawyers, who handled the questioning when she was on the stand, gave her ample opportunity to expound on her agricultural ventures, her airfield, her resort, and her many other activities. There were plans for more motel rooms, she told the court. The rodeos were getting "bigger and better. We had a lot of dreams and a lot of hopes and a lot of plans." After what amounted to almost eighty pages of testimony, Pancho told the court that she figured the value of her property at $1.5 million.

Now it was the government lawyers' turn. Their strategy was to show that Pancho's operation, although inarguably vast and various, was not, in fact, profitable. Because of her nonchalance about all matters financial and her disdain for record-keeping, Pancho helped the government's case more than the lawyers could have hoped.

"Was the operation of the motel profitable or unprofitable, Mrs. Barnes?" one of the government lawyers asked. He had tried to get at this point with more subtle questioning, but it hadn't worked.

"I can't say," Pancho replied, "because I don't know about those things. I don't know about the books of the ranch. I can't tell you where profits were made and where they weren't. They all tied together and I didn't pay too much attention to that." When pressured again and again about the profitability of the ranch, Pancho continued to hedge. She really didn't know where the money came from and where it went and how much of it there was. But in court, she sounded as if she were evading the question, as if she were trying to hide the fact that, as a business, Rancho Pancho was not worth much. The government lawyers, who could not have been more delighted with Pancho's vague answers, continued peppering her with financial questions. "All I know," she said finally, weary of the interrogation, "is that we have been living there for a long time, and we used to have money and go places."

For all her confusion about money matters, for all her flamboyance and lack of lawyerly skills, Pancho was irresistible in the courtroom, the maverick standing up for her rights, the private citizen refusing to be steamrolled by the government. The jurors saw a spunky woman who refused to be a victim, and they voted for her. Finally, after four lawsuits, she had actually won. It was then up to U.S. District Judge Gilbert Jertberg to decide how much money her property was worth. In November 1956, he issued his final judgment, setting fair compensation at $377,500 and charging the government interest that upped the settlement to $414,500—more than twice what had originally been offered.

Pancho should have been ecstatic. She had finally beaten the government and had done so on her own terms. The settlement was an enormous sum, at least as much (allowing for inflation) as the previous inheritances that had made her a wealthy woman. But Pancho could not leave well enough alone. She appealed the case to the Ninth Circuit, asking for a reversal on the basis of two technicalities. The justices were not only unconvinced, they also took the time to chastise her. "From the beginning of the proceedings until the present day, the record is replete with one legal maneuver after another by the Appellants," one judge wrote, obviously fed up with the case and Pancho's tactics. Pancho's joy in victory was further tempered by the realization that it had cost her almost $100,000 to win the lawsuit. Then there was the four years' worth of back taxes, owed to the federal government and the state of California, that would be deducted before she saw any money. Still, she cleared $300,000 from the deal and was a local heroine, the only homesteader to have challenged the government and won.

But Pancho would have given all the money back if she could only have reclaimed her land. She had lived with three husbands on that land, had raised her own son as well as Mac's, had weathered World War II and helped usher in the supersonic age, had entertained military brass, headline-making pilots, and scores of Hollywood celebrities. She had lost much more than 360 acres. She had lost a way of life.

Part Three

Ratlands

20

Down and Out at Gypsy Springs

North of Edwards, north of the scrubby desert town of Mojave, the landscape changed slowly and for the better. The high desert floor was still parched, flat, and almost featureless, the color of powdered bone, but here, to the west, there were rock canyons and sandstone cliffs. Here were the six-thousand-foot peaks of the Sierra Nevada—Cache Peak, Cross Mountain, Butterbread Peak—with their soft pleated folds of tawny brown and ocher. One road went through this country, a lonely two-lane highway that led north from Mojave, through the ratlands, skirting the cliffs and canyons for mile after uninterrupted mile. In the summer, the roadbed was so hot that it softened tires.

Pancho's new home was a mile or so off the highway, down a rutted old dirt road near a place called Cantil. She moved there in the 120-degree heat of the summer of 1954, taking up residence on land even more remote, even more sparsely populated than Muroc had been twenty years before. The region north of Edwards was undeveloped, with no services, no power, no phone lines, no nearby towns. Everything was twenty or thirty or fifty dusty miles away. But land was abundant, available, and cheap, and the moment Pancho started getting her settlement money from the government, she began buying it by the square mile.

First she bought the Gypsy Springs ranch, 485 undeveloped acres with an artesian well—the "spring" of Gypsy Springs—and a crumbling stone house that had been a stagecoach stop. So flat and so unencumbered by vegetation was the ranch that it had what Pancho estimated to be an eight-thousand-foot natural airstrip. The price was $13,500, about $28 an acre. Pancho put down $3,000 and took out a mortgage. Next she bought the run-down collection of shacks known as Cantil, actually a postal designation more than a town, along with some surrounding acreage. Here sat the Jawbone Café and Motel, the Cantil store, and the gas station, all in varying states of disrepair. The grocery store, windowless and jammed with shelving, was barely 250 square feet. The Jawbone Café was about as small. Whatever eating was done—and there wasn't much, because traffic was sparse in these parts—was done on one of two ancient picnic tables baking in the roadside dust. The gas station had two pumps that sometimes worked. She paid $10,000 cash.

Another $4,500 bought 640 acres up at Last Chance Canyon north of Cantil along with an adjacent mining claim. There were old gold and silver mines all through the hills, but they had been played out in the early part of the century. Now the land was being mined for its less glamorous minerals, gypsum, tungsten, and borax. She bought a 170-acre parcel and then a 120-acre parcel, and still the spree was not over. She bought a 160-acre alfalfa ranch near Cantil, hoping the crops would feed her horses. That cost her $30,000 down and encumbered her with a $3,500 payment every six months for the next five years. She bought several lots in Ridgecrest, a desert burg fifty miles to the northeast. Then, of course, she needed new machinery, tractors, trailers and trucks, gas pumps, wagons. And she needed new expensive playthings, the luxuries that had always been part of her life. Spending the settlement money almost before the government checks had time to clear the bank, she bought a Stinson airplane and, for weekends at a lake to the north, a twenty-four-foot cabin cruiser and a high-speed catamaran.

These wealthy woman's toys reflected something more than mere acquisitiveness, something more even than desire for the good times they would provide. They were proof that although she had been battered by five years of litigation, although she had lost what was most important to her, although she was no longer the doyenne of the desert, she was still Pancho. She was still in control. She was still living the life she wanted.

It was a momentarily heady time. But the huge purchases belied the day-to-day reality of her life. Cabin cruisers and catamarans aside, she was living in an old rock building with a collapsed roof. The walls had been fissured by earthquakes. The windows were broken. The floorboards were rotting. It looked exactly like what it was: a place that had not been lived in or cared for in many, many years. Pancho temporarily moved to an old house trailer on the property while employees removed the rotting floorboards in the house, then hosed down the dirt, stomped on it with their boots, and called the job finished. Pancho moved back in. The woman who had once lived in a thirty-five-room mansion now lived in a shack with dirt floors. But she didn't think of it that way. She didn't feel sorry for herself. She seemed incapable of feeling sorry for herself; it would have taken more introspection than she could muster. Besides, self-pity would have opened her up to the pity of others. To Pancho, the new place, with all its squalor, was an adventure. The dirt floor reminded her of Mexico and the adobe houses she had stayed in.

The house wasn't the only problem at Gypsy Springs. The artesian well promised much water, but there were no pipes from the well to the house, which meant no running water and no indoor plumbing. There was no irrigation system—not that that mattered anyway. The soil was so alkaline that no amount of water would have made it agriculturally productive. The area was, and always would be, scrubland dotted with clumps of tumbleweed and gnarled trees no taller than a short man.

There were also no outbuildings on the property, which meant that Pancho's beautiful horses had no shelter from the elements. They stood in corrals hastily hammered together by Pancho's employees.

The only shade came from an occasional tamarisk tree. Sometimes, when the heat was so ferocious that the horses might otherwise die, they were herded into the darkness of abandoned mines on the property.

The ranch hands who came with Pancho had no cabins or barracks here. There was no big ranch kitchen set up to feed them. They lived in old trailers hauled onto the property. No outbuildings also meant no shelter for Pancho's expensive toys. The airplane, parked in her front yard by some desert shrubs, was battered by sandstorms and baked by the sun. The cabin cruiser, sitting exposed to the elements on a trailer nearby, aged years in a matter of months. In some ways, Gypsy Springs was not unlike dozens of other hardscrabble desert outposts with their parched land, dilapidated buildings, and hard-luck stories. But few other desert rats had private airplanes in their front yards, or brand-new color television sets sitting on the dirt floor of their kitchens.

If Pancho worried over her present circumstance, it was not for long. She was far too busy with plans for the future, big, grandiose plans that would dwarf anything she had accomplished at Rancho Oro Verde. One plan was to use the water from the artesian well to create an enormous lake on the property. Pancho envisioned boaters and water-skiers skimming across the surface. She would build a marina, a sporting goods store, a gift shop. Another artificial lake would be a waterfowl refuge. She'd pump water into two in-ground swimming pools, part of a recreation complex that would include a lounge, cabanas, and a trailer court. "It will be like the old club, only better," she told her friends.

She had plans to get back into the aviation business, too. She would pave the eight-thousand-foot natural runway, line it with lights, build hangars, and create a bigger and better airport than she had ever had at Muroc. She told friends that she planned on hiring some young ladies to work for her. They would stand on the taxiway waving colored flags to guide airplanes on and off the strip. Apart from the flags, they would be naked. Pancho winked and chortled when she described this scenario to her friends, but they never doubted her sincerity. It was just what they expected from her. Gypsy Springs would be the Happy Bottom Riding Club and Pancho's Fly-Inn reincarnated, made bigger, showier, even more extravagant.

Out on the old highway, she had plans to turn the Cantil property into a roadside attraction. She would put in a trout pond by the Jawbone Motel. She would build stables, corrals, and rodeo grounds behind the motel and offer trail rides through Red Rock, Jawbone, and Last Chance canyons. There would be a free campground for people who brought their own horses. She had an idea to open four different cafés in one long, new building, each featuring a different cuisine— American, Mexican, German, and French. There would be a bar and, she hoped, gambling in the back room. She talked about constructing an entire city out on the highway, incorporating it and then legalizing gambling within its limits. She didn't expect much difficulty with the authorities. The twenty-by-forty-mile jurisdiction was policed by only one constable, and he didn't even have a telephone. Besides, Pancho intended to run against him in the next election. If that didn't work, she told her friends, only half joking, she would secede from the Union and proclaim the Independent Nation of Pancho.

Meanwhile, Pancho's life proceeded as it always had: fast, with little attention to detail and great attention to whatever made Pancho happy at the moment. She lost the election for constable but took it in stride, barely remembering it after the votes were counted. There were many other activities to keep her busy, the primary one being spending enormous sums of money on horses. She drove to Oklahoma and came back with six registered quarter-horse stallions, all from champion brood stock. Her favorite horse—as she told friends, "the best damn horse I ever owned"—was Jack Payne II, whose mother was a full sister of Fair Play. And Fair Play, as everyone in the horse breeding and horse racing world knew, had sired the famous Man O' War. Pancho envisioned overseeing a significant breeding operation at Gypsy Springs, but it was her passion for horses combined with the influx of cash—rather than any considered business plan—that kept her buying.

Her generosity was also unbridled. At the Jawbone Café, she would feed people who walked in the door with no money. If a fellow was hungry and he knew Pancho, or he knew someone who knew Pancho, or he'd ever flown an airplane, or he could tell a good dirty joke, or she just liked the way he looked, he'd get a free meal. At the Cantil store, she gave groceries away right off the shelves, asking for no IOUs, writing no names in a ledger. Commissaries at the base considered precut, prewrapped meat to be garbage if it didn't sell in three days. Pancho struck a deal to collect the unsold meat, then froze it in one of the several industrial-sized freezers she'd moved from the old place to the new one. The freezers were invariably full of roasts, chops, and steaks, and it seemed that every hobo, desert rat, and out-of-work ranch hand within fifty miles knew it. It was not unusual to walk into Pancho's dirt-floor kitchen on a late afternoon and find half a dozen down-and-outers eating T-bones at her table.

The flip side of Pancho's unabated generosity was her contentiousness. She loved a good fight, or even a bad one, and the years of litigation with the government had not cured her. When a foreman she hired to oversee her new alfalfa ranch slacked off on the job, she not only fired him, she sued him for more than $5,000, claiming he had ruined her crops. When a highway patrolman stopped her for driving on the wrong side of the road near the entrance to Gypsy Springs and made the mistake of threatening to take her to jail, she pulled a pistol from her pocket and challenged him to a gunfight right there. She didn't like to be told what to do, but her challenge was more theatrical than threatening. The patrolman didn't see it that way. He backed off, then called the dispatcher from his car radio. "What's the woman's name?" the dispatcher asked him. "Pancho Barnes," the patrolman said. "Just get in the car and leave," the dispatcher replied.

Another time, Pancho was cited for running a stop sign in Lancaster. The ticket would have cost her a few dollars. Instead of paying it, she hired a photographer to spend a full day set up out on the road next to the stop sign taking pictures of cars as they failed to stop. He also shot a series of photographs showing how far off the road the sign was and how increasingly difficult it was to see as the sun went down. Armed with a thick stack of photographs, Pancho had her day in court over a five-dollar traffic ticket. The judge, so she told the story, took one look at her walking into court with her stack of material and dismissed the case.

As the years went by at Gypsy Springs, Pancho became more and more of a character, more and more of a true desert rat. Alternately ornery and openhanded, disputatious and sociable, she was a woman who lived in a world of dirt and horse manure, her front "yard" a study in tractors and trailers, planes and boats, auto parts, pipes, steam boilers, and heavy equipment, all baking in the sun, paint flaking, parts rusting. Pancho didn't care about appearances. What she cared about was re-creating her desert dream, remaking her empire. That, it turned out, was not possible.

<hr />

For one thing, money stood in her way. As usual, she kept no books and few business records, paying cash for deliveries of food and other goods at the store and café, paying cash for wages and equipment out at the ranch, never noting or caring how much was going out and how little was coming in. Had she been paying attention, she would have known that the $300,000 she netted from the government settlement was too quickly lavished on large tracts of desert scrub and corrals full of expensive horses. She had paid as much as $20,000 for a single stallion. Even undistinguished quarter horses from unknown bloodlines were running upwards of $5,000. But it was not the initial cost that was hurting her now. It was the enormous sum she was spending to feed the horses. She could not grow alfalfa in the poor soil of Gypsy Springs, and the acreage she bought for the purpose of providing hay was mismanaged and lay fallow. She put herself in the position of having to feed fifty-four racehorses on trucked-in, baled hay at a cost of more than $60 a day. Tony King, who had been her ranch hand and then ranch foreman so many years before, came out to help her, simultaneously reveling in all the gorgeous horseflesh and shaking his head over

Pancho's lack of business—or even common—sense. He told her to sell off some of her stock, consolidate, take better care of what she had. She tried to follow his advice, putting a few horses on the market. But she could never quite bring herself to actually sell any of her beauties. Once a man drove down from Las Vegas and offered her an excellent price on one of her stallions. She had his check in her pocket. She watched him load the horse into his trailer. She couldn't stand it. "Put him back in the corral where he belongs," she told a ranch hand. Then she tore up the check.

For years, Pancho had made money with hogs, feeding them on garbage collected from the base, then selling them at market when they were sufficiently fat. To continue the operation at Gypsy Springs, she invested considerable money in feeding platforms, new pens, and a Health Department–required steam boiler to cook the garbage before it was fed to the hogs. She had about six hundred hogs on her feedlot when she contracted the business out to a local couple. By oral agreement, they were supposed to care for and feed the pigs, but somehow that never happened. Pancho went to court, sued them, and won $2,500, but in the meantime, the hog operation faltered. In 1957 she sold it all, which was a relief—the hogs were a major and malodorous responsibility—but was also a bad business decision. Fed on free garbage, the hogs were a steady source of income. Without that business, without the Happy Bottom Riding Club, the Fly-Inn, and all the attendant activities, Pancho's income was reduced to whatever she could clear from the tiny Cantil store and the Jawbone Café and Motel. She had no money to finance her grand plans, no money even to fix up the run-down buildings. Business was minimal six months of the year, when the desert sun kept temperatures consistently above one hundred and few cars traveled the long, hot back road to nowhere. As an income source, the Cantil highway properties were not doing well. Not only that, but Pancho discovered too late that the government held a lien against those properties for nonpayment of income taxes by the previous owner, a matter that should have surfaced when she first bought the property, but for some reason didn't. Now there was a chance she would lose her entire investment. At any rate, it might take years to disentangle the mess. Just a few years after she had received a fortune from the government, it was becoming clear, even to Pancho, that she was in serious financial trouble.

"As far as cash is concerned, at the moment I am strictly out of it," she wrote to one old friend. "We are struggling along," she wrote to another. "Almost everything is really in a bad way." To a third friend, she admitted: "We are land poor." To improve her situation, Pancho tried to sell some of the land she had so recently acquired. She wrote to several friends, asking them to put the word out that she had 160 acres to sell at $500 an acre, "a real swell buy," as she put it. But there were no takers. She also, while trying to clear up the tax problem on the Cantil highway property, tried to find someone to rent and operate it. She attempted to persuade Tony King to take over the operation of the bar, touting all her big plans for the trout pond and the rodeo grounds and the canyon trail rides. But Tony understood the situation better than Pancho and was not tempted, even for a moment.

As the situation worsened, Pancho finally resorted to selling some of her horses. But she had paid more than top dollar for them and had not kept them in top condition. There were no stables at Gypsy Springs, and horses were not fed and watered reliably. If Pancho was out of money, no hay was delivered. If she went away for a few days and forgot to leave money, the horses didn't eat. Rather than pay a veterinarian to care for them, she hired Tony King on the cheap. He loved horses and was knowledgeable, but these were fine, top-bred racehorses that needed consistent, professional care, and they weren't getting it. Their hooves badly needed trimming. "Their feet are practically turned up, they are so long," Pancho wrote to a friend, trying to enlist his services. She found few buyers.

Three years after the government settlement, Pancho was desperate for funds. Late in 1957, she even contemplated liquidating everything and moving to Mexico. She wrote to her old traveling companion Roger Chute that she wanted to buy a place with "a good view, good water, good sea breeze and good health conditions." Roger volunteered to do some scouting for her and suggested a friend who knew the Michoacán country, but Pancho never followed up. She had probably forgotten the matter as soon as she mailed the letter.

⊷ ⊨✦⊨ ⊶

Even if money had not been a problem, her dream of reincarnating Rancho Pancho was doomed. Even if she had succeeded in building the airport and the ranch house, the swimming pools and the marina, she would have had considerable trouble attracting customers. The men at Edwards were no longer desperate for entertainment now that the base was a thriving, self-contained city with homes, stores, clubs, and even its own golf course. The Blow and Go pilots who had made Pancho's their unofficial headquarters and had brought the club both notoriety and business were no longer daring young men looking for a good time. They were colonels and corporate executives, married men with children. They had responsibilities and reputations to uphold. There was now an excellent highway over the San Gabriels into Los Angeles, a mere ninety miles away, an easy hour-and-a-half drive. The Happy Bottom Riding Club had been just three miles from the base. Her new place was thirty or forty miles away. The location made no sense.

And the timing couldn't have been worse. In the fall of 1958, in the midst of all the schemes and dreams, Pancho found what no woman wants to find. It was there, in her right breast, a small lump no bigger than a pea. Her local doctor couldn't feel anything but sent her down to the Los Angeles Tumor Institute to have it checked out. There doctors performed a biopsy, removed the lump, and sent the tissue to the lab for examination while Pancho recovered in her hospital room. Three days later, she received the good news: It was not cancer.

The relief was like nothing she had ever felt before. The world came back into focus. She could breathe again. She had to celebrate and celebrate big. She and Mac stayed in Los Angeles several days, hitting their favorite hot spots and carousing with friends. But when she came home, there was a letter from the Institute waiting for her. It said that, after further analysis, the lump in her right breast had been determined to be malignant. She should return to the hospital immediately.

Hearing that news is about as tough as it gets. But for Pancho, the situation was even tougher. She had just been on that roller coaster. She had just lain in a hospital bed for three days, trying not to think about the only thing she could think about. She had been told she was in the clear. Now this. The letter said to report to the hospital immediately, but Pancho couldn't bring herself to go. Her spirits were lower than they had ever been. She needed time to recoup the emotional stamina she would need. Pancho, being Pancho, didn't go about this in an ordinary way. She had Mac drive her all around Los Angeles to visit friends. At Santa Ana Airport, she met up with Russ Schleeh, a former Blow and Go pilot who had turned to boat racing. As a test pilot ten years before, he had landed on Muroc Dry Lake with his craft on fire, then literally broke through the side of the plane to save the lives of seven crew members. He had broken his back in the process and battled back to health. This was the kind of fighter she needed to talk to, the kind of story she needed to hear. After her visits, Pancho finally showed up at the hospital—at eleven that night.

Breast cancer treatment in the late 1950s meant one thing, surgery, and surgery meant one thing: radical mastectomy. At the Tumor Institute, doctors removed not only her breast but the underlying pectoral muscles, everything, Pancho said, "from the beginning of my ribs right straight up into the armpit." The surgery left not only significant scars, but a deep, deformed concavity where the breast used to be. The doctor warned her that because of the muscles he had to cut, she might lose the use of her right arm. That scared her more than what she saw in the mirror. Her physical strength had always been a source of pride. Even in her late fifties, Pancho would take any occasion to roll up her sleeve, flex her biceps and insist that some friend or stranger feel how hard the muscle was. She would clench her thigh muscle and have someone beat on it with a fist. It was as hard as a wooden leg, she boasted. She could deal with the loss of her breast. She would have to deal with it. But she could not tolerate the loss of her strength. She went home and, as soon as she could, she started swinging Indian clubs and chopping wood. She exercised the arm until it hurt, and then she exercised it some more. It took time, but she regained and kept full use of her arm.

The whole ordeal was terrifying. Pancho showed her scar to anyone who wanted to see it—and many who didn't—but she would be damned if she would show her fear. She answered her door dressed in a man's undershirt, daring visitors to be shocked. She would trump their pity with immodesty, with forthrightness that took their breath away. "A couple of physical problems came along and I had to have my tit cut off" is how she told a new friend about her cancer. People shook their heads and talked about what a character she was. "Most people are as alike as rabbit turds," Roger Chute wrote to one of his friends. But "no system of conformance, no all-embracing plan of regimentation, no demented concept of unvarying mediocrity ever produced a human phenomenon such as Pancho."

In the midst of the land dealings and the income problems and the big plans that sounded good but went nowhere, Pancho somehow managed to recover. By 1960, her strength, both emotional and physical, was back. But so was her cancer. This time there was a lump in the left breast, and another trip to Los Angeles and another disfiguring surgery and another long recovery. Pancho was fifty-nine by then, and after the second surgery, she felt every year of it. Her life was no longer good. It was no longer even interesting. She was isolated at Gypsy Springs. Her old friends from the base had moved on or moved up. Pancho was a closed chapter in their lives, a lively anecdote to tell their friends. There were no parties at Gypsy Springs, no banquets, no rodeos, no flying treasure hunts, none of the social activities that Pancho thrived on. There was only Pancho, her horses, and her husband. And not much of him.

21

Deserted

After that first summer at Gypsy Springs, the summer of 1954, things were never the same between Pancho and Mac. The move was tough on both of them, not just physically—although the hard labor of moving the entire operation in the August heat was considerable—but emotionally. They were leaving the only life they had known together. They were leaving the place where they had first lived together with that initial fervor of new lovers; the place where they had gotten married; the place that, for all the daily annoyances and ongoing concerns that were part of running such a diverse business, for all the financial and legal hassles, had been the wellspring of energy and excitement in their lives. Had they been different people, more introspective people, they might have sat down with each other that summer and talked things out, or tried to. But neither of them knew the meaning of reflection. The move was thus even more emotionally dislocating than it needed to be. Pancho's reaction to the stress was to spend money as fast as she could. Mac's was to retreat.

Life at the new ranch was so much harder, more primitive, and more isolated than life had been at Oro Verde. There were big plans, of course, but the reality was that their new home was a crumbling stone stagecoach stop with a dirt floor and no running water. Their new ranch was a square mile of arid alkali scrubland with no outbuildings, no facilities. Their new life was devoid of Hollywood visitors and hot-shot pilots. The tedium of hard work was broken only by Pancho's buying sprees: the hundreds of acres of land, the corrals full of expen-sive racehorses that everyone, including Mac, thought she was crazy to buy. But after a while, there was no money for that. There was just Pan-cho in and out of the hospital, battling breast cancer, barely achieving one recovery before being hit by another problem, her energy sapped, her confidence shaken not only in her invincibility but, even more im-portant, in her sexuality. She had always been a homely woman, but she had had a vitality, a sexual energy that had made her attractive to many men well into middle age. Now she felt that ebbing. Mac began spend-ing more and more time away from Gypsy Springs, traveling to their various landholdings, sometimes staying at the Cantil property on the highway. A woman named Lenora, who cooked at the Jawbone Café, lived in a trailer behind the restaurant. Pancho felt abandoned when she needed help the most. She also felt, for perhaps the first time in her life, jealous.

Meanwhile, things at Gypsy Springs were getting worse. Pancho, most often alone with her horses, two burros, and a few dogs, was liv-ing in increasing squalor. Her few visitors couldn't help but notice that she was filthy and unkempt, that her house smelled of the manure she tracked in on her boots and of the remains of weeks' worth of meals that littered the counters, the table, and even the floor of her kitchen. As bad off as she was, the horses were worse. They were starving. They were dehydrated. There were dead horses lying in the dirt of one cor-ral. There was no water in the troughs. Tony King and his wife drove out to help, as did her old friend Bob Fetters. They would bring hay and feed the horses. They would start the pumps to water the animals. But when they came back later, they discovered that Pancho had done nothing in the interim. It was all getting to be too much for her.

The woman who had owned Cadillacs her whole life was now driv-ing a Volkswagen Beetle. When she hit a railroad track that crossed her land, blowing both tires and damaging the hood, two friends repaired the car with junkyard parts. The woman who had been bathed and dressed by servants as a child and who had been surrounded by dozens of hired hands at Rancho Oro Verde now had no help. She could no longer afford employees. After a while, she could not even afford phone service. Sometime in the late 1950s, she stopped paying property taxes. She began defaulting on mortgage payments. The owners of some parcels of land in Ridgecrest took legal action, claiming she hadn't made payments since a year after she bought the property. The state threatened to take 640 acres of land because Pancho hadn't paid property taxes on it for several years. She also owed back taxes on the Cantil property and was being sued for nonpayment by the company that provided gas to the service station out there. By the early 1960s, her "idiotic squandering," as Roger Chute described it, had brought her to the verge of bankruptcy. Her property was now being auctioned off at sheriff's sales, or she was selling it as quickly as she could to stay ahead of foreclosure. In 1961, she sold part of the Cantil land and another fifty-acre parcel. In 1962, she lost the Cantil store and 160 acres at a sheriff's sale. In 1963, she sold additional acreage north of Cantil.

But she wasn't about to give up. In the middle of her property tax problems, potential foreclosures, and forced sales, desperate for cash, she mounted yet another suit against the U.S. government, this one to attempt to recover almost $5,000 she had been forced to pay the IRS in 1959. Like most of Pancho's legal and financial dealings, this one was a mess. It concerned taxes the IRS claimed she had owed since 1940 on income from the Richard Dobbins trust, her inheritance from her maternal grandfather. Pancho claimed, among other things, that her uncle Horace, the executor, was mismanaging the trust. The income she had been taxed on, she claimed, was not real but rather the result of creative bookkeeping. As usual, Pancho handled the case herself, squaring off against three U.S. attorneys who deluged her with a dozen requests for legal papers and then criticized her for submitting "handwritten documents . . . which purportedly contain your reply." She expended time, energy, and money on the case, and lost.

Life was further complicated by Pancho's involvement in at least ten lawsuits filed in Bakersfield and Los Angeles. She was suing or being sued for various deals gone sour—horse deals, airplane deals, complex real estate arrangements. The state of California sued her for stiffing three workmen on their wages. A landowner sued her for back rent and damages to land she was leasing, and won a $20,000 judgment. A man sued her over ownership of a quarter horse. Another sued her over charges incurred when he stored airplanes on her property. Yet another creditor sued her for more than $30,000—and won, precipitating the sale of some of the Cantil land to satisfy the judgment. Pancho instigated several suits herself, one claiming that a couple owed her more than $6,000 for renting farm equipment (she won a $772 judgment and was ordered to pay her own court costs), another against the local constable for towing away three of her trucks. She claimed $6,100 in damages and won nothing. She appealed and lost. In the most disturbing case, Mac sued Pancho to keep her from selling her interest in the Jawbone Café. That was how badly their relationship had deteriorated.

——◄◆►——

On a summer day in 1962, Pancho asked Mac to drive her into Bakersfield, telling him that they needed to look at records at the Kern County courthouse to prepare for one of their many pending lawsuits. While Mac was standing at one of the counters reading over documents, Pancho excused herself. "Back in a minute," she said. "Keep on looking."

When she returned a few minutes later, she had a sheriff's deputy in tow.

"That's the son of a bitch," she said to the deputy, pointing at Mac. "Serve him." The deputy shoved some papers into Mac's hands, and that was how the fourth husband of Pancho Barnes found out he was being sued for divorce. The legal papers, filed in mid-August, claimed abandonment. In those days before no-fault divorce, someone had to be the villain, and Pancho had no trouble listing for the record what she viewed as Mac's many failings. The complaint for divorce called Mac a "neurotic procrastinator" who "leaves the plaintiff alone practically all of the time." He "fraternizes with . . . people of an inferior standing" and is "guilty of habitual intemperance." Mac had "willfully deserted and abandoned" Pancho, causing her "great mental anguish."

A few months later, Pancho followed up with an affidavit claiming that she was destitute, "without funds to feed myself or my livestock," without heat, without phone service, and "completely out of touch with anyone to take care of me." She asked the court to order Mac to sell a 1953 Cessna they jointly owned and apply the proceeds of the sale to past-due mortgages, notes, and taxes on a number of properties. In another affidavit, she claimed that Mac was preventing her from selling peat moss from one of the ranches they owned, thus depriving her of income. Their real estate holdings were a mess. Some property was jointly owned, some individually owned; some property had been deeded over from Pancho to Mac, some he owned but she held the first trust deed. Taxes were delinquent; mortgages were in arrears. They were being sued by creditors. The judge read Pancho's pleas but ordered that neither party sell anything until a divorce settlement was reached.

That would take some doing. Both Pancho and Mac were fighting for their financial futures, and both of them were fighting hard. California was a community-property state, meaning that the spouses were entitled to share equally in the assets of the marriage. Generally, that acted as a protection for wives, who in those days were likely to have spent their marriage taking care of the home and children and not adding income to the family coffers. A community-property settlement meant the wife was awarded half the assets, regardless of whether she had brought in half the income. In Pancho and Mac's case, the result was just the opposite. Pancho was—or had been—the wealthy one. It was she who had owned the land, Rancho Oro Verde, bought with money from her own inheritance; she who started the dairy and the hog business, the airport and the Happy Bottom Riding Club; she who had parlayed an eighty-acre alfalfa ranch into a 360-acre desert oasis. Therefore, she claimed in her divorce complaint, "there was not actually ever any community property." If Mac had any money when he came to live with Pancho in 1946, "the plaintiff was not cognizant of such," read the complaint. Pancho claimed that she had placed some of her property under Mac's name "to hold for her" because she "had been informed by doctors that she was not expected to live and she believed it." She was referring to the stroke she suffered soon after Mac moved in.

In her various complaints, affidavits, memoranda, and briefs, Pancho was busy rewriting history, or at least editing it heavily. In this revised narrative, Pancho cast herself in the role of an older woman who, faced with failing health in 1946, allowed herself to be taken advantage of by the young Eugene McKendry. When she met Mac, she stated in her trial memorandum, she "had had two major operations, was very depressed, blind in both eyes, unable to walk and bedridden." While she was in that compromised state, "defendant won her confidence and trust." Certainly Mac had won her trust after he helped her through that difficult period, but the fact was that she had met and started living with him before her stroke. Far from being bedridden, she was, when they first became lovers, a sexually vital woman with prodigious energy, a whirlwind of activity, the focal point of much attention, and a businesswoman of renown. After the operations at the Mayo Clinic, she was indeed temporarily incapacitated, but she was not so depressed or bedridden that she couldn't rouse herself to attend, and be fêted at, an air show just a few weeks later. Mac, who came to the relationship "with little or nothing," according to Pancho, had "lived off her ever since, and the only work he has ever done is work she put him to."

Mac, of course, saw their shared past quite differently. His version of history was that the two of them had bought property and run the business together, that their "mutual and joint efforts" made the estate what it now was, that Pancho had deeded him property as payment for his many services, that whatever property Pancho had owned at the time of their marriage had "long since been commingled and reinvested with community property." He claimed everything was community property. She claimed nothing was. Neither would compromise.

As the fight dragged on, Pancho became more and more interested in what Mac was doing when he stayed in Cantil. She became more and more interested in Lenora. In early 1963, angry, jealous, and fully aware that a charge of adultery would enhance her case, she hired a private investigator. Staking out the rear of the café on the night of March 9, the investigator noted that Mac went into the trailer and emerged some eighteen minutes later. Pancho amended her divorce complaint to include "adultery with Lenora A. Armstrong" on March 9, 1963, and "on numerous other occasions." As the legal bickering continued, more land was lost to tax liens, and Pancho's health worsened.

Pancho had never taken decent care of herself. When she got sick, she had to be coerced into seeking medical attention. But now, alone at Gypsy Springs, she had no one to coerce her. There was no one to see that she was becoming increasingly fatigued and mentally sluggish, no one to remark on her weight gain or her sudden chills, no one to notice that every day it became more difficult for her to rouse herself from bed. She didn't know it, but her thyroid had almost completely shut down. She was dying.

That was how Ted Tate found her one afternoon in 1963: alone, sick, and unable to crawl out of bed. Ted had been on the outskirts of the Happy Bottom Riding Club crowd when he was stationed at Edwards during the war. Years later, he met and befriended one of Pancho's old buddies and former lovers, the stunt pilot Ira Reed, who filled him with stories about the old days, wild tales of Pancho in her Mystery Ship, Pancho flying for Howard Hughes, Pancho and her legendary Laguna Beach parties. For Ted, a married man with four children, a mortgage, and a desk job at General Dynamics, this was heady stuff. Be sure to look her up if you're ever out that way again, Ira Reed told him. Ted didn't need much encouragement.

In 1963, he was sent to Edwards to deliver a lecture on flight safety and immediately started asking about Pancho. No one on base seemed to know exactly where she lived, but one of the pilots who knew her in the Happy Bottom days said he heard she might be up at an old ranch somewhere near Cantil. Ted jumped in his car and drove out the Sierra Highway looking for someone who could tell him where to find the ranch. After numerous inquiries, he finally located an old desert rat, an assayer who used to be a movie cameraman, who said he knew where Pancho lived. "But I wouldn't recommend going out there," he told Ted. "She's been having a lot of trouble with her husband, and she is threatening to shoot him and anybody else that tries to come in." Ted was insistent. The assayer directed him to an old dirt road blocked by a barbed-wire gate. Ted unhooked the gate and walked the long, dusty road to the house.

"Who the hell is it?" Pancho yelled through the door when she heard the knock. Ted told her his name.

"Who the hell are you?" yelled Pancho.

"I'm a friend of Ira Reed's," Ted yelled back.

"Are you going to visit formal or informal?" Pancho asked through the door.

"What's the difference?" Ted wanted to know.

"I had an operation," Pancho said, "and for anything formal I put on my rubber tits. If you don't care, I'll leave them off." As sick as she was, Pancho was still Pancho, still getting in the first licks.

Ted, who hadn't known quite what to expect, certainly hadn't expected this. What could he say? He told her he didn't care what she was or wasn't wearing, and she let him in. The place was in bad shape, but not as bad as its owner. Ted was appalled. This could not be the Pancho Barnes he had heard so much about. This was an old, sick woman. He soon became an important part of her life. When he was transferred out to Edwards two months later, he began visiting Pancho regularly, bringing food and water, doing the chores that needed doing, staying to talk. Things improved somewhat at Gypsy Springs, but Pancho herself got worse. Ted finally realized that if he didn't get her out of there and get some help, she would die.

He took her to the hospital in Lone Pine, a small town to the north, where her thyroid condition was immediately diagnosed and she was put on medication. "I was very nearly dead," she wrote to her old friend and fellow flier Bobbi Trout. "Now I take little pink pills." She stayed in the hospital for two weeks, slowly recovering her strength as the thyroid-hormone pills recalibrated her metabolism. Meanwhile, Ted was spreading the word on base that Pancho Barnes was alive but not well. It had been only ten years since the demise of the Happy Bottom Riding Club, but all that seemed part of another era. It *was* part of another era. Men who had known her back in those days were surprised to learn she was still around. People who had never known her, people who had heard the wild stories, people who had forgotten her years ago, all started talking. They should do something to honor her, especially now that it looked as if she might not be around much longer.

When Pancho was well enough to leave the hospital, Ted Tate was there in his '55 Thunderbird convertible to take her home to Gypsy Springs. He was also there to tell her that the Air Force Flight Test Center at Edwards—her boys, the pilots—were proclaiming May 23 "Pancho Barnes: The First Citizen of Edwards" Day. Pancho had not been on base for years. But that Saturday in May, professionally coiffed and dressed well for the first time in ages, she held court at the officers' club, where, as the program stated, "darn right—the bar is open." More than a hundred people came to pay tribute, including a number of her old friends: Major General Al Boyd, the stunt pilot Paul Mantz, and a contingent of test pilots from the supersonic days—Bill Bridgeman, Tony LeVier, "Fish" Salmon, and her erstwhile pal Chuck Yeager, now a colonel. General Jimmy Doolittle sent a letter from Alaska. Paul Mantz, who owned her old Mystery Ship, promised to rebuild it and let her fly it one more time. The base commander toasted Pancho as "America's living heritage of the good old wood-and-wire days." For Pancho, the most social of animals, a woman who thrived in the spotlight, this was far better medicine than the little pink pills.

⊷ ⩗⧫⩘ ⊷

Her old acquaintances from the Happy Bottom Riding Club days may have feared she would soon die, but a combination of the thyroid medicine, the renewed attention orchestrated by Ted Tate, and her abiding, energizing anger at Mac led to a strong recovery. She told a lawyer who was helping her with her real estate problems that she would "get even with Mr. McKendry if it was the last thing she ever did." As soon as she was well enough, she threw herself back into the divorce proceedings, which had already dragged on for more than two years. Mac, perhaps learning a litigious lesson from Pancho, countersued for divorce, claiming that "Plaintiff failed to prove her case for divorce by reason of the inherent untrustworthy nature of all her testimony." Pancho's legal memorandum was "strong on length," but "wanting for foundation since it is built upon 'shifting sands,' to wit: the completely untrustworthy testimony of Mrs. E. S. McKendry." In a six-and-a-half-page trial brief, Mac bolstered his community-property claim while disputing Pancho's allegations of adultery. He did not directly deny the allegation, but rather insisted that her evidence had not proved it. He was entitled to a divorce from her, not the other way around, his lawyers argued in the countersuit. "It would be hard to name a person more entitled to a divorce on the ground of extreme cruelty than the cross-complainant," stated the brief. In a support document, Mac claimed that Pancho had threatened, in front of customers, to break all the windows of the Jawbone Café, had kicked in the café's front door, and was spreading "untruthful rumors and gossip throughout the eastern Kern county area." The lawyers argued that Mac should pay no alimony and should have clear title to the Cessna airplane, whatever interest remained in the Jawbone Café, and some additional parcels of property. The rest of the property should be considered community property and "awarded in a fair and equitable manner between the two parties."

The countersuit only strengthened Pancho's resolve. Although she was representing herself in the case, she hired a lawyer, a Mr. McFarland, to depose Mac, and the man did a bang-up job, grilling Mac for hours about the particulars of the financial arrangements between him and Pancho. Mac was resistant to any implication that he had lived off Pancho. It took McFarland more than a dozen questions to force him to state that money he used to buy clothes and other personal items came from the operation of the ranch. The questioning went like this:

McFarland: "After you started taking care of her full-time, did she give you any spending money in any form?"

Mac: "I don't think so."

"Do you smoke?"

"No."

"Do you drink?"

"Yes. Well, a little."

"If you wanted to buy a drink somewhere, where did you get the money?"

"I didn't go anywhere. I mean, I was with her all the time."

The going was slow and frustrating, but the lawyer kept at it.

McFarland: "Let's put it this way: You got clothes somewhere, didn't you?"

Mac: "Yes. About what I have today, yes."

"Where did you get the clothes?"

"I bought them."

"With what money?"

"At J. C. Penney's."

"With what money?"

"With the money that came from the operation of the ranch."

Moving from that hard-won admission, McFarland labored to show that the ranch, the couple's sole source of income, was entirely Pancho's property, bought and developed before she and Mac even met. Then he began quizzing Mac about later loans that helped finance the acquisition of additional land and the further development of the ranch.

"Was this on a personal signature of your own?" the lawyer asked, about a loan for $6,500.

"No," Mac replied. "This was borrowing on a boat."

"Whose boat was that?"

"My boat."

"Did you have that when you and Pancho started living together?"

"No," admitted Mac. "We acquired the boat at a later date."

"Who paid for it?"

"We did."

"We paid for it," the lawyer repeated. "How much did you contribute to that?"

"I wrote the check that paid for it," said Mac.

"That was not my question," said the lawyer. "Where did the money come from that you paid for . . ."

"Came out of our bank account," said Mac.

But the lawyer would have none of that.

"What monies were put into this bank account when it was opened?" he asked. When Mac deflected the question, he asked again: "Where did the money come from?"

"The first money came from a—some money that was due in Pennsylvania."

"From whom?" asked McFarland.

"I mean, from her uncle." Score another for the lawyer. He had shown that an item "they" bought and later used for collateral had been purchased with Pancho's inheritance money.

The deposition went on like this relentlessly. When it was over, McFarland had made the best case he could that Mac brought little money and no property into the marriage, that the money he spent during the marriage came from the operation of Pancho's ranch, and that improvements and additional acquisitions could be traced to Pancho's money.

As the case went forward, three successive judges asked to be relieved of duty. All had been involved in previous suits mounted by or against Pancho. She was such a fixture in the Bakersfield courthouse that there was talk of a change of venue. But finally, Kern County Superior Court Justice P. R. Borton agreed to hear the case. It went to trial on November 29, 1965, Pancho serving as her own attorney. The questioning went on for four days, with Pancho and Mac the star witnesses for their own sides, repeating what they had stated in their briefs, memoranda, and depositions. Each called four other witnesses on his or her own behalf, the focus being almost entirely on who owned what, when, and how.

It took Judge Borton almost six months to sort out the details and ponder the case. On June 3, 1966, he ruled decisively for Pancho, stating that she was entitled to a divorce from Mac on the grounds of extreme cruelty and adultery. In sorting out the various property claims on both sides, Borton ruled that property acquired since the marriage, regardless of whose name was on the deed, had all been bought with funds from the same source: the proceeds from the sale of the ranch Pancho owned before her marriage. Borton awarded Pancho all the real estate held jointly and individually by the couple at the time, 941 acres of it, plus the cabin cruiser, a Stinson airplane, trucks, tractors, and all the farm equipment, the horses and tack, and any money on deposit with the county clerk. To Mac, "in lieu [*sic*] of his negligible contributions to this marriage," he awarded the Cessna airplane, which had not been flown in years and had suffered considerable damage after tipping over in a windstorm, and the eleven-year-old Cadillac coupe he was currently driving.

Pancho couldn't have done better with the settlement—on paper. In reality, she owed so much money in mortgage payments and property taxes, judgments, and liens that she was as close to broke as she had ever been. Judge Borton would have awarded her alimony, as was usual, but, as he stated in his decision, he saw no way for Mac to pay it. "Although plaintiff is elderly and in poor state of health and the defendant is still a man in the prime of life and in robust health, he obviously has been trained to live only upon the property of foolish women and has no visible means of support," he stated.

Matters should have ended there, but they didn't. Three months after the divorce decree, Pancho was charged with cruelty to animals and hauled before a judge in Lake Isabella, a little town to the northwest. She was convinced Mac was behind the charge, and she said as much to the judge in her argumentative, confrontational style. Dressed as usual in dirty jeans and an old shirt, spouting accusations about Mac pouring cement down her well and hiring men to hit her horses on the head with hammers, Pancho, it seemed to the backcountry judge, was a paranoiac old woman. The judge, apparently one of the few people in the area who wasn't acquainted with either the person or the legend of Pancho Barnes, suspended the proceedings because he had "serious doubts as to the present sanity of said defendant." He ordered her to undergo two psychological evaluations in October 1966.

She told both of the Bakersfield psychiatrists that she was completely innocent of the charges and that Mac was to blame, both for the deaths of her horses and for the filing of the complaint against her. It wasn't their job to figure out if she was right, only if she was sane enough to stand trial. One doctor took the opportunity to note that she had "very poor feminine gender identification, some asocial trends . . . and no insight." Another, who found her more acceptable, concluded that "she is aware that she does not always behave in a most endearing fashion." Both found her loquacious, colorful to the point of eccentricity—and sane. She was not convicted, nor did she convince anyone that Mac was at fault. But she believed it, and the bitterness against her ex-husband stayed with her.

She was sixty-five years old, alone, in questionable health, and close to broke. But she would start over again.

22

The Last Flight

Something had to be done. It was clear to Ted Tate and the few other friends who visited Pancho at Gypsy Springs that she could not take care of her property, her animals, or herself. It was not that she was ailing or infirm. Her thyroid condition was under control as long as she took her medication. Her high blood pressure had been cured by the operations at the Mayo Clinic. Her cancer had not come back. She was, in her late sixties, still a physically strong and active woman. But there were far too many chores at the ranch for one person, man or woman, of any age. And the primitive conditions—the lack of running water, the lack of outbuildings, the lack of a phone—made the job that much harder. Pancho had always enjoyed physical labor, but this was different. This was a seven-day-a-week commitment to chores both grueling and tedious: watering the horses, currying them, cleaning their hooves, cleaning out the corrals, hauling in alfalfa, caring for the dogs, mending fences, burning garbage, repairing machinery—the list was endless. Pancho couldn't do it all. She didn't *want* to do it all.

She could not even take care of herself. Accustomed to having a cook all her life, Pancho could do little more in the kitchen than open a can. Often she let days go by without having a regular meal. When her hunger was too great to ignore, she drove into Cantil or Mojave and ate at a diner, or she dropped in on a friend and raided the refrigerator. Without someone to pick up after her, the house was not merely a mess but a health hazard, littered with clothes, muddy boots, garbage, open cans of food, boxes of crackers, dirty coffee cups, plates, and dog food. Ted took it all in and knew he had to get Pancho out of there permanently. And Pancho, despite her fierce independence, knew it, too.

Help came by way of a woman she had known since the 1930s. Arlene Milhollin, whom Pancho had helped long ago during a time of need, owned a place ten miles down the road from the north entrance to Edwards, on the outskirts of a town called Boron. She offered it to Pancho, rent free. Boron, named for the nearby borax mine, called itself "the biggest little boom town" because the few hundred residents there claimed they heard more sonic booms than any other people on earth. On all other counts, it was hard to feel any civic pride about Boron, with its scabby hills, parched land slithering with Mojave green rattlesnakes, and street after street of small, sad concrete houses.

Pancho's new house was on the outskirts of town on a half-acre of scorched dirt stubbled with desert weed and brush, an old wooden barn in back, a big, misshapen tamarisk tree in front. The house was a squat, ugly, flat-roofed building, perhaps twenty by twenty-five feet, made of chunks of rock set in concrete troweled over chicken wire. The rock was the color of dried blood. At the front was a porch of sorts, a scrap-lumber-and-plywood extension roofed with a piece of sheet metal. Inside, it was dank and close, light coming in from a few small, grimy windows. A pit had been dug in the dirt floor, courtesy of the former tenant, a garage mechanic who used the building as a place of work, not a residence. Ted and one of his buddies cleaned the place, replastered the old walls, filled in the pit, and put in a floor. They hired a handyman to install wiring and build cupboards. It took weeks to make the place marginally habitable.

Pancho moved in. She was now just blocks from what passed for civilization in that part of the Mojave, close to a post office, a grocery, a diner, even a little hospital. The little stone shack was the humblest place she'd ever lived. It was more primitive than the cabins her hired help had stayed in at Rancho Oro Verde, cruder than the quarters for the stable hands who had worked for her in Pasadena so many years before. But she had running water in the house. She had a phone. She had neighbors. And she was living rent free. Pancho was happy to be rid of the responsibilities of a 640-acre ranch. Ted and the few friends who had watched Pancho's decline at Gypsy Springs were relieved.

Pancho told her faraway friends she was now living in a "little half-hacienda." She said it without irony and even without bitterness. She knew exactly what kind of a place it was, and although she didn't care in the least about appearances, she was not eager for others to know her true circumstances. She would live quietly in Boron with an unlisted phone number.

She would also live messily, as usual. Soon the yard of the little half-hacienda was home to an assortment of rabbits, goats, horses, and dogs. She milked the goats—enjoying the fresh milk she had acquired a taste for decades before when a doctor suggested her infant son would thrive on it—and treated them as pets too, often shoehorning one or two of them into the back of her Volkswagen when she went visiting. Her beautiful horses from Gypsy Springs had been stabled at a friend's ranch while she was in the hospital and during her recovery. But she could not stand to be away from them permanently. Once she was settled in the stone house, she had several trucked to Boron, even though a local ordinance made it illegal to quarter them in town. The sheriff came out to tell her so and fined her. Pancho paid as much attention to him as she did to most people in authority.

Inside, the tiny house was in permanent disarray. When Ted Tate came to check on her one day, he found a pile of opened cans in the corner of the kitchen area. "You've got to clean this place up," he told Pancho. "Look," she said, "where I grew up, I had people to wait on me and do these things. I never learned to cook and clean house, and I'll be damned if I'm going to learn it now." Ted shook his head. Then, at his own expense, he hired a housekeeper to come to Pancho's every two weeks and keep things from getting completely out of hand.

Pancho spent her days quietly. "I have been going along slowly," she wrote to a friend, "goofing off somewhat but not raising any cane [*sic*]." She took up knitting, an unlikely hobby for a woman so disdainful of domestic activities. But her mother had taught her to knit and embroider when she was a teenager, and she liked to have something to do with her hands as she sat at home or in the living rooms of the few friends she visited. She spent much of her day caring for her animals, expanding her menagerie to include Yorkshire terriers, which she began breeding with the idea of starting a business. Yorkies had a reputation as "old ladies' dogs" because they were small and cute and owners tended to put little bows in their hair. But they were also independent, assertive, and intelligent. Pancho doted on them, sharing her cramped quarters with dozens of them, letting them sleep on her bed at night, stashing them in the backseat of her car—along with the occasional goat—when she did her errands.

She might have made a go of her business, which she named PeeBee Kennels, had she not had such a hard time parting with the dogs she bred. She bought the first Yorkies as a business investment, or so she told herself, but they were soon her friends and loyal companions, just as dogs had been throughout her life, from the big police dog that had been by her bedside when she gave birth to Billy to the Chihuahua she outfitted with a parachute in the old days to the Dalmatian that flew with her to Mexico so many times. Her closest human friends these days, the ones she knew she could depend on, the ones who never tired of her stories, were two younger men: Ted Tate and an airplane nut named Walt Geisen.

Walt was a big, good-looking, mustachioed man who worked at Edwards as an engineering supervisor for General Electric. He had met Pancho in 1953 when, on a quick trip to the base, he visited the Happy Bottom Riding Club just before its demise. Five years later, he and his family moved to Lancaster, and Walt found himself working at GE with Pancho's son, Billy. Like Ted, Walt was fascinated by the old wing-and-a-prayer days, and it wasn't long before Pancho started coming to the Geisens' house to spin yarns. It was her habit to drop by at least once a week, seemingly by chance, but always at the dinner hour. June, Walt's wife, would invariably ask her to stay for a meal. Pancho would express surprise at being asked, as if, week after week, she hadn't planned it this way. But she repaid them with stories. All the Geisens got an education of one kind or another around the dinner table when Pancho was a guest.

One night she dropped by just as the family was leaving to go out to a Chinese restaurant for their son's fourteenth birthday. "I sure love Chinese food," Pancho told Walt when she heard their destination. Of course, she was invited along. At the restaurant, Walt accidentally spilled tea on her. "Oh, darn," she said, grabbing for a napkin. "Oh, hell," she said, a little louder. Then she turned to Tim, the fourteen-year-old. "Well, Tim," she said, "you're old enough to know I was really gonna say, 'Oh, shit.' "

Walt was accustomed to Pancho's language. It took him a bit longer to get used to some of her cruder ways. One afternoon, on a trip to Bakersfield—Walt took on the job of chauffeuring Pancho back and forth to attend to legal affairs—Pancho turned to him. "Pull over," she said, "I gotta take a leak." Then this seventy-year-old woman got out of the car, pulled down her dirty dungarees, and squatted by the highway. Walt couldn't believe it. He didn't know whether to gasp or laugh or maybe put his foot on the gas pedal and get the hell out of there. In the end, he accepted her behavior, as all her friends had to if they wanted to remain her friends. In the end, her antics were turned into stories he would tell for years.

Ted Tate and his family also had to learn to accept the rougher parts of their new friend. On a car trip Ted and his wife, Cecilia, took with Pancho to meet an old-timer who had been a cameraman for Howard Hughes, Pancho started telling some colorful story. When she came to the profane part, she stopped, and started all over again, looking for a way to clean it up in front of Ted's wife. Then she talked her way into the offending part again, and again stopped herself. "I've been around the Air Force for twenty years," Cecilia finally told her. "I've heard every word in the book, so you don't have to monitor your language anymore." Pancho gave her a sweet smile. "I'm glad to know that," she said, "because I've been having a helluva time cleaning up these fuckin' stories."

Ted spent a lot of time with Pancho, roaring around the desert in his convertible T-Bird, driving too fast, skidding around curves, spewing gravel as they went. They would stop for something to eat at the Wagon Wheel Café or just hunker down in the desert sand while Pancho spun the tales Ted never tired of hearing. One day he drove her into Los Angeles, where her movie connections got her into the commissary at Universal Studios. She was just tucking into a free meal when a big guy came up and put his hand on her shoulder.

"Pancho, you remember me?" the big guy asked. She looked up at him for a moment.

"Yes, you're Marion Morrison," she said.

"I'm more than that," the big guy said. "I'm John Wayne." The Duke had camped out at Pancho's Pasadena mansion back in the mid-1920s, when he was a USC student on a football scholarship. She gave him another quick look.

"Well, big fuckin' deal," she said. "Now let me finish my lunch."

Ted and Walt were Pancho's escorts whenever she needed one. Ted had spread the word around Edwards and throughout the local aviation community that Pancho was still around and still her old self. After her "rediscovery" at Pancho Barnes Day at the base, more invitations to speak started to come her way. Accompanied by one of her two handsome escorts, Pancho spoke at local banquets for the Society of Flight Test Engineers, the Silver Wings Club, and the Experimental Aircraft Association. She was the featured speaker at the fiftieth anniversary celebration of the McDonnell-Douglas Aircraft Company. Ted and Pancho worked out a shtick for these speaking engagements. He would introduce her gravely and formally, as one of the pioneers of the field. She would, gravely and formally, recite a bit about early flying. Then she would take a deep breath and launch into one of her outrageously raunchy stories. Ted, sitting next to the podium, would act shocked and flustered. He loved being part of the act. He loved watching the looks on the faces of the men and women sitting at the banquet tables. Usually, after a long moment of silence, the room erupted in laughter.

Pancho told good stories. She was, in her late sixties and early seventies, as quick-witted, funny, and foulmouthed as she had ever been. She loved to talk about her cross-country jaunts in open-cockpit planes, flying by dead reckoning and landing in pastures, or about her speed-racing days, when two hundred miles an hour was faster than any human being had ever traveled, or about her stunt-flying adventures, when pilots routinely risked their lives for fifty dollars. She was living history, and the audiences loved it. They sat, rapt, while she gossiped about the people she had known in her eventful life: Amelia Earhart, Howard Hughes, Erich von Stroheim, Kirk Kerkorian, Paul Mantz—friends to her, legends to her audience.

Soon Pancho began to be invited to less formal functions at the base: change-of-command ceremonies, promotions, parties to celebrate birthdays, arrivals, and departures. She attended a farewell party for the base commander and a number of going-away parties for officers leaving for tours of duty in Vietnam. At one such party at the officers' club in the spring of 1970, she decided to go all out and appear in a skirt for the first time in no one knew how long. She had her black curly wig done up in a fancy hairdo. She carefully applied blue eye shadow and clipped on long, spangled earrings. She wore a long, multicolored silk blouse over a dark blue five-inches-above-the-knee miniskirt. Her "false bosoms," as she wrote to a friend, were "wreathed in ornate chains," her legs "encased in silk elastic stockings which took out all the knotting muscles and veins." Everyone circled around, looking her over, making just the kind of fuss she had hoped they'd make. A general came rushing over. "I heard the news," he said, "and I had to come over to look at you." Later, when everyone was seated at the dinner table, the new chief test pilot, who was replacing a Vietnam-bound officer named Gus Julian, announced: "Pancho Barnes is here tonight, and she took off her pants for Gus Julian." The audience hooted and clapped until Pancho stood up, feigning modesty. She was at the top of her form.

One of the very best parties was Pancho's own seventieth birthday bash, thrown in the summer of 1971 at the commanding general's quarters, with Jimmy Doolittle, Buzz Aldrin, and a number of other famous pilots in attendance. It was a gorgeous night, with the August moon illuminating the deep, well-irrigated green of the base's golf course. There was drinking and conversation and much toasting of the honored guest. When it was Pancho's turn to say something, she looked out the window at the full moon. "Well," she said, "I never thought that on my seventieth birthday I'd be looking at the moon with the man beside me who walked on it." Aviation had come a long way since the Mystery Ship.

Pancho drew strength from all this attention. She took off in her Volkswagen, four dogs in the backseat, and attended three successive U.S. National Aerobatics championships in Fort Worth. She worked with Walt Geisen planning a major event to help raise $250,000 to build an aviation museum at the Lancaster airport, using her contacts to gather luminaries like Al Boyd and Jimmy Doolittle for the kickoff fund-raiser. She tried to reconnect with her son. Billy had gone on to marriage number three, this one to a Chinese woman named Shouling whom he had met overseas. He had started his own aviation business at the local airport. Mother and son rarely saw each other. Even when they lived together at Rancho Pancho for those many years, their relationship had been distant and sometimes stormy. Now, Pancho told Walt Geisen, Billy's birthday was coming up, and the mother wanted to do something for her son. Walt threw a party at his own home and happily presided over the reconciliation. The bond between Pancho and Billy further strengthened when the two of them, along with Shouling, attended an antique airplane auction in a hangar at the Orange County airport outside Los Angeles. Up for bid was Pancho's old Mystery Ship, the sleek, low-winged beauty that had once been the fastest civilian airplane in the world. Now it was a wreck, in need of hundreds of hours of repairs. But still, when the auctioneer put it up for bid, paddles went up all over the room, with the bidding continuing briskly for many minutes. Then, one by one, the active bidders dropped out, lowering their paddles as they looked toward Billy Barnes. The word had spread, person to person, row by row, among the five hundred gathered in the cavernous hangar that Pancho Barnes, the legendary Pancho Barnes, original owner of the Mystery Ship, was in the audience and that her son was bidding on the plane. When the auctioneer brought down the gavel on Billy's final bid of $4,300, the crowd stood and applauded.

With the old racing plane back in the family's possession, and Billy set to restore it to its former glory, Pancho got the notion that she would take to the skies again. She imagined flying the Mystery Ship to air shows all around the country. She signed up for lessons at Billy's Lancaster airport school, but the going was tougher than she had expected. There was new technology in the cockpit; there were new radio procedures, new FAA requirements, complex airspace regulations. Pancho struggled along, wearing out one instructor after another. A more opinionated, truculent student would have been hard to find. "I am having an unhappy time. . . ." she wrote to an acquaintance. "Also have to pass a written exam for my license. Hate to study!" It took Pancho months to get a new student pilot certificate. She would need to undergo medical tests to qualify for a regular certificate, and she balked at that, undoubtedly suspecting that she wouldn't pass. She never went for the physical exam. The lessons became more sporadic. Then they stopped altogether. Pancho's days of piloting were over.

<hr />

She may have been living a quieter life now, but her legal and financial dealings were as manic as ever. Pancho was a naturally, energetically contentious woman, and now she had time on her hands. In between the banquets, the weekly dinners with the Geisens, and the wild desert rides with Ted Tate, she was lonely, an aging woman living alone and close to poverty. All the property she had won in the divorce settlement did her little good. She couldn't sell it. It was too heavily mortgaged and had too many liens on it. All she could do was try to scrape together enough money to keep the mortgages afloat and feed her remaining horses.

What she needed was a cause to animate her, a battle that might net some cash. She found it in June 1971, when she filed suit against the Bank of America for stopping payment on a fifty-dollar money order. She insisted that she had paid for the money order. The bank claimed that a teller mistakenly did not charge her. Pancho parlayed this book-keeping confusion into an enormous civil lawsuit, asking for $135,000 in damages for "defamation of character, breach of contract, libel, slander and intentionally causing emotional distress." She also claimed in three succeeding causes of action that the bank issued the stop-payment order "with intent to menace, intimidate, frighten and in-jure . . . and that said acts were done maliciously and oppressively." But the claim that elevated the lawsuit to prominence was Pancho's de-mand for punitive damages of nine-tenths of one percent of the bank's net worth. That would have been in the neighborhood of $630 million. Pancho was being an opportunist here, no doubt, but she was also truly offended and embarrassed. When the bank teller determined that she had given Pancho too much change, essentially not charging her for the money order—that was, at least, the teller's story—she called Billy Barnes to help straighten out the matter, because Pancho had an un-listed phone number. On the phone, the teller implied that Pancho had "shortchanged the bank" or "robbed the bank"—or so Pancho claimed in court. Her financial situation was so precarious that she felt the stop payment hurt both her credit and her reputation.

The bank fought the case for three and a half years, spending thou-sands of dollars filing motions and countermotions in Kern County Superior Court. When the legal maneuverings were finally exhausted, the case went to trial with Pancho, as usual, acting as her own attorney. Legal briefs were duly filed, and although the judge had up to ninety days to consider the matter, it took him only a few to hand down his de-cision. Judge P. R. Borton, the same man who had ruled for Pancho in her divorce, now ruled for her again—but in a very limited manner. The bank's action was "a flagrant violation of a properly executed and performed contract," Judge Borton ruled. On that score, he awarded Pancho $500, but he dismissed all the other complaints. There would be no enormous settlement, no tapping the net worth of one of the wealthiest institutions in California. "I wish I had gotten $50,000, $100,000, $1 million or $3 million," Pancho told a newspaper reporter after she heard Judge Borton's decision. But, she quickly and characteristically added: "At least I took the Bank of America to court and beat them. That'll deflate them some!"

She could have used the money. Unable to support herself from week to week, she entered into a complex deal with Mount Shasta Mining Company, giving the company title to all the property and mineral rights she owned in exchange for a small monthly stipend. That was what she lived on. She borrowed money from Billy to buy the Boron house. Occasionally she would win some judgment or another in county court—her legal machinations were constant—but whatever money came her way she spent immediately and impulsively. Driving home from Bakersfield with Walt Geisen after learning she had won a judgment, she instructed him to stop at a car dealership. Minutes later, she had put a down payment on a station wagon. When she won another small judgment, she spent it all on a television set for Billy.

Pancho may have given up on her dream to fly the Mystery Ship again, but she had not given up dreaming. She planned to buy a big horse trailer and raise a special kind of quarter horse. She planned to buy land in Mexico and raise papayas. She planned to build a self-contained desert city with its own airstrip and a tram to take guests to a five-sided restaurant perched atop a butte, a project worthy of the granddaughter of Thaddeus Lowe. She had the ambition. She had the ideas. All she needed was the money. She hired a lawyer named Jack Bohan to sue Mount Shasta to get back the titles to her property. If she could do that and somehow—she hadn't figured out how, yet—pay off the liens, she would be on her feet again.

Arguing that Pancho had deeded away her land out of desperation and that Mount Shasta had taken advantage of her grave circumstances, Bohan managed to win the case in 1972. But she knew that as soon as the state and her other creditors learned the property was hers again, they would go after her. She was in immediate danger of losing to foreclosure and forced tax sales all that she had just regained. She needed to get those taxes paid off fast. In stepped her loyal friends Walt and Ted. Between them, they took out $10,000 in personal loans and turned over the money to Pancho for her taxes. In exchange, she deeded over to them a few parcels of land as security. She deeded over other parcels to Billy and Shouling and another local couple, trying to stay one step ahead of foreclosure on those properties. At the same time, she was supposed to deed over land to her lawyer, Jack Bohan, to cover his legal fees. The two had signed an agreement back in 1969 that Bohan would receive a 20 percent interest in any damages received and any property recovered. With the case won, Bohan hand-delivered the paperwork to Pancho, forms she would need to file to transfer the deeds. Pancho apparently rewrote the paperwork before she handed it in, cutting Bohan out of the deal. He took her to court immediately and won a major judgment, receiving for his services the deed to the 640-acre Gypsy Springs parcel.

Pancho used her $10,000 loan to pay off debts on some of the property, then sold some of the remaining property to raise money to repay Walt and Ted. After all the litigation, after winning the divorce case against Mac, after winning the case against Mount Shasta, Pancho ended up with a few small parcels of land. She had been a wealthy woman when the government settled her condemnation suit fifteen years before. Now, for the third time in her life, she had run through a fortune. But this time, she hadn't had much fun doing it.

— ⚑ —

Late in her life, people enjoyed the legend of Pancho Barnes, but most shied away from the person herself. She was a daunting figure in her early seventies, filthy and unkempt unless there was a party to go to, a startlingly black wig perched oddly, often backward, atop her head, her skin mottled with age spots and almost forty years' worth of sun damage, her neck extraordinarily full and fleshy, sagging below the second button on her Western shirt. She had all her mental faculties, but age had made her more argumentative. It seemed she quarreled with just about everyone except her few loyal friends. She was truly happy only when tooling around the desert with Ted or eating dinner at the Geisens' or on those special occasions when she attended banquets and parties. Otherwise, she didn't like people coming around the house and often either didn't answer the door or shouted them away. On the other hand, when she went to the grocery store in Mojave, she was, out of loneliness, a little too talkative, a little too eager to bend someone's ear, alienating strangers, who backed away and then went home to regale their friends with stories about the great Pancho Barnes whom they had just seen in person over at the Safeway. She remembered the people who were no longer part of her life, her erstwhile buddies from the Happy Bottom Riding Club days, the men who had depended on her good and generous nature to make it through anxious times, the men who had long ago forgotten her. She didn't talk about it, but she felt the betrayal keenly. It came out in her contentiousness. It came out in her inability to truly trust anyone but her dogs.

But in many ways, Pancho's behavior in her seventies was just as it had been in her twenties. She was brash and outspoken, profane and impulsive, deeply self-centered yet generous beyond her means. She reveled in ownership—land, horses, dogs—but so neglected the concomitant responsibilities that she continually sabotaged her own efforts. She was, as she had been since her days as a rebellious teen at Bishop School in La Jolla, a character, a woman who cut a wide swath through life, a person who lived as if life had no consequences. When she was young and wealthy, the darling of the Los Angeles press, the confidante of exciting and powerful men, her brash ways were often admired, her uniqueness was her charm. But now that she was old and living in a shack with only dogs for company, the same character traits were interpreted differently. Now she was a crazy old lady. Now some people thought she was drunk or on drugs or getting senile.

When the Mount Shasta suit was settled and she had a few dollars in her pocket, she took an extended trip to Mexico, staying in Guaymas as in the old days. It was August and beastly hot, but she wrote to Walt that she was having a great time. It was hard to come home. When she did, she seemed to have left something behind, some vital life force. She sequestered herself in her house. Sometimes no one saw her for weeks.

⊰✦⊱

Toward the end of March 1975, Pancho drove herself to the little thirteen-bed hospital in Boron, complaining of chest pains. But she walked out before the doctor on duty had a chance to examine her. A week or so later, she was set to speak at a luncheon sponsored by the Officers' Wives Club on base. She had spoken to the group several times before, wisely reining in her profanities, entertaining the women instead with tales of stunt flying and speed racing. She was such a popular guest that, for the first time in its history, the club had opened the luncheon to husbands as well. There was a good crowd waiting for her, every seat at every table taken. They waited for ten minutes, twenty, a half-hour, an hour. But she never showed. When the luncheon was over, one of the women called Billy Barnes, asking him if he knew where his mother was. Few people had Pancho's unlisted phone number. Billy said he didn't know, but he'd call over there and see what was going on. The phone at Pancho's stone shack rang and rang. Finally, Billy called the local sheriff's deputy, asking him to drive by the house.

The deputy saw her car out front and some sick-looking animals out in the yard. When he knocked, there was no answer. He circled the small house, peering in the windows as he went. He saw dogs everywhere and something lying on the bed. He went back to his cruiser and radioed Pierre Poudevigne, the county's animal-control officer. There was no way the deputy was going to break into a house full of dogs. Poudevigne arrived, assessed the situation, and broke a window to get into the house. As soon as the glass shattered, as soon as he stuck his head and shoulders through the opening, he knew something was wrong. He shimmied back out of the opening, waiting for air to circulate in the house. He lit a cigar to mask the smell. Then he went back in.

Someone had turned up the heat above eighty degrees. The kitchen faucet was running. The sink was overflowing, and three inches of water covered the floor. Pierre slogged through it, stepping around and over dogs, more than fifty of them. Fifteen had starved to death. He made his way to the tiny bedroom where Pancho's body lay on the bed. At least he thought it was Pancho's body. He could hardly recognize human features. There was dried blood all over the bed. Pancho's right arm, below the elbow, was gone. The dogs, he thought. Dogs are loyal and true, but when they get hungry, very hungry, they eat. He figured Pancho had been dead for at least a week, more than enough time for a dog to get very hungry.

After the autopsy, the coroner declared heart disease the cause of death, clinically noting the "advanced decomposition" and the "traumatic fracture of forearm, right." The death was ruled a natural one, but a number of people questioned the findings. Poudevigne was one of them. He didn't pretend to know what had happened, but the whole situation struck him as strange. If a person wanted to decompose a body as quickly as possible, turning up the heat and flooding the place was the way to do it. Was there foul play? He thought so. Richard McKendry, Mac's son, whom Pancho had helped raise, told everyone who would listen that "they did her in," "they" being transients she had hired to do some work around the place. Others concocted theories about the Mafia sending hit men out to Boron, about Pancho threatening to publish the names of certain men who had frequented the hostesses' quarters at the Happy Bottom Riding Club, men who might not want to read about their exploits two decades later. Few were willing to believe that this colorful, eccentric woman had just clutched her heart and fallen, dead, on her bed. But despite the stories, there was no further investigation.

Pancho had been scheduled to be a guest of honor at the fifth annual Barnstormers Reunion on April 5, 1975. This was the group Walt Geisen had put together, with Pancho's assistance, to help establish a local aviation museum. Now that banquet became Pancho's unofficial funeral service, with her old friend Lieutenant General James H. "Jimmy" Doolittle delivering the eulogy. Pancho, he said to the quiet and respectful crowd, had a "heart as big as a ham." She "put great store by courage, honor, and integrity. . . . She was outspoken and she said exactly what she thought and believed." Then Doolittle paused a moment. "You know," he said, smiling, "I can just see her up there this minute. . . . She is probably remarking to some old and dear friend who preceded her, 'I wondered what the little old bald-headed bastard was going to say.' " The crowd laughed. That would be Pancho, all right. They could just hear her. Then everyone in the room stood for a toast.

After the eulogy, the scheduled program dragged on, with a drunken stand-up comic from Las Vegas laying bombs. Ted Tate, the master of ceremonies, sat disconsolately, thinking about how different the event would have been had Pancho been there to tell her stories. Then he had an idea. He'd do the shtick without her, in honor of her. He stood at the podium, hands holding the rostrum, head bowed. Everyone quieted down, expecting another eulogy. As dramatically as he knew how, Ted told how Pancho had planned to tell the crowd a very special story that night. "I know it's late, and we're all getting a little tired and a little drunk, but would you like to hear Pancho's story?" The crowd roared *yes*. Then Ted launched into one of the filthiest, most profane stories in Pancho's repertoire, a story involving naked women and peach ice cream and words most of the men in the room had never uttered aloud. There was silence, then titters, then loud and nervous applause. In a tight knot, the directors of the new museum marched up to the podium and demanded Ted's resignation from the board.

The morning after what he came to think of as "this indiscretion," Ted called the commanding officer at Edwards asking him for clearance to fly over the site of the Happy Bottom Riding Club. He and Billy wanted to scatter Pancho's ashes there. That's what she had said she'd wanted. The general, Bob Rushworth, gave the okay. But later in the day, one of the men involved in the museum project called the Los Angeles media and told them of the plans. Network reporters quickly descended on Edwards, asking permission to enter the old club site to take photographs. Rushworth called Ted in a huff. "I was going to let you do this as a personal favor," he told Ted. "But it's right in the path of our low-altitude flight test corridor and you can't do it." Ted drove to the base and begged the general. Okay, he finally said, but just one pass.

Billy fired up his little Cessna, and with Ted in the passenger seat, he flew out of Fox Airport in Lancaster. "Let's fly the old gal around the valley one last time," Billy said. They did. Then they radioed the base for permission to make their one pass. They got it, and began to bank into a turn. As Billy flew, Ted tried to get the top off the brass urn that held Pancho's ashes, but it was stuck. Billy kept circling while Ted struggled with the urn. Now Edwards was on the radio telling them that their time was up, that they needed to get out of military airspace right away. "I can't read you," Ted said into the mouthpiece. Billy kept flying. From the side window, he saw the huge, flat expanse of the dry lake, the flattest place on earth, disappear behind him. Directly below was what used to be Rancho Oro Verde. He could make out the ruins, the four-tiered stone fountain that used to be in the motel courtyard, the remains of the corrals, the crumbling foundation of the old dairy building. The desert was reclaiming it.

Finally, Ted got the top off the urn and slid the window open. Edwards was screaming at them to get out of there. He raised the urn and upturned it. The ashes were the same color as the desert floor. They fell slowly, like snowflakes. Then a crosswind caught them, and Ted and Billy watched as the remains of Pancho Barnes flew back through the Cessna's window and into the cockpit.

Epilogue

Pancho lived like a pauper for the last years of her life, but it turned out that there was enough money and property in her estate to be worth a fight. Her last will and testament, dated January 8, 1958, left everything to Mac. Pancho had written it four and a half years before she served him with divorce papers.

But it was more than the money—about $70,000 worth of real estate, personal property, and money she was owed—that motivated her son, Billy, to hire a lawyer and file a six-part objection contesting the will. It made little sense to Billy and to many of Pancho's friends that the man she had publicly reviled for the last fourteen years of her life, the man she had accused in court of defrauding her, threatening her life with a gun, and committing adultery, should now be entitled to her estate. As Billy pointed out, anger clearly showing through the legalese, a California Superior Court judge had ruled unequivocally against Mac years before, during the divorce hearings. Mac had not gotten his hands on Pancho's estate then. Why should he benefit now?

Billy also claimed that his mother had destroyed a duplicate copy of the 1958 will with the intent of revoking it and had handwritten a new will in February 1970. But that will, if it ever existed, was never found.

After more than a year and a half of legal wrangling, the son and the ex-husband settled out of court. Mac retained his status under the 1958 will and paid Billy $22,500 to stop legal action.

Less than four years later, Billy Barnes was flying a World War II–vintage fighter plane from Fox Airport in Lancaster to Edwards Air Force Base when the ship suddenly and inexplicably nose-dived into the desert northwest of town. It exploded on impact, starting a fire that burned more than ten acres before it was controlled. Billy was killed instantly. He was fifty-eight years old.

In the spring of 1980, five years after Pancho's death, Edwards Flight Test Center Commander Major General Philip Conley and his wife, Shirley, began what has become an annual tradition by hosting a party out on the ruins of Pancho's old place between the two dry lakes. Chuck Yeager, Pete Everest, "Fish" Salmon, and many of Pancho's old Happy Bottom Riding Club buddies were there to eat barbecue and drink to her memory. The next year, more than four hundred people attended the party.

In November 1980, Secretary of the Air Force Hans Mark officially dedicated the Pancho Barnes Room at the Edwards Air Force Base Officers' Club.

A few months later, the ruins of Pancho's desert oasis, which sit in the middle of the Edwards Air Force gunnery range, were placed on the National Register of Historic Places.

Source Notes

Prologue

I was able to re-create the Experimental Aircraft Association banquet and the events leading up to it with the considerable assistance of Walter Geisen, who kept personal logs of his activities during the time, made an audiotape of the event itself, and later self-published a memoir, *A Story of the Life and Times of Walt Geisen.* My correspondence and interviews with Geisen throughout 1997 and 1998 provided additional information. Geisen also provided a photograph of Pancho at the podium. Additional detail comes from a Dec. 8, 1980, interview conducted with one of Pancho's friends, Lois Hubbard, by James Young and Ted Bear of the Air Force Flight Test Center (AFFTC) History Office, Edwards Air Force Base (AFFTC History Office collection, Edwards Air Force Base, Edwards, Cal.).

Chapter 1: To Whom the Future Belongs

Information on the Dominguez Hills aviation show comes from posters, pamphlets, and ephemera in the private collection of Jon Wm. Aldrich as well as author's interview with Aldrich (Jan. 17, 1998).

The life of Pancho's grandfather, Thaddeus Lowe, is detailed in Russell J. Brownbach, "Commentary on Life and Achievements of T.S.C. Lowe," *The Bulletin of the Historical Society of Montgomery County,* vol. XX, no. 1 (Fall 1975), pp. 3–32; George Wharton James, "One Man's Life," *National* magazine, August 1908; William Jones Rhees, "Reminiscences of Ballooning in the Civil War," *Chautauquan,* June 1898, pp. 257–62; J. A. Vye, "Thaddeus S. C. Lowe" (undated, typed manuscript in Pasadena Public Library Lowe/Barnes collection); and Thelma Clark and Patricia Copley, *Pasadena Oral History Project,* interviews with Dorothy Dobbins Freeman (Pasadena: Pasadena Historical Society, 1980, 1982).

The best material concerning the building of Mount Lowe Railroad can be found in Charles Seims, *Mount Lowe: The Railway in the Clouds* (San Marino, Cal.: Golden West Books, 1976) and Maria Schell Burden, *Professor T.S.C. Lowe and His Mountain Railway* (Los Angeles: Borden Publishing Co., 1993).

Newspaper accounts, both contemporaneous and historical, were also helpful: Pasadena *Star-News*, June 9, 1886, Jan. 29, 1894, May 5, 1912, Aug. 23, 1924, and July 7, 1951; Los Angeles *Express*, Jan. 16, 1913.

Pasadena is a much written about city. The following books were of enormous help in reconstructing the past life and times of this place: Jane Apostol, *South Pasadena 1888–1988: A Centennial History* (South Pasadena, Cal.: South Pasadena Public Library, 1987); Thomas D. Carpenter, *Pasadena: Resort Hotels and Paradise* (Pasadena: Castle Green Times, 1984); Lon Chapin, *Thirty Years in Pasadena* (Pasadena: Southwest Publishing Co., 1929); Jennie Hollingsworth Giddings, *I Can Remember Early Pasadena* (privately printed, 1949); Maureen R. Michelson and Michael R. Dressler, eds., *Pasadena: One Hundred Years* (Pasadena: New Safe Press, 1985); Joyce Y. Pinney, *A Pasadena Chronology 1769–1977* (Pasadena: Pasadena Public Library, 1978); Ann Scheid, *Pasadena, Crown of the Valley* (Northridge, Cal.: Windsor Publications, 1986); Elizabeth R. L. Vail, "Pasadena's Crown Jewels" (typewritten manuscript, 1941, Pasadena Public Library).

Chapter 2: An Overexuberance of Spirit

Pancho chronicles some of the events of her childhood in the untitled, typed notes she compiled in the 1960s, with an eye toward writing an autobiography (AFFTC History Office collection). She also testified about some details of her childhood when she took the witness stand in *U.S.A. v. 360 Acres of Land* (case no. 1253-ND, U.S. District Court, Southern District of California, Northern Division; full files located in National Archives and Records Administration's San Bruno, California, repository). Taped interviews with Pancho (interviewer unknown) in 1970 (private collection of David Chisholm) also proved very helpful, as did the Dorothy Dobbins Freeman oral history transcript and an untitled biographical sketch of "Mrs. Florence Lowe Barnes," 1930, in the Pasadena Public Library collection.

Throughout her life, Pancho told writers stories about herself. Some of the best anecdotes about her childhood can be found in Barbara Mitchell, "Pancho Barnes: A Legend in Our Lifetime," *Hi-Desert Spectator/Antelope Valley Spectator*, part I (vol. 2, no. 1, Jan.–Feb. 1963); Don Kuhns, "Pancho Barnes: A Legend in Her Own Time," *VA Aviation*, Oct.–Dec. 1980; and Grover Ted Tate, *The Lady Who Tamed Pegasus: The Story of Pancho Barnes* (n.p.: Maverick, 1984). Tate's book was a particularly rich source, as it is a series of rollicking anecdotes, complete with off-color dialogue, that Pancho told Tate toward the end of her life. I am also indebted to the work of Barbara Hunter Schultz, who preceded me as Pancho's biographer. Her *Pancho: The Biography of Florence Lowe Barnes* (Lancaster, Cal.: Little Buttes Publishing Co., 1996) provides an excellent chronology of Pancho's life.

Details on Pancho's schooling came from the Westridge School for Girls fall 1981 catalog; records and ephemera provided by Sister Rose Frances of Ramona Convent; Johnson Heumann Research Associates, "Alhambra Historic and Cultural Resources Survey" (Alhambra, Cal.: Alhambra Public Library, 1985); and a memoir written by the woman who roomed with Pancho at Bishop School, Ursula Greenshaw Mandel, *I Live My Life* (New York: Exposition Press, 1965).

Chapter 3: An Imaginable Future

The best sources of information on Pancho's early married life are her own typed aubiographical notes and the stories she told Ted Tate, which he later published in his book, *The Lady Who Tamed Pegasus.* Schultz's *Pancho* repeats many of those stories and adds a few. News of Pancho's prenuptial celebrations and marriage can be found in the Pasadena *Evening Post,* Dec. 10, 1920, and Dec. 23, 1920, and in *California Southland,* January 1921.

Chapter 4: Becoming Pancho

Details of Pancho's married life, amorous adventures, and Hollywood work can be found in her autobiographical notes; the 1970 taped interview in the David Chisholm collection; Mitchell, "Pancho Barnes: A Legend in Our Lifetime," part III (vol. 2, no. 3, April 1963); and Tate's *Pegasus* and Schultz's *Pancho.*

Pancho's South American trip is chronicled in part IV of Mitchell's series, *Hi-Desert Spectator/Antelope Valley Spectator* (vol. 2, no. 4, May–June 1963); Don Kuhns, "The One and Only Pancho Barnes," *In Touch* (Lancaster, Cal.: Antelope Valley College, 1969–70); and Schultz's *Pancho.* The love poem from Don Shumway Rockwell, from the William E. Barnes collection, is quoted in Schultz.

Pancho offers her own account of her Mexico adventure in the 1970 taped interview. Roger Chute, her companion, offers his account in "The Unknown Island," Spokane *Spokesman-Review* magazine, March 11, 1951, and in his autobiographical notes in the Roger Chute collection at the Washington State Historical Society. Chute's letter to Pancho, Feb. 16, 1930 (Aldrich collection), also supplied details. The Mexico adventure is perhaps the most written about part of Pancho's life. Virtually every article about her mentions it. Particularly helpful were Mitchell, "Legend," part I, and Kuhns, "The One and Only Pancho Barnes."

Chapter 5: Flying

I am indebted to Diane Ackerman's lovely book *On Extended Wings* (New York: Charles Scribner's Sons, 1988) for its insights into what it means to be airborne. Numerous books on aviation history, and particularly women's role in it, enriched my understanding. Most include biographical information and/or references to Pancho. Notable are Jean Adams and Margaret Kimball, *Heroines of the Sky* (Garden City, N.Y.: Doubleday, Doran & Co., 1942); Elizabeth S. Bell, *Sisters of the Wind: Voices of Early Women Aviators* (Pasadena: Trilogy Books, 1994); Wendy Boarse, *The Sky's the Limit: Women Pioneers in Aviation* (New York: Macmillan, 1979); John Burke, *Winged Legend: The Story of Amelia Earhart* (New York: G. P. Putnam's Sons, 1970); Mary Cadogan, *Women with Wings: Female Flyers in Fact and Fiction* (Chicago: Academy Chicago Publishers, 1993); Amelia Earhart, *The Fun of It: Random Records of My Own Flying and of Women in Aviation* (New York: The Junior Literary Guild and Brewer, Warren & Putnam, 1932); Dean Jaros, *Heroes Without Legacy: American Airwomen, 1912–1944* (Boulder: University Press of Colorado, 1993); C. V. Glines, "The Remarkable Life of Amelia Earhart," *Aviation History*, July 1997; Henry M. Holden and Lori Griffith, *Ladybirds II: The Continuing Story of American Women in Aviation* (Mount Freedom, N.J.: Black Hawk Publishing Co., 1993); Valerie Moolman, *Women Aloft* (Alexandria, Va.: Time-Life Books, 1981); Charles E. Planck, *Women with Wings* (New York: Harper & Bros., 1942); Doris L. Rich, *Amelia Earhart: A Biography* (Washington and London: Smithsonian Institution Press, 1989); David Roberts, "Men Didn't Have to Prove They Could Fly, but Women Did," *Smithsonian*, Aug. 1994; Elinor Smith, *Aviatrix* (New York: Harcourt, Brace, Jovanovich, 1981); Donna Veca and Skip Mazzio, *Just Plane Crazy: Biography of Bobbi Trout* (Santa Clara, Cal.: Osborne Publishers, 1987). Additionally, the author's interviews with pioneer women aviators Bobbi Trout (Nov. 6, 1997; Jan. 8, 1998) and Fay Gillis Wells (Feb. 5, 1998) were very helpful.

Pancho offers numerous anecdotes about learning to fly in her autobiographical notes and her 1970 taped interview. The author's interview with George Griffith, the brother of one of Pancho's early flying friends, was helpful. Additional details are found in a 1930 biographical sketch in the Pasadena Public Library Barnes file; part III of Mitchell's series, *Hi-Desert Spectator/Antelope Valley Spectator*, vol. 2, no. 3; Kuhns, "The One and Only Pancho Barnes"; Don Downie, "Fabulous Pancho Barnes," *Flying*, March 1949; and Tate, *Pegasus*.

My understanding of Pancho and Rankin's unusual relationship comes from numerous letters they wrote to each other in the late 1920s and early 1930s, all found in the Aldrich collection.

Chapter 6: One of the Boys

For a lively social history of the time and insights into the zeitgeist of the 1920s, I am indebted to Frederick Lewis Allen's *Only Yesterday: An Informal History of the 1920s* (New York: Harper & Bros., 1931).

Pancho offers details of her amorous adventures in her autobiographical notes. The details of her flying adventures come from both her autobiographical notes and her Pilot's Log Book, which provided information about every flight she took from 1928 through 1931 (AFFTC History Office collection). She also testified about her early flying experiences during the *U.S.A. v. 360 Acres* case and spoke about them in the 1970 taped interview. The author's interviews with Fay Gillis Wells, Bobbi Trout, and Elinor Wagner (Jan. 14, 1998) also provided information on flying—and hangar flying—in those days. The Dec. 8, 1980, oral history interview with Lois Hubbard (AFFTC); Morrie Morrison's remembrances, "Florence Lowe Barnes—Aviatrix Known to the Guys as Pancho" (undated, AFFTC History Office collection); anecdotes from Tate's *Pegasus* and Downie's "Fabulous Pancho" (on the Short Snorts), and chronology from Schultz, *Pancho,* all contributed. Pancho comments at length on her stormy relationship with Erich von Stroheim in the 1970 taped interview.

Details of Pancho's experiences as a test pilot and Union Oil promoter are found in her testimony in *U.S.A. v. 360 Acres* (where she also talks about the first time she saw the Muroc homestead she would later purchase), and in Downie, "Fabulous Pancho"; Mitchell, "Legend," part IV (*Hi-Desert Spectator/Antelope Valley Spectator*, vol. 2, no. 4); and Holden and Griffith, *Ladybirds.* Coverage in the *Los Angeles Times* detailed her maximum-load tests and attempts to better the solo endurance record: March 26, 1929; March 28, 1929; March 30, 1929; April 1, 1929.

Pancho wrote about her active social life in both San Marino and Laguna in her autobiographical notes. Schultz, *Pancho,* and Downie, "Fabulous Pancho," have details on her San Marino parties. Descriptions of activities at her Laguna Beach home come from the author's interviews with former Hollywood stuntman John Weld (Dec. 13, 1997), Laguna Beach historian Liz Quilter (Dec. 11, 1997), and George Griffith (Dec. 9, 1997). Weld's *Fly Away Home: Memoirs of a Hollywood Stuntman* (Santa Barbara: Mission Publishing, 1991) added detail. Stories in the *Los Angeles Times* provided a history of the property: "Homes to Be Built on Site That Gave Voice to Roaring 20s," *Los Angeles Times,* Sept. 11, 1995, and "From Estate to Subdivision," *Los Angeles Times,* Nov. 11, 1992. Pancho wrote about her goings-on to a friend, Frank Hawks, on Oct. 30, 1931 (letter in Aldrich collection).

Concerning Pancho's problems with her grandmother over the airport on the Laguna property, see letter, Southern California District Manager Edison Electric Co. to Pancho, July 21, 1928, and Pancho to Laguna Chamber of Commerce, June 22, 1928 (Aldrich collection). The accident is reported in the *Los Angeles Times,* July 7, 1930.

The opening of Grand Central Airport was a major local news story at the time, noted in the *Los Angeles Times,* Feb. 22, 1929, and recapped in a *Los Angeles Times* story on Aug. 23, 1993. Veca's *Just Plane Crazy* has details about the airport opening and the first speed race. The author's interview with Bobbi Trout added material about the event. Mitchell, "Legend," parts III and IV, contains summaries of the race. Details about Roscoe Turner come from C. V. Glines, *Roscoe Turner, Aviation's Master Showman* (Washington, D.C.: Smithsonian Institution Press, 1995). The anecdote about Pancho and Roscoe Turner is told in many places, including Downie, "Fabulous Pancho," and Schultz, *Pancho.*

Chapter 7: Flying Faster

The first Women's Aerial Derby is colorfully and dramatically chronicled in Terry Gwynn-Jones, *The Air Racers* (n.p.: Landsdowne Press, 1983). Pancho writes about her participation in a letter to Glenn Buffington, Feb. 2, 1934 (International Women's Air and Space Museum collection), and to her husband, Rankin, Aug. 29, 1929 (Aldrich collection). Mitchell, "Legend," part IV (*Hi-Desert Spectator/Antelope Valley Spectator*, vol. 2, no. 4), Downie, "Fabulous Pancho," and Schultz, *Pancho,* all contain versions of the story of the race. Burke, *Winged Legend,* focuses on Earhart's participation, but offers general details as well, as does Earhart in *Fun of It.* Text and reproduced newspaper clippings in Veca, *Just Plane Crazy,* helped trace the progress of the race, as did coverage in the *Los Angeles Times,* June 13, 1929, Yuma *Morning Sun,* Aug. 20, 1929, and Wichita *Eagle,* Aug. 25, 1929.

Information about the Travel Air Mystery Ship came from Edward H. Phillips, *Travel Air: Wings Over the Prairie* (Eagan, Minn.: Flying Books International, 1994). Pancho's receipt for the Mystery Ship is in the Aldrich collection, and coverage of the sale is in the *Los Angeles Times,* June 25, 1930.

Pancho's record-breaking 196.19-mile-per-hour flight was covered by the *Los Angeles Times,* Aug. 5, 1930. Newspaper clippings reproduced in Veca, *Just Plane Crazy,* added details, as did an account of the flight in Moolman, *Women Aloft.* On page 61 of the Moolman book is a color reproduction of a magazine advertisement for Union Oil entitled "Fastest mile ever traveled by a Woman . . . !" that capitalizes on Pancho's flight.

Chapter 8: Much Here Revolves Around Me

Details about Pancho's flying adventures in the early 1930s are found in her Pilot's Log; her testimony during *U.S.A. v. 360 Acres;* in her letter to Buffington; in her letters to her husband, May 1, 1931; Nov. 20, 1931; and Sept. 25, 1931 (Aldrich collection); and in the *Los Angeles Times,* Feb. 26, 1930; Oct. 22, 1930, March 31, 1931; and May 4, 1931; and in the Pasadena *Star-News,* Aug. 11, 1930, and Aug. 24, 1931.

Evidence of Pancho's literary efforts was found in the Aldrich collection, which contains notes for the beginning of a book about an airplane pilot, an unpublished two-thousand-word magazine story, several incomplete manuscripts for stories and a poem.

A number of books were helpful on the subject of Hollywood stunt flying: Don Dwiggins, *Hollywood Pilot: The Biography of Paul Mantz* (Garden City, N.Y.: Doubleday, 1967); Don Dwiggins, *The Air Devils: The Story of Balloonists, Barnstormers and Stunt Pilots* (New York: J. B. Lippincott, 1966); Jim and Maxine Greenwood, *Stunt Flying in the Movies* (Blue Ridge Summit, Penna.: Tab Books, 1982); and H. Hugh Wynne, *The Motion Picture Stunt Pilots and Hollywood's Aviation Movies* (Missoula, Mont.: Pictorial Histories Publishing Co., 1987). Richard Griffith, ed., *The Talkies, 1928–1940* (New York: Dover Books, 1971) helped me understand the impact of Howard Hughes's *Hell's Angels*. Thomas Schatz, *The Genius of the System: Hollywood Filmmaking in the Studio Era* (New York: Pantheon, 1988) was an important historical source.

Pancho wrote about her own experiences in the movies and with her fellow stunt pilots (both professional and intimate) in her autobiographical notes. Her testimony in *U.S.A. v. 360 Acres* and the 1970 taped interview also contain details and anecdotes. An article she wrote, "Motion Picture Pilots Formed by Necessity," *The Airline Pilot*, vol. 1, no. 7 (July 15, 1932), details the founding of the Association of Motion Picture Pilots. Don Dwiggins's letter to the *Los Angeles Times*, Dec. 8, 1985; Downie, "Fabulous Pancho," and Kuhns, "Pancho Barnes," are also good sources.

Pancho and Rankin's relationship is reflected in the many letters they sent to each other during this time, especially Pancho to Rankin, Sept. 25, 1931, and Nov. 20, 1931; undated telegram addressed to Rankin at Gramercy Park Hotel, New York; Rankin to Pancho, May 15, 1931, and Nov. 11, 1931. Also, Pancho to Billy, Oct. 22, 1931, and Pancho to Magnus Thomle, March 17, 1931 (all in Aldrich collection).

Pancho's spending habits, her attitude toward money, and her money worries during the Depression are reflected in a variety of receipts for goods and services and several monthly budgets found in the Aldrich collection. Pancho wrote about her money problems to Rankin (May 1, 1931; July 3, 1931; Sept. 19, 1931) as well as to others: Pancho to Cliff Henderson, Aug. 20, 1931; Pancho to H. F. Stowe, March 27, 1931; Pancho to W. A. Hammond, April 15, 1932 (all in the Aldrich collection).

Pancho's health problems are documented in her letter to Rankin, July (?) 1931; her letter to Roger Chute, Feb. 16, 1930; a letter to Rankin from unknown writer, June 17, 1931 (all in Aldrich collection); and stories in the Pasadena *Star-News*, Aug. 8 and 24, 1931.

Chapter 9: Love and Politics

Pancho's political aspirations are documented in the *Los Angeles Times* of May 7, 1932; May 20, 1932; and Aug. 6, 1932. Her campaign brochure (AFFTC

History Office collection) spells out her philosophy and goals. A telegram from Sig Grauman to Pancho, Aug. 11, 1932 (Aldrich collection), mentions her skywriting campaign. Both Tate, *Pegasus*, and Downie, "Fabulous Pancho," provided additional information.

Pancho wrote extensively about her trip to Mexico with Buron Fitts, devoting more than a dozen typewritten pages of her autobiographical notes to these exploits. Other sources include Don Dwiggins, "Happy Bottoms Here We Come!" *The Argosy*, September 1963, and Tate, *Pegasus*.

Information about the formation and various activities of the Women's Air Reserve are preserved in WAR membership lists, rules and regulations, memos, efficiency reports (Aldrich collection), a WAR roll book (AFFTC History Office collection), and contemporaneous newspaper coverage, particularly the Pasadena *Star-News*, Aug. 13, 1935. Veca's *Just Plane Crazy* is an excellent source for information about the group. The author's interviews with Bobbi Trout complemented the written material. Dwiggins, "Happy Bottoms," Holden and Griffith, *Ladybirds II*, and Downie, "Fabulous Pancho," were also helpful.

Chapter 10: Lady of the Dry Lake

Pancho's various property deals are recorded in deeds and transactions housed at the County Clerk's Office, Kern County Courthouse, Bakersfield, California. She talks about her land acquisitions in her testimony during *U.S.A. v. 360 Acres*. The Antelope Valley *Ledger-Gazette*, March 7, 1935, announced (somewhat tardily) Pancho's arrival in the desert.

Information on Granny Nourse came from Schultz, *Pancho*, based on that author's interviews with Nourse in 1989 and 1990.

The early history of Muroc has been thoughtfully preserved by the Muroc Community Inventory (a Legacy Resource Management Project), a collection of transcripts of oral history interviews with many former Muroc homesteaders, conducted in 1994 and 1995 under contract to the AFFTC History Office at Edwards (AFFTC History Office collection). The interviews with Ray Hisquerido, George Adair, Harry Mertz, and Margorie Fourr were especially instructive. Also see Roger G. Hatheway, "Muroc and the Homesteaders," section III, *Historical Overview of Edwards AFB and AFFTC* (undated, AFFTC History Office collection).

The early history of the Muroc airfield is well chronicled in James O. Young, "The Golden Age at Muroc-Edwards," *Journal of the West*, Jan. 1991 (vol. 30, no. 1), and summarized in Steve Pace, *Edwards Air Force Base Experimental Flight Test Center* (Osceola, Wisc.: Motorbooks International, 1994). I owe my understanding of this era, as well as my appreciation of the geography and ecology of the area, to the patient tutelage of Raymond Puffer, AFFTC historian.

The material about Pancho's early years in the desert, how she ran the ranch, the businesses she started, and other topics comes from interviews I conducted. Tony King was an extraordinary source (Dec. 29, 1997; Jan. 3, 1998; Jan. 29, 1998), as was Al Houser (Oct. 14, 1997; Dec. 1, 1998). Other important sources were Mary Fetters (Sept. 21, 1997), Phyllis Walker (Nov. 29, 1997), and Grace Logan (Sept. 21, 1997). Lois Hubbard offered useful information. Pancho herself went into great detail about her early ranch experiences in her testimony during *U.S.A. v. 360 Acres.* Secondary sources include Mitchell, "Legend," part IV (*Hi-Desert Spectator/Antelope Valley Spectator*, vol. 2, no. 4.); Holden and Griffith, *Ladybirds II;* Kuhns, "Pancho"; and "Pancho Barnes: An Original" (typed manuscript, March 1982, produced by the AFFTC History Office and in the Barnes collection there).

Chapter 11: Something Out of Nothing

My interviews with Mary Fetters and Al Houser and correspondence with Carl Bergman were rich sources of information about Pancho's relationships with her desert neighbors. Oral history transcripts of interviews with Betty Morris, Norm Graham, and Bob Jones (part of the Muroc Community Inventory) were also helpful.

Pancho's property transactions and financial difficulties can be traced through deeds, civil suits, and actions all recorded and on file at the Kern County Courthouse, Bakersfield. The sale of her San Marino home is recorded in Los Angeles County records, Los Angeles.

Caroline Dobbins's will, the contests of it, and the record of final distribution (case no. 147937) are on file at the Los Angeles County Archives, Los Angeles. The Pasadena *Star-News*, Aug. 3, 1935, reported on the disposition of the case.

My interviews with Tony King and Otto Tronowsky (Jan. 29, 1998) provided important information about Pancho's participation in the Civilian Pilots Training Program. Pancho outlined the operation herself when she testified in *U.S.A. v. 360 Acres.* Transcript of an oral history interview with Irma "Babe" Story (part of the Legacy of Pancho Barnes, Oral History Program, carried out by Computer Sciences Corporation under contract to the AFFTC) added important detail. Secondary sources included Mitchell, "Legend," part V (*Hi-Desert Spectator/Antelope Valley Spectator,* vol. 2, no. 5); Kuhns, "Pancho"; Schultz, *Pancho;* and Chuck Yeager, Bob Cardenas, Bob Hoover, Jack Russell, and James Young, *The Quest for Mach One* (New York: Penguin, 1997).

Pancho and Rankin's divorce decree (no. 101652) is on record in Los Angeles County.

Chapter 12: The War

The growth of Muroc Air Base during the war is well chronicled in Young, "The Golden Age," and Pace, "Edwards Air Force Base." AFFTC historian Ray Puffer was an invaluable source of information about everything from wartime activity to the personalities of different commanders. The AFFTC History Office has numerous files detailing that history, including such helpful documents as "Military Units at Edwards AFB," which lists year by year the various squadrons and groups assigned to Edwards. Pancho related anecdotes about this time during her 1971 speech before the Experimental Aircraft Association (Geisen collection).

Concerning the activities at Pancho's place during this time, my interviews with Dorothy Woods (Sept. 24, 1997), Bob Fetters (Sept. 21, 1997), Mary Fetters, and Tony King were extremely helpful. Correspondence from Martin A. Snyder and Helen Fulmer-Steager provided important details, as did Pancho's testimony in *U.S.A. v. 360 Acres.* Transcripts of oral history interviews with Bob Jones, Walter Williams, and Irma "Babe" Story (Barnes Legacy Program) enriched my understanding. Both William Bridgeman and Jacqueline Hazard, *The Lonely Sky* (New York: Henry Holt, 1955); and Chuck Yeager and Leo Janos, *Yeager: An Autobiography* (New York: Bantam Books, 1985) provide detail. Yeager et al., *Mach One;* Tate, *Pegasus;* and Schultz, *Pancho,* were additionally helpful.

Pancho's money problems are well documented in the half-dozen civil suits filed against her in Kern County (Kern County Courthouse, Bakersfield). Details about the estate of Richard J. Dobbins come from the R. J. Dobbins file at the Orphan's Court of Montgomery County, Pennsylvania, and from other documents and records (including the original Dobbins will) that are part of *Pancho Barnes v. U.S.A.* (case no. 63-1097-PH, U.S. District Court, Los Angeles).

Details about Don Shalita's life come from my interviews with his niece, Nancy Simonian (Dec. 15, 1997), and photos and ephemera she provided. Interviews with Dorothy Woods and Bob Fetters also contributed. Tom Regan provided details about the Broadwood Hotel.

Chapter 13: Pancho's Fly-Inn

Once again, Pancho is the best source of information about the growth and activities at her ranch. She testifies about them at length in *U.S.A. v. 360 Acres.* My interviews with Ray Urick (Dec. 4, 1997), Bob Fetters, and Tony King were very helpful. Eugene McKendry talks about this time in Yeager et al., *Mach One.* Most interesting of all were the brochures, pamphlets, and advertisements for Pancho's Fly-Inn produced during this time and happily preserved by the AFFTC History Office. A number of people who visited or worked at Pancho's shared their memories for the Barnes Legacy Program. Notable were Walter Williams, Jack Ferdinand, Irma "Babe" Story, and Ruth Russell. Joe Pauly's oral history transcript (Muroc Community Inventory) also provided information.

Concerning the Blow and Go test pilots and their relationship to Pancho and her place, several secondary sources provide interesting details, including "Ad Inexplorata: The Evolution of Flight Testing at Edwards AFB" (Edwards AFB: AFFTC History Office, 1996); Young, "Golden"; Pace, *Edwards;* Dwiggins, "Happy Bottoms" and "Florence 'Pancho' Barnes: Aviator's Companion" (on-line biography written by AFFTC historians at www.edwards .af.mil/cover/pancho/html). But the richest material comes from the pilots and engineers themselves. Chuck Yeager devotes an entire chapter to Pancho's place in his 1985 autobiography. Pilots Bill Bridgeman, *Lonely Sky;* R. A. "Bob" Hoover, *Forever Flying* (New York: Pocket Books, 1996); and Tony LeVier, *Pilot* (New York: Harper & Bros., 1954) all tell stories about these days. Bob Cardenas and Bob Hoover offer additional memories in Yeager et al., *Mach One,* which devotes a chapter to Pancho's place. My interview with Barney Oldfield (Sept. 11, 1997) and correspondence with Martin Snyder were helpful. Other men went on record about these times as part of the Barnes Legacy Program. Notable were Pete Everest, Paul Brewer, and Donald Thomson.

The expert on Yeager himself is Yeager. His autobiography is rich with personal anecdotes and sprinkled with insightful comments from his wife, Glennis. Yeager's comments in Yeager et al., *Mach One,* are also important. Correspondence from Helen Fulmer-Steager added good detail. Aileen Pickering's oral history transcript (Barnes Legacy Program) was helpful.

Chapter 14: Blow and Go

Yeager tells the story of his riding accident the night before the historic flight as well as his run-in with General Boyd in his autobiography.

Material on Eugene McKendry comes from Pancho's testimony in *U.S.A. v. 360 Acres;* documents relating to his birth, job experience, and military service in the Barnes file at the AFFTC History Office; conversations with Bob Dennis (Sept. 19, 1997) and Richard McKendry (Sept. 20, 1997); correspondence with Phyllis Walker; and Daryl Murphy, "Thirty Years with Pancho Barnes," *Flyer,* Jan. 23, 1998. Material concerning Billy and Betty comes from author's interviews with Betty's sister, Dorothy Woods.

Chapter 15: Did She or Didn't She?

Pancho gave a long, detailed narrative account of her stroke and subsequent operation in a story she wrote, presumably for publication in the *Reader's Di-*

gest: "How the *Reader's Digest* Saved My Life" (unpublished, in AFFTC History Office collection). Her medical history, including this episode, is well summarized in a letter from F. A. Matychowiak, a Bakersfield psychiatrist, to Judge J. Kelly Steele, Oct. 18, 1966 (AFFTC History Office collection). I am indebted to Dr. Ron Cirullo for his help in understanding hypertension and sympathectomies.

Everything that has ever been written about Pancho has something to say about the Happy Bottom Riding Club and its activities. Important secondary sources include Dwiggins, "Happy Bottoms"; Dwiggins, *They Flew the Bendix Race* (Philadelphia: J. B. Lippincott, 1965); Holden and Griffith, *Ladybirds II;* Schultz, *Pancho;* and Tate, *Pegasus.* But the people who lived this era tell the story best. Pancho gave her own version of the goings-on at the Happy Bottom Riding Club in her *U.S.A. v. 360 Acres* testimony. Both Chuck and Glennis Yeager reveal much in Yeager's autobiography. My interviews with Al Houser, Tony King, Ray Urick, Grace Logan (Sept. 21, 1997), Richard Bortner (Oct. 21, 1997), and especially Bob Logan (Sept. 21, 1997) supplied a wealth of information. Letters to me from Martin Snyder, James Bardin, Helen Fulmer-Steager, and Phyllis Walker were important sources as well.

A number of men and women interviewed as part of the Barnes Legacy Program had anecdotes and insights to offer. Especially helpful were the interview transcripts from Mary Ellen Masters, Mary Pittman, Aileen Pickering, Paul Brewer, Ruth Russell, Tony LeVier, Walter Williams, and Cliff Morris. Several informants in the Muroc Community Inventory Project also contributed their memories—and opinions—of Pancho's operation, notably Harry Mertz, Norm Graham, and William Fourr.

Finally, interesting and important ephemera from the Happy Bottom Riding Club heyday still exists. Several rodeo flyers and treasure hunt flyers are in the Aldrich collection. A copy of the "official" rodeo newspaper, the *Happy Bottom Blister,* is in the AFFTC History Office collection, as is a typewritten list of "Hostesses Rules . . . Regulations." Letters and advertisements related to the recruiting and hiring of hostesses are reproduced in the pages of the Barnes Legacy Program transcripts.

Chapter 16: Just Do It

Roger Chute, who accompanied Pancho on various trips to Mexico, wrote about them in a letter to his mother: Chute to "Moms," Feb. 12, 1951 (Chute collection, Washington State Historical Society). Cliff Morris, another traveling partner, described the trips in interviews conducted as part of the Barnes Legacy Program. Transcripts of interviews with Morris, Ted Tate, and Paul Brewer supplied material about the moviemaking activities at Pancho's. Pancho testified about this in *U.S.A. v. 360 Acres.* Both Yeager et al., *Mach One*, and Mitchell, "Legend," part IV (*Hi-Desert Spectator/Antelope Valley Spectator*, vol. 2, no. 4) are good sources as well. The sheet music for several of Pancho's songs is in the Barnes files at the AFFTC History Office.

Pancho and Mac's relationship was much speculated upon at the time. The memories, thoughts, and insights of Grace Logan, Dorothy Woods, Bob Fetters, and Al Houser (all author's interviews) helped to reconstruct this. Pancho and Mac's wedding invitation is preserved in the AFFTC History Office files. Detailed coverage of the wedding appeared in the Antelope Valley *Ledger-Gazette*, July 3, 1952; Pasadena *Star-News*, June 30, 1952; and *Los Angeles Times*, June 30, 1952.

Chapter 17: The War of the Mojave

The changes at Edwards in the early 1950s are well summarized in the Air Force's official biographical sketch of General J. Stanley Holtoner (AFFTC History Office). Other important details were provided by General Holtoner in a letter to the author. The AFFTC historian Ray Puffer was an invaluable source. Oral history transcripts from interviews with Cliff Morris, Ted Tate, Pete Everest, and Don Thomas (Barnes Legacy Program) also contributed. Veca's *Just Plane Crazy* contained important insights into the way aviation itself was changing.

Author's interviews with Grace Logan, Bob Fetters, Mary Fetters, and Al Houser supplied rich detail about the way the Muroc community reacted to and was affected by the expansion at Edwards. Joe Pauley, in an interview for the Muroc Community Inventory (AFFTC History Office), also spoke to this point. Pancho discusses the threat to her own property in particular in an affidavit filed in *U.S.A. v. 360 Acres*. Cliff Morris talks about it in his Barnes Legacy Program interview. General Boyd's letter to Pancho, April 6, 1953 (AFFTC History Office), and Pancho's letter to General Schuler, April 13, 1952 (quoted in Schultz, *Pancho*), are also important documents. Dwiggins, "Happy Bottoms"; Mitchell, "Legend," part V (*Hi-Desert Spectator/Antelope Valley Spectator*, vol. 2, no. 5); Tate, *Pegasus;* and Holden and Griffith, *Ladybirds II*, all relate stories about Pancho's dealings with the Air Force and Army Corps of Engineers over her land.

All the court documents relating to Pancho's first lawsuit, *Pancho Barnes v. U.S.A.* (case 1146, District Court of U.S., Southern District of California, Northern Division) are on file at the National Archives and Records Administration's San Bruno, California, repository. The papers include Pancho's original complaint, her amended complaint, the affidavit of bias and prejudice, and transcripts of the hearing. Coverage of the case appeared in the *Los Angeles Times*, March 11, 1952, and the Pasadena *Star-News*, March 11, 1952.

Chapter 18: Pushing the Envelope

All the court documents relating to Pancho's second case, *Pancho Barnes v. U.S.A.* (case no. 1221, District Court of U.S., Southern District of California, Northern Division) are on file at the National Archives and Records Administration's San Bruno, California, repository. Pancho's FBI file (no. 77-57149, Serials 1, 10, 12, 13, and 21) was obtained by the author through Freedom of Information Act request no. 426206-2. Coverage of the case appeared in the *Los Angeles Times* (undated clippings in the Barnes file, AFFTC History Office).

Pancho's third case was filed as *Pancho Barnes v. Joseph Stanley Holtoner and Marcus B. Sacks* (case no. 15403-C, District Court of U.S., Southern District of California, Central Division). I was unable to locate that entire case file, but the official Findings of Facts were in the *U.S.A. v. 360 Acres* case file. Pancho's troubles with Holtoner are expressed in her March 1952 letter to General Partridge (quoted in Schultz, *Pancho*). Cliff Morris tells the story of serving papers on General Holtoner in his interview for the Barnes Legacy Program. Mary Ellen Masters, a witness called in the trial, tells her story in the Legacy interviews as well. Coverage of the case appeared in the *Los Angeles Times*, April 23, 1953; New Orleans *Item*, April 23, 1953; Los Angeles *Herald Express*, May 19, 1954; and Riverside (Cal.) *Daily Press*, July 14, 1954. Secondary sources include Dwiggins, "Happy Bottoms"; Tate, *Pegasus;* and Schultz, *Pancho*.

Chapter 19: Goodbye to All That

The devastating and mysterious fire was covered in the Los Angeles *Express*, Nov. 15, 1953, and the Antelope Valley *Independent*, Nov. 17, 1953. My interview with Dorothy Woods provided important details. The transcript of the AFFTC History Office interview with Lois Hubbard was also helpful. Mitchell, "Legend," part V (*Hi-Desert Spectator/Antelope Valley Spectator*, vol. 2, no. 5), is the best secondary source.

The *U.S.A. v. 360 Acres* case file contains the complete trial transcript, including almost eighty pages of testimony by Pancho. Other helpful documents included the Declaration of Taking, the List of Witnesses, and the Questions for Jury. Pancho appealed the District Court's decision in *McKendry v. U.S.A.* (254 F2d. 659, U.S. Court of Appeals, Ninth District, April 21, 1958). Additional judicial judgments on the case can be found in 174 Federal Supplement 576.

For details concerning Pancho's move, see "Factual Situation," a document filed in *U.S.A. v. 360 Acres*, the "Final Judgment" from that case, and a historical overview published in the *Antelope Valley Press*, March 30, 1989.

Chapter 20: Down and Out at Gypsy Springs

Pancho's buying spree is well documented in deeds, titles, and transactions recorded at the Kern County Courthouse, Bakersfield. A detailing of what she owned, land, machines, and other items, can be found in Eugene McKendry's deposition in the couple's divorce case, *Barnes v. McKendry* (case no. 84552, Superior Court of California, Kern County, Kern County Courthouse) and in the Plaintiff's Memorandum in that case.

In interviews with me, Joe McKinstray (Feb. 7, 1998), Everet Forten (Jan. 11, 1998), Rob Pollack (Nov. 5, 1997), and Tony King all provided important details about Pancho's Gypsy Springs and Cantil properties. In their interviews for the Barnes Legacy Program, Ted Tate and Richard Ledwidge provide good material on this subject. Pancho discusses her plans for the new ranch in letters written in 1960 to L. W. Browne and Tony King (AFFTC History Office). Her plans are outlined in newspaper stories in the Los Angeles *Examiner*, May 7, 1960, and Pasadena *Star-News*, March 5, 1960, and later summarized in the *Antelope Valley Press*, April 20, 1975, and July 1, 1983.

Evidence of Pancho's money problems can be found in the civil actions against and by her on record at the Kern County Courthouse. She wrote about her problems to Roger Chute in October 1962 (Chute collection). She also wrote letters to Lee Purcell, Paul dePietro, and L. W. Browne (AFFTC History Office) in 1960 asking for their help in selling off property. Tony King, Joe McKinstray, and Everet Forten supplied additional information about Pancho's money problems. Robert McDougle, in correspondence with the author, was particularly helpful concerning Pancho's penchant for expensive horses. Eugene McKendry is on record on this subject in the *Antelope Valley Press*, March 30, 1989.

Pancho tells the story of her breast cancer in the unpublished "How the *Reader's Digest* Saved My Life." She also gave Ted Tate some details, which appear in *Pegasus*. My interview with Carl Bergman (Dec. 17, 1997) supplied additional information. Roger Chute's comments about Pancho's extraordinary character are contained in a letter from Chute to unknown, June 1959 (Chute collection).

Chapter 21: Deserted

Pancho is the best source of information about the unraveling of her life at Gypsy Springs. See her amended complaint in the divorce case, *Barnes v. McKendry*. Mac McKendry's deposition in that same case is also a good source. Other details are contained in a psychiatrist's report on Pancho: Antonio Perelli-Minetti, M.D., to Hon. J. Kelly Steele, Oct. 17, 1966 (AFFTC History Office). Her problems can also be traced through the changes of titles and deeds, notices of foreclosure and sale, and more than a dozen civil actions against her filed during this time (Kern County Courthouse). My interviews with Tony King and Bob Fetters contributed important information. Tate, in his oral history interviews for the Barnes Legacy Program, was a good source. Roger Chute's letter to unknown, Oct. 29, 1962 (Chute collection), was helpful. Pancho's misbegotten suit against the government to try to recover taxes she paid in 1940 is *Barnes v. U.S.A.* (no. 63-1097-PH, U.S. District Court, Southern California, Central Division).

The story of how Pancho served her husband with divorce papers comes from my conversation with James Young, director of the AFFTC History Office, and from Mac McKendry's own account in the *Antelope Valley Press*, March 30, 1989. A variety of court documents relating to the case itself (Kern County Courthouse) were extremely important, including affidavits, memoranda, complaints, amended complaints and cross complaints, judgments and decrees, and, most especially, the transcript of the hearing.

Pancho's health problems and the entrance of Ted Tate into her life is documented by Tate himself in his Legacy interviews. Pancho also talks about it in her taped 1970 interview and in a letter to Bobbi Trout, reproduced in Veca, *Just Plane Crazy*. My interview with David Chisholm was very important in understanding Ted Tate and his attraction to Pancho; my interview with Al Houser added detail. The program for "Pancho Barnes: The First Citizen of Edwards" Day is part of the Barnes collection at the AFFTC History Office. Schultz, *Pancho*, offers additional details about this celebration.

The misdemeanor case against Pancho for cruelty to animals (no. 12044, Kern County) was not particularly enlightening. But the letters from two Bakersfield psychiatrists ordered to examine her because of the charge were. Perelli–Minetti to Steele, and Matychowiak to Steele are both in the AFFTC History Office collection.

Chapter 22: The Last Flight

Pancho's house in Boron is still standing. Walt Geisen was a major source of information about Pancho's life in Boron, both through his self-published memoirs and in numerous interviews with me (Oct. 9, Oct. 13, Nov. 20, 1997; March 4, 1998). Tate relates stories about this time in his oral history interview for the Barnes Legacy Program and in *Pegasus*. Pancho wrote about her activities at the "half-hacienda" to Bill Campbell, May 24, 1970 (AFFTC History Office).

Material concerning Pancho's "rediscovery" and renewed public activities comes from the AFFTC History Office interview with Lois Hubbard, Tate's Legacy interviews, Geisen's memoirs, my interview with Tony King, and a letter to me from Gene Soucy. There is also a postcard from Pancho to Walt and June Geisen, Aug. 24, 1973 (Geisen collection). A story in the *Antelope Valley Press*, Aug. 8, 1971, provided some details.

Records of the Bank of America lawsuit, *Barnes v. Bank of America* (no. 114572, Kern County Courthouse), document the case. Stories in the Antelope Valley *Ledger-Gazette*, Nov. 27, 1974, and Jan. 10, 1975, have considerable detail, including direct quotes from Pancho. The Mount Shasta case—actually a series of legal actions, all recorded in the Kern County Courthouse—is best understood by reading the deposition of Jack Bohan, Pancho's attorney, in a subsequent case: *Bohan v. Barnes, Barnes, Geisen and Tate* (no. 119683, Kern County Courthouse). The deals between Pancho, the Geisens, and the Tates are well documented in loan papers, quitclaims, deeds, bank statements, and letters in the possession of Walt Geisen.

A number of people had insights and opinions concerning Pancho's death, including Mary Swann, Al Houser, Richard McKendry, Doug Keeny (all in interviews with me) and Hubbard in the AFFTC History Office interview. The most credible and detailed information came from Pierre Poudevigne (interview Oct. 2, 1997, and correspondence with me), the first person to see Pancho's body. The autopsy report (AFFTC History Office) was an important source, as was the death certificate (in my possession). General Doolittle's eulogy is in the Barnes file at the AFFTC History Office. Ted Tate tells the story of his own involvement in the evening's events in *Pegasus*. My interview with Bob Fetters, and especially Tate's Legacy interviews, provided information about the scattering of Pancho's ashes.

Epilogue

Information about the battle over Pancho's will comes from the Last Will and Testament of Pancho Barnes McKendry (on file, Los Angeles County Archives), Second Amended Objections to Probate of Will in the *Matter of the Estate of Pancho Barnes*, Superior Court of the State of California, Kern County, case no. 27083 (on file, Kern County Courthouse), letter from Kenneth Hastin (Billy Barnes's attorney) to Robert Self (Eugene McKendry's attorney), Nov. 10, 1976 (Kern County Courthouse).

Billy Barnes's death was reported in the *Mojave Desert News*, Oct. 9, 1980, and the Antelope Valley *Ledger-Gazette*, Oct. 6, 1980.

The first party at the ruins of the Happy Bottom Riding Club was covered in the *Antelope Valley Press*, July 8, 1980. The second party was covered by the *Mojave Desert News*, May 7, 1981. The *Antelope Valley Press*, Nov. 25, 1980, reported on the official dedication of the Pancho Barnes room at the officers' club. AFFTC historian Ray Puffer provided additional details.

Index

300   Index